DYING   RVE

SOUTH ASIA IN MOTION

EDITOR
 Thomas Blom Hansen

EDITORIAL BOARD
 Sanjib Baruah
 Anne Blackburn
 Satish Deshpande
 Faisal Devji
 Christophe Jaffrelot
 Naveeda Khan
 Stacey Leigh Pigg
 Mrinalini Sinha
 Ravi Vasudevan

MARIA RASHID

DYING TO SERVE

Militarism, Affect, and the Politics of Sacrifice in the Pakistan Army

STANFORD UNIVERSITY PRESS
STANFORD, CALIFORNIA

Stanford University Press
Stanford, California

© 2020 by the Board of Trustees of the Leland Stanford Junior University. All rights reserved.

No part of this book may be reproduced or transmitted in any form or by any means, electronic or mechanical, including photocopying and recording, or in any information storage or retrieval system without the prior written permission of Stanford University Press.

Printed in the United States of America on acid-free, archival-quality paper

Library of Congress Cataloging-in-Publication Data

Names: Rashid, Maria, author.
Title: Dying to serve : militarism, affect, and the politics of sacrifice in the Pakistan Army / Maria Rashid.
Other titles: South Asia in motion.
Description: Stanford, California : Stanford University Press, 2020. | Series: South Asia in motion | Includes bibliographical references and index.
Identifiers: LCCN 2019028963 (print) | LCCN 2019028964 (ebook) | ISBN 9781503610415 (cloth) | ISBN 9781503611986 (paperback) | ISBN 9781503611993 (ebook)
Subjects: LCSH: Pakistan. Army. | Militarism—Social aspects—Pakistan. | Military casualties—Pakistan. | Families of military personnel—Pakistan. | Military ceremonies, honors, and salutes—Pakistan. | War and society—Pakistan.
Classification: LCC UA853.P18 R37 2020 (print) | LCC UA853.P18 (ebook) | DDC 306.2/7095491—dc23
LC record available at https://lccn.loc.gov/2019028963

Cover design: Rob Ehle
Cover illustration: From a commemorative plaque placed in Chakwal by the British Government In India.
Typeset by Motto Publishing Services in 11/15 Adobe Caslon Pro

For my father,
who loved me regardless

Dear father, when you're standing over my grave
old and tired and childless and lonely,
and you see them lowering me into the dirt
and, father, you're standing above me.

Don't stand there so proudly,
and, father, don't hold your head high,
you and I are now standing flesh to flesh
and, father, now's the time to cry.

So let your eyes cry over mine,
and don't mourn in silence for me,
something more important than my honour
father, is now lying dead at your feet.

And don't say that you've made a sacrifice,
because the one who's made the sacrifice is me,
and don't use any more lofty words
because, father, I'm already buried deep.

Dear father, when you're standing over my grave
old and tired and childless and lonely,
and you see them lowering me into the dirt
then, father, ask for forgiveness from me.

From *Queen of the Bathtub* by Hanoch Levin, translated from the Hebrew by Naaman Tamuz. Reprinted with permission from the Hanoch Levin Institute of Israeli Drama.

CONTENTS

	Acknowledgments	xi
	List of Abbreviations	xv
1	Technology of Rule	1
2	A Calculated Dose of Grief	23
3	The Land of the Valiant	55
4	Manufacturing Soldiers	87
5	Grief and Its Aftermath	111
6	The Value of Loss	139
7	The Bodies Left Behind	161
8	Pro Patria Mori	177
9	A Post-Military World?	207
	Notes	219
	Glossary	239
	Bibliography	241
	Index	255

ACKNOWLEDGMENTS

The realization that I should have meticulously recorded along the way the rather extensive list of people who have in some way or another contributed to the completion of this book rests heavily with me as I try to write this section. I also realized that it is not just people but also situations, events, conferences, articles, books, and films that have contributed to what I have been able to produce in the pages that follow. To use the words of one of my favorite fiction writers, Elena Ferrante, this book, like most acts of writing, is the result of "the many collateral effects of an active life." Hence, at the outset I state my inability to do justice to the acknowledgment of the myriad influencers that have made this possible.

I begin by thanking Dr. Laleh Khalili, who from the outset was supportive, encouraging, and, most of all, keenly interested in my initial, somewhat garbled attempt to put forward the subject of my inquiry. She remains the single most important supporter of this project, and I must acknowledge her unfaltering mentorship. The study has been shaped by and benefited immensely from her theoretical acumen, her attention to detail, and her deep insight into and knowledge of the subject at hand. Dr. Khalili's immense energy and fierce interest in research, in inquiry, and perhaps in life itself have been an inspiration to me. This—along with her unwavering faith in my ability to produce something that was good, perhaps even significant within studies on militarism—sustained me through many meandering and daunting periods of writing this book.

I would also like to acknowledge Dr. Matthew Nelson, who provided an immensely grounded perspective on a number of chapters. The incredible speed with which he responded to my emails and persistent requests for guidance is something I am grateful for. A special thanks also to Natalya Kamal, who helped me decipher legal terminology as I researched cases related to compensation offered for death in military service. Ahmed Salim's generous access to his wonderful archives in Islamabad is greatly appreciated as well. And I am grateful to Drs. Saba Khattak, Rahul Rao, and Ambreen Ahmad and to Nighat Said Khan for taking the time out to talk with me as I struggled to give shape to my ideas.

I am immensely lucky to have a wonderful set of friends whose support I could count on to carry me through the various phases of the project: Sameen Mohsin, Asha Bedar, Shahpar Bakhtiar, Shabana Arif, Saffi Ullah, Zehra Kamal, Anjum Piracha, Sharay Saeed, Mariam Salik, Shadab Zeest Hashmi, Veronica Ferreri, Emanuelle Degli Esposti, and Sena Galazzi Lian. Some provided me with useful distractions when needed, others a regular dose of much-needed brutal honesty, and still others with direly needed copyediting or help with translations. They kept me sane and kept me on the path that I often threatened to wander from. They offered to read my work, and even though not all came back with comments, their ongoing engagement with my ideas and insights were immensely useful as I waded through the wonderful mess that is data. Some may remain unnamed; for that I seek forgiveness in advance and also look forward to them reminding me of this oversight for years to come!

To my boys, Emir and Ali, who put up with my many absences—some physical and others mental—while I remained chained to my computer, I say a special thank-you! Their oft-repeated comments to me, said with loving yet somewhat edgy weariness, that I could do this and that I needed to stop feeling anxious still make me smile. For Adil, my husband, who was (un)fortunate enough to meet me halfway through this project and who impressed me with his ability to get to the heart of what I was trying to say, sometimes in words clearer than my own, I am grateful. His ability to see the big as well as the small picture and thus keep me grounded in everyday life sustained me. A special thank-you goes to my mother, Farzana, who, like most South Asian grandmothers, stepped in time and time again to mother my children in my absence. I have taken her presence for granted, as we often do with mothers, an expectation of comfort and support that has enabled much of what I have achieved in my life. Her support for me has never faltered, and for this I am immensely grateful.

My gratitude for my father, Rashid Ali Malik, a proud third-generation army man, is perhaps more complicated. My father was alive when I began working on this project and then passed away a few months after I completed the first draft of the manuscript. That he got a chance to read some of this work is comforting to me, because the seeds of the project started in our many heated discussions. Initially I was baffled by his acceptance of the fact that I was researching and studying militarism within the Pakistani context. That was a subject he held close to his heart, with his views lying at the opposite end of the spectrum from mine. My only answer is that he loved me and believed in my right to stand apart from him. For a father as authoritative as he was, this was challenging. And for this I thank him, because it is the single most important gift that he left me. It is ironic that the book deals with death and its accompaniment, mourning of those left bereft and incomplete—feelings that I now struggle with. I am grateful that I finished this work before he left us, for I would not have had the courage now to allow myself the intimacy with grief and loss that was necessary for the project.

I would like to thank the members of the Pakistan Army who facilitated my access to various military institutions and events. Some in this group were refreshingly honest and insightful, and I am grateful for the glimpse they offered me of the world within and around them. Although some may not agree with all that is said here and, more importantly, may not want it to be said openly, I hope that, like my father, they will recognize the value of and the right to deviating analyses and opinions. To my interlocutors who opened up their homes, patiently sat through my conversations with them, and accepted my desire to know and understand, I am forever indebted. As will be obvious in this book, without their voices and their silences, I would never have been able to put together my thoughts and insights about this subject.

ABBREVIATIONS

AFIRM	Armed Forces Institute of Rehabilitation Medicine
COAS	chief of army staff
DASB	District Armed Services Board
DSB	District Soldiers Board
FATA	Federally Administered Tribal Areas
GHQ	General Headquarters
ISPR	Inter Services Public Relations
JCO	junior commissioned officer
KP	Khyber Pakhtunkhwa
MC	master of ceremonies
NCO	noncommissioned officer
NoK	next of kin
PA Directorate	Personnel Administration Directorate
PASB	Pakistan Armed Services Board
SRO	Selection and Recruitment Office
TTP	Tehreek-e-Taliban Pakistan
WO	welfare officer
WOT	war on terror
WWP	war wounded person
YeD	*Youm-e-Difah*
YeD/S	Collectively refers to YeD (2015–present) and YeS (2010–2014) national ceremonies
YeS	*Youm-e-Shuhada*

DYING TO SERVE

CHAPTER 1

TECHNOLOGY OF RULE

IT WAS A pleasant, balmy evening, with countless rows of chairs laid out in meticulous symmetry on the green expanse of a perfectly manicured lawn at the Pakistan Army General Headquarters (GHQ). The green Pakistan Army emblem lay nestled between the majestic white marble triangles of the *Yadgar-e-Shuhada* (Martyrs' Memorial) monument lit in national colors for the evening. The monument rested on a resplendent stage surrounded on all sides by giant elevated screens. Familiar patriotic anthems blared from large speakers, while smartly dressed men and women in army uniforms ushered in an audience of a couple thousand people. The 2015 *Youm-e-Difah* (YeD; Defense Day), a national military commemorative ceremony, was about to commence.

Having arrived early, I was seated in the press area and noticed that the last enclosure on my right was already full of people. I knew even before I saw the sign reading "NoK" (next of kin) that this was where the families of dead soldiers would be seated, largely because the enclosure was dominated by people from villages—men and women in *shalwar kameez* (traditional dress consisting of a long shirt over loose trousers) and women with white *chaddars* (large, often white, cotton cloth) covering their heads and upper bodies. Seated here was the group from the village of Palwal,[1] which had lost five young men in military service, three in the ongoing war in northwest Pakistan. They saw me before I saw them, maybe because I stood out from the crowd with my uncovered head and colorful clothes. I went over to say hello, and they seemed pleased to see a familiar face.

Backstage, the scene was somewhat chaotic; some celebrities were getting their makeup done, while others stood to the side, smoking and discussing poetry. There was nervous laughter and some last-minute instructions and script changes. An elderly Baluch man wearing a flowing white traditional headdress was seated silently on the side. He was the father of a dead soldier and was to give his testimony onstage that day. An army officer asked him if he wanted some juice and then told a soldier to make sure he was looked after, as he was their most honored guest. The father seemed very gracious but did not speak much. After a while, he was joined by a middle-aged woman, another dead soldier's mother, who was also to give her testimony. She too seemed aloof from the rest, who were talking and joking among themselves. Maybe they were tense, maybe they were sad, or maybe they were rehearsing their lines? I wondered if I should sit with them or continue to stand with the organizers and celebrities. I decided instead to leave the now darkened backstage, as the show had begun, and sit with the families from Palwal for the rest of the program, because our locations and vantage points determine not just the scope of what we see but also the atmosphere we breathe.

Near the end of the ceremony, the colorful stage and larger-than-life screens went dark. The music stopped playing, and the master of ceremonies announced to the hushed audience that next onstage would be the mother of a *shaheed* (martyr). Fathers, widows, daughters, and sons of dead soldiers had already appeared onstage, and the finale in this commemorative ceremony had been reserved for the testimony of the mother. She walked onto the stage and stood confidently at the dais. Her eyes glistened with tears as she spoke lovingly of her son. At times she stopped, took a breath, and visibly steadied herself, but when she spoke her voice did not waver. She spoke with pride and poise, her head held high. Her grief hung in the air, but more touching to watch was her resolve, her ability to stand firm and resolute against the overwhelming loss that this death had brought her. It was a powerful moment. The camera lingered on it and then swung to the audience, where some watched in awe, while others sobbed or cried silently.

I sat with Yasmin, the mother of Nawaz, a young soldier who had died in Wana, South Waziristan, in 2009. As Yasmin watched the mother speaking onstage, I remembered the conversation we'd had back in her village about these testimonies. It had been a sleepy summer afternoon, with the monotonous sound of the village tube well in the background, the mundanity of the scene far removed from the grandeur and drama of our current surroundings. We had been sitting in her courtyard, a house built with money received as compensation for her son's death, when Yasmin said to me, "The army leaves after the funeral; it doesn't look back. It throws innocents into battle and says go fight. What do they care? How would they know what happens inside the walls of the home? It is not so easy to accept this; women will say we will send another son into the army." There was a short silence and then her voice had floated through the haze of the warm sun. "I don't know who these women are."

When the mother onstage made the predictable offering of another son, Yasmin turned to me with a raised eyebrow and a shake of her head and said, "Look how easily she says it." Her smile was rueful, and I wondered if she too remembered our earlier discussion. Here, within the hush of the NoKs enclosure, the rhetoric of continued sacrifice for the nation—the section of the show that held the most resonance for the rest of the audience—seemed to reverberate the least and invoked cynicism.

I felt surprised, a sense of uncanniness heightened by the dramatic affective register onstage and the response it seemed to invoke within spectators in enclosures that watched these performances (and wars) from afar. The surprise was directed not at what was unfolding before me, for tales of glory, heroism, and willing sacrifice woven around the dead in battle are nothing new. What intrigued me instead was not just the recognition of the farce-like nature of the spectacle before us within the row upon ceaseless row of the families of the military dead but also the impulse of these families to lend themselves to these orchestrations around death.

How does the military retain its power when it all but guarantees the death of its subjects? What compels grieving families to stand within these commemorative spaces? What does an investment in these spectacles of mourning, which demand the affirmation of militarism from subjects who have suffered a substantial loss, tell us about the nature of modern militarism? These questions not only allude to statecraft and the utility of these spectacles in sustaining militarism but also bring into focus subjects of militarism and the uneven, seemingly antithetical practices that define them. Answering these questions demands an investigation of the YeD shows and what lies beyond their blinding stages—the discourse, policies, and practices of the military that tie soldiers, their families, the nation, and the army together in a narrative that channels affect and sensibilities. This book is my effort to conduct such an investigation.

The current world climate is marked by the ordinariness and banality of war and conflict. Militarism is no longer just the more distinct experiences of war and political violence—distinct in that they can to an extent be temporally and geographically bound—but altogether a more pervasive phenomenon. It is now defined by the existence of massive armies, paramilitaries, and military contractors; production and accumulation of arms; growing state ability for surveillance; use of militarized imagery in popular culture; militarization of university and research agendas; making of national histories to glorify military action; and belief that military efficiency is integral to state survival and security.[2] The ease with which wars can be waged in the modern world demands an extension of the study of militarism to beyond macrolevel analyses that traditionally have looked for grand narratives and explanations in historical, political, economic, and technological shifts.[3] Catherine Lutz's work on the permeation of military life into contemporary American society nudges us in this direction.[4] She suggests that we live in a state of "permanent war," with the citizenry and state always prepared and in which the war terrain is not just the battlefield but also the home front that requires "cultural deployments, affective munitions and mental recruitment."[5] The relentless expansion of the military to newer domains of life that are informed by a military worldview and by military values and technologies would suggest that militarism diffuses and thus shapes lives and spaces around it. A sociological phenomenon, it penetrates social structures, relations, and practices including popular culture, modes of economic production, and hierarchies of race, class, gender, and sexuality.[6]

In trying to trace this process of infection outward, this book affixes its gaze on to the military as an institution, the affective bonds it cultivates with soldiers and their families, and the function of these relationships in fashioning the appeal and presence of militarism in modern society. The study of militarism in this book foregrounds an intimate aspect of war preparation, namely the production of the instruments and then subjects of violence: military soldiers and their families. The figure of the mother on the magnificent stage at the YeD ceremony offering another son as cannon fodder and the overflowing mass of people in the NoK enclosure hint at the tragedy of death in war as well as at the casualness of life, the apparent ease with which it is offered to the military. These are subjects of violence that are willing to endure violence not only to their bodies but also to the bodies of those they love. For any definition of militarism to hold, it must consider the complicity of large numbers of soldiers and their families in these projects of war and their apparent willingness to suffer violence. This attention to the complicity of subjects of militarism is important for obvious instrumental reasons, because standing armies are integral to the ability of militarism to thrive, and they will be for some time to come. Understanding this complicity is also necessary for grasping the symbolic significance of these relationships and associated claims for the need to sacrifice and die for the nation state. The YeD ceremony also holds thousands who watch as spectators and through their affective responses become locked in an emotive relationship with war, violence, and the military. These soldiers and their families are then subjects of militarism who stand at the center of war, making it not only possible but also worthwhile.

MILITARISM AND THE INSTITUTION OF THE MILITARY IN PAKISTAN

The nation-state of Pakistan has had its fair share of wars—internal and otherwise—since its formation after the partition of British India in 1947. This has included four cross-border wars with India, countless anti-insurgency operations within the country, covert involvement and support of the Afghan Mujahideen during the 1980s, regular deployment of troops in combat missions abroad, and the more recent conflict within its own northwestern regions as a key ally in the global war on terror (WOT). This penchant for war demands a ready and replenishable supply of troops, and yet the Pakistan Army has never had to resort to conscription and remains an all-volunteer force. According to 2004–2013 Pakistan Army Induction Data, an average of over 130,000 young men apply every year, of which only 38,000 are selected.[7] The voluntary nature of enlistment in the nonconscription military of Pakistan has often been explained as a function of economic desperation. In the rain-fed hilly tracts of Punjab—famed martial districts cultivated by the British Indian Army and subsequently by the Pakistani military—historical proclivity has also been cited as reason.[8] Successful patterns of military recruitment in other provinces and districts post the national integration policy announced in 2001, and, most importantly, the Pakistani military's emphasis on maintaining a certain appeal and image of the force hints at other explanations as well.

This desire to enlist and the apparent enthusiasm for war have been carefully honed over the seventy-one years since Pakistan's genesis. The military in Pakistan—more specifically, the Pakistan Army[9]—has ruled directly for roughly half of Pakistan's existence and indirectly for the rest of the time through the domination of defense and foreign policy and the manipulation of domestic politics. The boundaries between military and civil-political institutions is ever shifting, although rarely in favor of civilian dominance, and the military continues to stand as one of the most powerful institutions in the country, where it has had a de facto role in politics whether it is directly in power or there is civilian rule.[10] The military's ability to take up political space has been attributed to a number of factors, including its postcolonial history, with its hyperdeveloped Punjabi military apparatus that has been strengthened above and at the cost of other state institutions; its geostrategic importance during and after the Cold War; and its growing economic empire.[11]

To understand the Pakistani military's hold over the imagination and loyalty of Pakistani society requires changing our focus from the coercive power of the military that's on display every time a military regime takes over to its ability to shape sympathy and opinion during as well as *after* military regimes leave. This is not to suggest that coercive power is not a primary determinant in the Pakistani military's hold over populations or that resistance to the military's intrusion into civilian domains does not exist. The intent here, though, is to identify the more insidious ways that the military and its norms and aesthetics make their way into Pakistani society. This allows for an examination of how the military "*produces* politics rather than how it is related to it" (emphasis in original).[12] In doing so, the book turns away from attempts to decipher the much-studied and debated *whys* of the military's dominance in Pakistan and instead contributes to an understanding of the *hows* by which the military creates its image as an institution that demands reverence and allows docile populations to emerge.[13]

Militarism's forays into Pakistani society are visible in social studies textbooks that glorify war and valorize Muslim warriors of an imagined past as well as military soldiers who seek martyrdom and to defend their country against traitors looking to dismantle the nation.[14] Popular culture, songs, images, and literary texts further exalt militarist nationalism, and national rituals are replete with military symbols.[15] A well-known war song popularized in the 1965 war with India glorifies the military dead in battle:

Oh, martyrs in the path of righteousness
pictures of faith
the daughters and mother of the land salute you[16]

Imaginings of the soldier and model citizen are heavily gendered. Masculine men protect the nation and the women, who are repositories of national honor. The latter in turn serve the nation by not only producing these soldiers but exalting and praising the men who die in wars to protect the nation.[17] Rubina Saigol suggests that "this form of complementary visualization of masculinity and femininity *enables* warlike nationalism to be imbibed by the citizenry which feels empowered by vicarious participation in the state's nationalist triumphs" (emphasis in the original).[18]

The militaristic state is scripted not just in songs and literature but also in physical spaces. Killing machines such as guns, missiles, fighter jets, and submarines, including the hills where Pakistan conducted its first nuclear tests, are inscribed into the daily lives of people as monuments in civilian public spaces.[19] Pakistan Day is commemorated by holding a military parade every year on March 23, which marks the anniversary of the passing of the Lahore Resolution in 1940 by the All India Muslim League. The practice of commemorating a designated national day that has little to do with military force or war by holding a military parade lends itself to a reading of how the state and society within Pakistan are militarized. The event—a display of military strength with troops from all three forces, the Pakistan Army, Navy, and Air Force—also includes an air show depicting the prowess of fighter jets and other military aircraft and a showcase of diverse arenas of military technology, including telecommunication, arms, and ammunition. It is attended avidly by civilians and telecast live across the nation. Other, even more visible faces of the military in civilian society are its involvement in rescue operations after natural disasters and in law-and-order assignments in which they are tasked with controlling political upheavals. (Civilian governments in the past have called on the military instead of on civilian law enforcements to do this job.)[20] The Pakistan Armed Forces are also called on to use their superior organizational and technological resources for public-welfare projects such as building roads, bridges, and so on.[21] In 2018, the military, on the request of the Election Commission of Pakistan, dispatched as many as 371,000 troops (including reservists and retired soldiers) to over 85,000 polling stations across the country to assist with the election process.[22] All this and more, including the military's propensity to set itself up as a religiously motivated force, allows the military to bill itself as the defender of Pakistan's physical borders as well as its "ideological frontiers," an ethos that is often repeated within military discourse.[23] The role of the military in Pakistan extends and spills over into political and social spaces in which it positions itself as a savior, the ultimate guarantor of the permanence and continuity of the state, while various democratic and military regimes come and go.

Sociological and anthropological accounts of the military institution in Pakistan are rare. Scholarship has attempted to shed light on the military's internal mechanisms, such as recruitment and training practices, but this focus has been at best tangential to the commentary on its political positioning.[24] This book is a study of the complex ideological processes that fuel and sustain the appeal of the military in the general public, namely, how the hegemonic power of the military diffuses through the lives and deaths of people that are made visible and notable within national imaginings. Building on Foucauldian notions of governmentality, the book foregrounds affect as a technology of rule in which statecraft is invested in governing both the polity and the affective selves of subjects.[25] It contends that the Pakistani military's ability to access political space depends in part on its ability to produce certain kinds of political and affective subjects such as Yasmin, Nawaz, and the sentimental audience of the YeD shows. These subjects of militarism are made possible through a set of gendered governing policies around recruitment, training, and the management of death and compensation. These policies are formed within military strongholds such as the General Headquarters (GHQ) in Rawalpindi, Pakistan, and subsequently play out in a series of intimate exchanges with the soldiers and their families, within military recruitment training centers and the rural environs in which the military recruits its seemingly inexhaustible workforce. Although the military uses many ways to capture the imagination and loyalties of its subjects, this book examines the role of affect—such as grief and its accompanying notions of death, dying, and sacrifice as well as feelings of attachment, pride, and fear— in maintaining the military's hegemony in Pakistan.

SENTIMENT AND THE STATE

The presence of sentiment within state and military narratives has been explained as ruse, propaganda (to fuel war rhetoric), or a form of paternalistic governance that uses familial analogies to define the relationship between the rulers and ruled.[26] These theorizations, which situate affect within governance as an embellishment, only partially explain the critical role of affect as a medium that allows power to diffuse through society.[27]

In this book, I offer affect as an analytical lens to understand subject formation or, more specifically, as a technology of rule that can be employed by the military to create subjects both immediate (soldiers and families) and secondary (civilian populations). The state in this reading is not averse to sentiment but actively produces affective subjects[28] that imbibe the state's (and in this case, the military's) concerns and aesthetics through the control of both affective excess (such as intense grief) and affective absence (such as apathy toward military dead). The military controls, suppresses, or invokes all sorts of affect, such as grief, fear, attachment, and loyalty, in its subjects through a host of meaning-making processes including commemorative spectacles as well as policies and practices of recruitment, training, and compensation. Governmentality becomes an exercise of power that involves "the conduct of conduct" by which subjects are produced through the management of individual behavior[29] and in which consent to domination is made possible "by shaping appropriate and reasoned affect, by directing affective judgments, by severing some affective bonds and establishing others, . . . in short, by educating the proper distribution of sentiments and desires."[30] These gendered governing practices are pivotal in sustaining collusive relationships between those who stand to suffer significant losses (soldiers and their families) and those who stand to gain (the military institution)—relationships cultivated not only to replenish rank and file but also to serve as conduits for communication with the citizenry.

A number of terms have been used within scholarship on affect, including *feelings, sentiments, passions*, and the two most commonly used, *emotion* and *affect*.[31] Capable of contagion and less easily externally driven, *affect* is used as a broader framework within the study and concerns the more embodied, unformed, autotelic, abiding, and labile aspect of human feeling.

Reading the relationships between the military and its subjects through the lens of affect makes visible the ways that subjects negotiate the overwhelming power of the institution. That these relationships also allow for *disengagement from the project of militarism*, defined as thoughts or acts by soldiers or families that challenge or deny the demands of the nation-state for sacrifice, is apparent in the opening vignette.[32] I encountered many such moments in my fieldwork: when a mother in *vaen* (a Punjabi mourning ritual) sat at her son's grave and wished he had died when he was a baby, when a soldier in training discussed the conscious process of becoming a mindless automaton, and when a father said to me that he told the colonel he would send his other son to the army because he felt *he had to*, almost like a platitude. These were hard-earned testimonies, for as I started my fieldwork in villages in Punjab and institutes of the military, the cacophony of voices that reached me was full of familiar narratives of willing service and sacrifice. During my fieldwork they seemed like significant moments, moments in which I felt I was hearing the *authentic* from my interlocutors, but over time their remarkableness lessened for me, and I became more interested in how pieces of narratives were joined together. The intricate lacing together of complicit and subversive narratives allowed the emergence of an ambivalent subject in which contradictions are experienced not as discordant notes but instead as a mosaic of affective experiences and states that these subjects identify with and accept as their lives.

The study of such ambivalences and disengagement within the operation of hegemonic power, the ability of the soldier to be the *knowing* automaton and of the father and mother to be both sacrificing *and* cynical, requires a theorizing of affect that can explain them. Reducing this analysis to theoretical positions that suggest the possibility of affective freedoms and see affect either as a prediscursive state existing outside social signification or as a straightforward mechanism that consolidates hegemonic power would be a disservice.[33] The book sets up the potential of affect to both affix relationships of oppression *and* provide cathexis to resist or oppose these relationships. For this, we may need to reimagine relations between human beings and space as irreducible to the interpretations that we as human beings project onto them. A more object-centered perspective would allow us to acknowledge the existence of something beyond human imagination that rests within the environment and material objects that produce an affect experienced by us.[34] This view challenges the traditional psychoanalytical association made between affective realm and human subjectivity, in which "affective possibility and potentiality" lie only within the inner world of human beings.[35] The alternative to this is the suggestion that the psyche is constructed and resides within discourse in the Foucauldian sense, in which the inside is reduced to an effect and subjectivity is an outcome of practices of governmentality that produce the subject. Perhaps the answer lies in placing ourselves between the traditions and disciplines that turn inward and theoretical frameworks that extend outward. In doing so, as Yael Navaro-Yashin suggests, "the purpose is not to privilege a new theory of affect against previous constructions of subjectivity but to develop a perspective that could be called the affect-subjectivity continuum, one that attends to embroilment of the inner and outer worlds, to their co-dependence and co-determination."[36] The study of affect must include attention to the interiority of affect and to various governmentalizing practices that form the subject. Positioning affect as not purely interior, even as it is not merely bounded within the realm of subjectivity, allows it to also be about affective transmissions between human subjects and their environment, so that interiority and exteriority become indistinguishable. Subjects that embody both disengagement from and complicity with the project of militarism are made possible by the potential of affect to linger and haunt. This allows affect to be produced and harnessed by disciplinary frameworks and at the same time exist outside them, residing in the interiority of the subjects *and* in their relations with each other and with their physical spaces.

GENDERING SUBJECTS FOR WAR

Within Pakistan, the appeal of military service to a large section of men as an attractive and idealized form of masculinity lies scattered among historical antecedents and sociocultural settings and institutions. The all-volunteer Pakistan army continues to draw with ease from the "sword arm" of the British Raj—militarized districts in Punjab.[37] But the history of militarism in Pakistan is tied to its colonial roots in other ways as well. British rule in India was heavily invested in the binary categories of the manly, scientific Englishman and the primitive, effeminate native in order to justify racial privilege. This in turn influenced the narrative of the nation that emerged in this postcolonial setting, in which resistance to colonial rule was invested with the politics of masculinity and the reclamation of male honor.[38] This resistance also played out along religious lines, with Hindu and Muslim identities being formed in the crucible of nationalist movements. This involved a recasting of Muslim and Hindu womanhood and manhood, which remained patriarchal in its possibilities.[39] Allama Iqbal, a Muslim nationalist poet, bemoaned the loss of Muslim masculinity and honor under colonial rule and campaigned for the reclamation of this loss through the hypermasculine Muslim, *Mard-e-Momin* (the Male Believer).[40] The woman in this discourse was cast as the "emotionally laden signifier and symbol of nation, self, the inner spiritual world and the home," to be shielded from Western influence, modern values, and secular education.[41] The postpartition Pakistani nation-state invented Pakistani nationhood through the forced homogenization of a culturally diverse geographical area under the banner of Islam. It constructed a Pakistani selfhood based on the physical and cultural purging of the other: the Hindu and the Hindu Indian State.[42] This required a certain aggressive posturing, which was provided by the strong Pakistani Muslim male figure who would defend the nation from the *other*, who was often portrayed as effeminate and thus polluting. The primary tropes of the nation-state, family, and religion were fused such that any attack on Pakistan was an attack on Islam and on the entirety of a citizen's family and kinship structure.

It has been suggested that the soldier in Pakistan is made outside the military, where "half of the army's work is done for it," and rural communities in Punjab and Khyber Pakhtunkhwa (KP) honed by the British for the project of war construct their men as hardy, valiant, and concerned with such primordial notions as *ghairat* (honor) and *izzat* (prestige).[43] Several theorists of masculinities suggest that these militaristic and masculinist subjectivities emerge from a conscious effort to create a distance from the other, seek to erase what is perceived as nonmasculine, and are fragile, insecure, and open to anxiety.[44] The book situates this *conscious effort* not within these districts but within military training institutions in which the soldier is meticulously and exhaustively disciplined. The manufacture of the soldier-subject requires the establishment of distance from former objects of affection and ways of living and the continuous control of sadness, fear, and shame. It involves the destabilization of stubborn familial attachments seen as feminine and as threats to the soldier's ability to stay in service. In place of such attachments, the military pulls in feelings of mastery, of masculine and rational superiority, and of attachment to one's army battalion and comrades.

Militarism's complicated relationship with its women subjects deserves scrutiny if we are to better decipher military's governing practices.[45] At one end of the spectrum we have women who are pacifists, resistors of war. At the other end are militarist mothers who willingly give up their children in support of war. The mother that I describe in the opening vignette oscillates between these two representations, and in this oscillation, she registers her refusal to settle in any simple subject position. The unclear margins of her subject position hint at the intense yet contradictory technologies of rule employed by the military that pull in the female subject and attempt to seal her compliance. This book documents how masculine subjectivity nurtured on the idea of separation and difference (in military training and in mourning rites) struggles with fear, which is expressed as a disdain for the feminine and the female subject's perceived lack of control over destructive affect. Her affect is exalted in other spaces in which the suffering mother and helpless wife, in need of protection from the masculine military, is the ideal subject because of her ability to express and invoke grief in the nation that watches her. This ambivalence within policies and practices that attempt to control her life and affect is mirrored in the female subject, and she stands as a possible resistor of militarism in one space and an active abettor of it in another. What are the disciplinary policies and practices that draw in women and men (for these technologies work in complementary ways) as subjects of militarism? And what can an analysis of affect contribute to these understandings of male and female subjectivities, including the possibilities of disengagements it affords subjects? As such, this book seeks to examine these technologies of rule that set up the female subject as central to militaristic imaginations involving both an espousal and repudiation of the feminine.

STUDYING THE MILITARY

Military discourse, policies, and practices that craft the subjects of militarism act as windows through which we can understand how symbiotic relationships between the military and its subjects are made possible. The persistent cultivation of loyalty and attachment in districts through incentivizing service; the meticulous claiming of the mind, body, and soul of the living and dead soldier through training and death rites; the skillful discipline of grief attached to the soldier's death through national and local spectacles of commemoration; and the mechanics of monetary compensation are all ways that the military interpellates its subjects. These are sites in which the state (that is, the military) sets out its expectations regarding how events are to unfold and emotions are to be distributed. This book describes how these subjects respond to this interpellation and how in doing so they sometimes move away from simple compliance. The technology of rule that I foreground in this study plays out through the affective interiority of subjects, which allows for moments of disaffection. It is a political ethnography that allows for a reversal of the usual top-down view of power, representing instead a view from below or, more aptly, a perspective that brings into focus "the myriad ways the state comes into view."[46] In so doing, I posit subject formation as a mutually constitutive process between subjects and the powers that form them and a process in which "subjectivity is not just the outcome of social control or the unconscious; it also provides the ground for subjects to think through their circumstances and to feel through their contradictions."[47] It is this meaning making, a potential for subjects to sense their condition, the flair for knowing, that I privilege as important to capture.

I study the instruments and subjects of war and violence: the *sipahi*[48] and the families of *sipahis* (dead and alive) of the Pakistani military, traditionally drawn from rural Pakistan. The subjectivities of those who are at the ideological and physical front of war in Pakistan—the junior commissioned officers (JCOs) and noncommissioned officers (NCOs) and mothers and families of dead soldiers—have often been missing from discussions in which the focus of attention has nearly always been on the officer corps. Perhaps this failure of attention can be attributed to how the soldier in the mass standing army of the modern military has often been painted as an automaton, or simply as a sheep willing and ready for slaughter. Underlying this assumption is the belief that the poor in rural areas of Pakistan are prone to being managed and are unquestioning in their loyalty to the military. When I started this inquiry, I was aware that sheep seldom act subversively, especially in the context of the Pakistani military (and even if they did, I did not think my fieldwork would be able to uncover this, for the military and its subalterns guard their secrets well). My interest was in finding out if the automaton or sheep could think. In other words, did the web of the military's disciplinary power break at any point, and if so, how did it reconstitute itself?

Much of my investigation examines the Pakistan Army. As the largest (in terms of manpower) and most influential (in terms of political clout) of the three forces[49] constituting the Pakistani military, I contend that many of the arguments in this study about militarism in Pakistan are best represented by this institution. The study is based on fieldwork conducted in five villages in the Chakwal district Punjab (a popular recruiting ground for the British Indian Army and the Pakistan Army) and formal encounters between the state and its subjects in military or semimilitary institutions.[50] The data in this study is drawn from ethnographic participant observation over a period of thirteen months and from more than one hundred interviews.[51] My primary interlocutors remained sipahis (NCOs and JCOs) and family members (mothers, fathers, and wives) of soldiers (dead, serving, and retired)[52] as well as civilians[53] from the villages or the city of Chakwal. I interviewed military officers and other personnel who were significant because of their association with soldiers.[54] Throughout the book, the names and identifying information of my interlocutors has been changed or sometimes withheld to preserve anonymity. Anonymity was a condition requested also by military officers and as such I only share their rank and department and have withheld information regarding location or date of interview.

Much of the ethnographic work was limited to Palwal village, located in Chakwal Tehsil. It lies in the Potohar belt, which is largely rain fed and is where agricultural land holdings tend to be small. The area relies primarily on service in the military and police as well as migration of unskilled labor to the Gulf States for its livelihood.[55] Pension records obtained from the nearest post office show that around 60 percent of households in Palwal have someone who has served in the military. This does not include soldiers currently serving, so the number of households with a direct relationship to the military is likely to be higher.

In my interviews, I engaged with sets of families rather than with individuals alone. I spoke with five sets of families, all of whom had lost a son in military service in the last sixteen years, one as recently as a month before I first talked with them. Many of these interviews were held in the courtyard of the family house, with my interlocutors walking in and out of the space as they went about their daily chores. The lived experience that I set out to capture was collective, not private, and was also highly affective. There was jubilation at the coveted acceptance of the son into the military, distress at his physical condition when he returned home after his initial training, pride at his recruitment parade, rising fear and anxiety when he was posted to a combat area, dread when the phone rang, numbness when the coffin arrived, helplessness when they found it nailed shut, awe at the grandeur of the funeral, and the rawness of grief when the military left. And there were tears, always tears. Some hovered behind wet eyes and others just rolled out unexpectedly, never wiped away but leaving traces as they dried. I worried initially about the lack of privacy and hesitated when initiating conversations about what I felt were sensitive or painful moments, but it seemed that the stories and experiences I sought had been discussed and talked about often. Thus, it was not so much that I was reopening painful moments for these families but that I was being let into conversations that were already happening.

The women, especially the mothers, went back to that time with little effort on my part, as if these were memories that they lived and breathed every day. Fathers, too, spoke to me, but that took longer. Some were reluctant or hesitant, and yet my regular presence in the village and in their homes drew them to speak, even though I did not intend to have that effect. Others continued to remain silent and suspicious. I maintained an uneasy relationship with these fathers, being respectful (of their space), grateful (that they still allowed me into their homes, where I spoke to another family member), and conscious of my location as a researcher (and the desire to know).

My initial visits caused little or no surprise in the villages. These villages were used to visitors from the city: journalists, filmmakers, and military personnel who wanted to know the stories of the *shuhada* (martyrs). What aroused a certain amount of discomfort and trepidation was that I wouldn't go away. By the second month it was clear that I was regarded with some bemusement and at times open suspicion. I attribute this in part to the naturally skeptical reaction in these areas to the somewhat nebulous notion of ethnography. Villagers were initially uncomfortable with these continued encounters that allowed the gaze of the researcher into everyday moments and the development of an attachment between the researcher and the subject, especially when the researcher represented a subject position that was removed by class and sometimes gender. Some were reluctant to engage. I believe this reluctance was also partly due to the subject of my inquiry. Many had questions; some were posed directly, and some were conveyed through others. I was watched, people were curious, and my motives were often questioned. *Why did I need to come in again and again when they had already told me all that I wanted to know? Did the military know I was there? Was I perhaps from the military sent to spy on people? Was my purpose to find out why people enlisted and discourage them from enlisting?* The village of Palwal was loyal to the military and felt uncomfortable with this stranger who came morning after morning and said she wanted to listen to people's stories. What was obvious to me was their hesitation, and their awareness of what could and could not be said and what might be said if I came again and again. It was a hesitation born out of increasing familiarity, out of the beginnings of an intimacy between researcher and researched that was uncomfortable, because it might allow an exchange that went beyond the script that is acceptable not just to the military but also to the self. To allay these suspicions and my own sense of frustration as I felt people withdrawing, I taught English in the village's only public school three times a week for a period of three months. Besides the somewhat useful distraction this provided for my own nerves, which were sometimes overwhelmed by the substance of my talks with families, it was instrumental in developing a number of enduring contacts. Most of all, although it did not change my identity as the woman *from the city researching the military*, it did allow the village to place me in a role in which I became more relatable and less alien.

A sense of what can and cannot be said comes out at different points in my study. It emerges in the narratives of villagers as well as in interviews with officers and soldiers. There was an avowal that *this is how it is*, but that it could not be said openly, and that there were open secrets that nonetheless needed to be guarded from outsiders (researchers) who may not understand. My interviewees expressed that in the interests of state security, the institution must be protected from those who wished to malign it. Clearly the topic of my research was considered sensitive enough to necessitate this warning, because the image of the institution was sacrosanct and was to be protected at all costs, even if truth had to be compromised from time to time. This was the message repeated by my military interlocutors, and it became louder as I went up the ranks to the generals, brigadiers, and colonels in more formal institutional settings such as the GHQ and Inter Services Public Relations (ISPR).

Interviewing was a dialogical process in my study, in which I was present and in which my personal biography intruded upon the social world I sought to interrogate. I situated myself as both an insider and an outsider within this research frame. I come from a military family, and clearly this subject position afforded me a familiarity with what I was studying. My childhood was spent within army cantonments, and much of my school life involved studying in educational establishments run by the army for the families of troops and officers. This allowed me an intimacy with army rules and norms, with its vocabulary and ethos. Pride in service and sacrifice was a narrative that I grew up with. My association with the army also brought some comfort to my interlocutors, not so much because they thought I was an insider and they could trust me but because I believe I could resonate their sense of dissonance from military scripts and at the same time also understand their appeal for them. I was also an outsider to the world I chose to study, the world of the subaltern military soldiers who were ever present in my life yet were silenced and separated by a deep chasm of class and gender. Reflexivity in this instance required more than vigilance; I had to acknowledge the attending self as a resource, one that stops me from generalizing about and simplifying other people's lives.[56]

As I proceeded with my fieldwork and the analysis of my data, I became increasingly conscious of my imbrication within the research frame. This was perhaps an inevitable consequence of the subject of my study, with an affect as powerful as grief. I could not situate myself outside the stories I heard for two reasons. The first was that simply listening to mothers and fathers talk about their loss was an emotive experience, and the second was that I was immersed as a subject of the military through tropes of grief and sacrifice even before this research began. Hence, tears would flow when I heard the families talk about their children, in the silences between our conversations, or as we sat by the graves of their dead sons. My own affective response to the stories became a site of observation; I developed an intimacy with the affect I sought to study, which was at times both exhilarating and exhausting.

CHAPTER ORGANIZATION
The book is organized into chapters that address the underlying argument in the context of ethnographic scenarios and fill in historical and contextual information necessary to ground the study. The text traces the affective bonds between the military and its subjects and follows them through various spaces and critical moments, with a dramatic first look into this relationship beginning in chapter 2, an examination of national military commemorations. The book shifts its focus in chapter 3 from the national stage to Chakwal, a famed martial district in Punjab, and offers a historical reading of the policies of the British Indian Army and of the postcolonial trajectory of the Pakistan Army's national recruitment policies and their impact on present day Chakwal. The relationship between the military and its subjects thus proceeds in chronological order from recruitment to training and disciplinary mechanisms that transform the soldier-peasant into the soldier-subject (chapter 4), to the death of the soldier and its reception in rural Chakwal (chapter 5), and to the rolling out of compensation policies offered against loss endured for the nation (chapter 6). The last two chapters on soldier disability (chapter 7) and on religion and the war on terror (chapter 8) discuss critical moments in which the relationship between the military and its subjects is tested. The ensuing dynamics reveal how narratives of sacrifice continue to hold valence despite strain. The concluding chapter recapitulates the centrality of affect in the relationships that the military crafts with its subjects—both immediate (soldiers and families) and secondary (the nation)—and suggests that a deeper examination of affective technologies deployed by the institution of the military can be a powerful political act used to challenge the appeal of militarism to its subjects.

This book is a journey that marks its start at the most logical point, an intense concentrated expression of militarist (national) ideology as framed by the military. In the next chapter I deconstruct military commemorations of soldiers that die in wars as sites at which the military and its subjects perform a heady mix of grief and ceremony for the larger nation.

CHAPTER 2

A CALCULATED DOSE OF GRIEF

IN 2010, the Pakistan Army declared April 30 as *Youm-e-Shuhada* (YeS)—Martyrs' Day—to pay tribute to the soldiers who died in the war in northwest Pakistan, a corollary of the war on terror. Since then, YeS commemorations have been held annually on this day within army garrisons. For the next five years, a large national commemorative ceremony was also held at the army General Headquarters (GHQ) in Rawalpindi, the heartland of the Pakistani military, and broadcast across the nation on state television and private channels.

I begin the book with an examination of these televised spectacles of mourning for two reasons. First, these spectacles define the master narrative, one that purports to shape and discipline citizens' perception of the military and its role. These ceremonies of light and shadow showcase performances that valorize military service, speak for the dead and their families, and construct the manly soldier and his family as willing, nationalistic beings who rally, stand firm, and offer more despite their immense hardship, pain, and suffering. The military-framed national ideology presented here is not some static contraption fixed in time and space, like literature, visual art, a song, or a history book. Instead, it is a performance, altogether more fluid and in which intended audiences or spectators seemingly become participants through shared affect. Second, these ceremonies represent a site for the examination of relationships—between soldiers, families, and the institution of the military—that lie at the heart of militarism. This encounter between the military and its subjects is perhaps the most dramatic, for it is staged for the benefit of the *qaum* (nation), the third vector in these relationships.[1]

The televised national commemorations aim to entertain and to inspire, through scale and color as much as through what is actually presented on stage. The entire performance is built around death that is often brutal and violent, and grief and loss are central themes. A spectacular stage performance choreographed down to the last detail and planned for effect, it is a visual and audio treat, one that tugs at the heartstrings, makes you weep, and then makes your heart swell with pride. It plunges you into deep, wretched sadness as you watch the mother of a dead soldier smile through her tears, and then it pulls you up within minutes on waves of pride with visions of smiling young muscular men in combat clothes, sounds of machine-gun fire, and tales of development and prosperity and of a nation that is at peril but resilient. In every scene, there are liberal splashes of the military and of a sovereign country that stands on the blood of the predominantly khaki-clad martyr. These visceral registers play through the bodies of the mothers, fathers, wives, sisters, brothers, and children of the dead and produce and shape the responses of the audience—the nation that watches them. The spectacle involves a harnessing of affect, a pulling of scabs to invoke a response of awe, gratitude, and empathy for the military.

A way to study these ceremonies is to understand them as an investment by the state in the management of grief through carefully crafted commemorative rituals of mourning and memory making.[2] Grief is managed in order to curtail dissent that may arise due to conditions of mass bereavement, and vigilance is required to construct grief and discipline mourning in ways that create support and reduce possible challenges to the state's inclination for war. Katherine Verdery's work on the political appropriation of dead bodies alerts us to what she calls the "strong affective dimension of dead-body politics." Bodies cannot speak but can be spoken for, an ambiguity that makes them useful. They can be utilized to invoke nationalist images that ask for unity around a hero of the nation or religious images that emphasize sacrifice and continuous life. Bodies also inspire awe as they bring up questions and fears about the meaning of life and death. Most importantly, they allow an engagement with affect and emotion through identification with the self and through invoked kinship relations, such as brothers and sons. All of this makes bodies "good symbolic vehicles."[3] I extend these claims to include the families of dead soldiers, whose bodies also become vehicles to display and invoke affect. Grief then becomes not an inconvenient fact of war that needs management but a resource to be deployed. Commemorative events go beyond mourning and tribute making; they also provide symbolic capital for the military that legitimately spills over into domains that strengthen its hegemony and control over the state. This is hardly surprisingly in the context of Pakistan, in which direct and indirect military interference in foreign policy and politics is an accepted fact. What is interesting for the purpose of this analysis is the nature of the platform used for this expansion, a platform that commemorates the dead. The military has other national stages at its disposal. The Pakistani military commemorates the Pakistan Day Parade on March 23 every year. The parade displays military prowess and discipline through the showcasing of military manpower, arms, and ammunition. Inasmuch as these events also seek to invoke a sense of national identity through tropes of loyalty and pride in the military, the military, as I show below, chooses the commemorative space in which to project its narrative on war, enemies, politics, and governance.

THE WAR IN NORTHWEST PAKISTAN AND ITS DEAD

The war on terror (WOT) and Pakistan's participation in it has been a contentious subject nationally and within the military. Especially at issue is the nation's alignment with the United States and the fact that the designated enemy is Muslim.[4] Much of the WOT, or at least the army operations, has been concentrated in the northwest parts of the country, including districts such as Swat and Federally Administered Tribal Areas (FATA). North and South Waziristan, sites of fierce combat between the Pakistan Armed Forces and the Taliban, are located in FATA, which borders the provinces of Baluchistan and Khyber Pakhtunkhwa (KP). Under British rule, FATA was loosely governed and used as a buffer zone between Afghanistan and colonial India. Postpartition, the Pakistan state used FATA as a base for resistance against various Soviet-supported governments and as a base for the subsequent Soviet invasion of Afghanistan in 1979. The site also provided support to Mujahideen groups fighting for Kabul in the 1990s and later to the Taliban and other militia in maintaining strategic depth in Afghanistan.[5] After the 9/11 attacks on US soil, Pakistan had to review its hitherto largely unquestioned alliance with the *jihadi* forces it had nurtured with US support and aided during and after the Afghan-Soviet war.[6] Although some small-scale operations and troop deployments in the WOT began in South Waziristan as early as 2002, it was not until 2004 that the military initiated more concerted operations in these areas. These have escalated steadily over the years, with Operation Zarb-e-Azab launched in North Waziristan in June 2014, followed by Operation Radd-ul Fasaad in February 2017. The numbers of law enforcement personnel, including military, police, and paramilitary soldiers, who have been killed or maimed in these operations have been high. Conservative estimates from the South Asia Terrorism Portal suggest that between 2003 and 2016, over 6,623 security personnel died in the WOT, and well over two times that number were maimed.[7]

The military's ability to garner support for this war has been hampered by contestations from right-wing political and religious parties largely regarding the military's claim to *shahadat* (martyrdom in the name of Islam) for its dead soldiers. Because of the heavy appropriation of religion by the Pakistani state and the military, this issue had not previously been contentious.[8] Hence, a soldier in the Pakistani military was considered a soldier of Islam, and when he died in the battlefield he became a *shaheed* (martyr). In 2004, Maulana Abdul Aziz, the Lal Masjid (Red Mosque) cleric in Islamabad,[9] issued a *fatwa* (ruling on a point of Islamic law) declaring the South Waziristan operation by the Pakistan Armed Forces un-Islamic and prohibiting the burial of soldiers in Muslim graveyards. There were media reports of disaffection among lower-ranking troops and resignations by commissioned officers posted to South Waziristan.[10] There were also reports of villagers refusing to participate in military funerals held in villages. In 2007, there was an armed confrontation between the Pakistan Army and clerics and students of the seminary attached to the Lal Masjid. The state officially acknowledged only the military dead as shaheed, while many religious parties also labeled the students who died during the army operation as shaheed. This period marks a distinct phase in which the military's claim of martyrdom for Islam began to be challenged in more organized and visible ways.

When a US drone killed the leader of Tehreek-e-Taliban Pakistan (TTP), Hekimullah Mehsud, in November 2013, the head of the Jamaat-e-Islami party, Syed Munawar Hassan, made two declarations:[11] first, that Mehsud was a shaheed, and second, that the Pakistani soldiers killed fighting Islamic militants in North Waziristan were not, because they were aligned with the United States.[12] In response to Syed Munawar Hassan, there was condemnation from the military; a delayed but resolute reaction from the civilian leadership, with Prime Minister Mian Nawaz Sharif going to GHQ to pay homage at the *Yadgar-e-Shuhada* (Martyrs' Memorial) monument; a retraction by the Jamaat-e-Islami; and subsequent debate in newspaper editorials and on television talk shows.[13] Conversation revolved around two primary themes: (1) theological speculation on what constitutes true shahadat and the reassertion of state policy on the right to claim shahadat for its armed forces and (2) possible injury to the morale and sentiments of soldiers and their families. The first was debated on television talk shows and in newspaper editorials, and the discussion that ensued was sometimes unresolved, but the need to protect the feelings of soldiers and their families received unequivocal support from both military and nonmilitary quarters.

What was at stake in these debates was the right of the military to claim shahadat in the service of Islam, a claim that had so far been synonymous with dying in military service. Anxiety on part of the military in response to this challenge from right-wing political parties and religious groups revolved around a practical fear of disaffection. Troops and their families in Pakistan reside in areas where mosques and *madrasas* (religious seminaries) are aplenty and ambivalent state policy has allowed extremist and sectarian ideologies to seep into neighborhoods, school curricula, and the media. The reported desertions from the army after the 2004 fatwa suggest that this anxiety is founded in reality, but not all men deserted or revolted; in fact, disaffection was dealt with swiftly. This may have been managed partly through court martials[14]—the 1952 Pakistan Army Act details strict procedures for court martials in cases of mutiny, desertion, and disobedience—but the Pakistani military did not sustain any serious damage and was able to continue recruiting and functioning. This can be attributed in part to economics; the comprehensive pension and welfare schemes offered by the military to officers and enlisted personnel continue to be some of the most exhaustive of any public-sector employer in Pakistan.[15]

Anxiety also revolved around the possibility that the military narrative of sacrifice and service to the state (and to Islam) would be weakened. This moral card is dear to the military, for it is a terrain on which the military is able to command blanket acceptance by both civilian populations and military personnel, as was obvious in the debates that followed the controversy generated by Syed Munawar Hassan's remarks. The military was able to win unreserved support in these debates due to appeals made on behalf of the sentiments of soldiers and families of the dead. The status of the dead was swiftly and unequivocally defended in the national landscape, not just by the military but by the media and civil-society activists, spaces where more open criticism of the military has been possible. The registers through which this debate unfolded almost always included a reference to the sentiment and feelings of troops and their families as sacred and revered. This sacredness, it could well be argued, is bestowed not by Islam, because that very association was under attack, but by the power of affect. These are sentiments that have been deliberately cultivated within the national imagination and have come to be associated with this kind of death. These feelings enable the militaristic narrative of service and sacrifice for the nation to come alive, stay alive, and stay relevant.

BRAND MARTYRDOM

The Pakistani military's declaration of April 30 as Youm-e-Shuhada in 2010, close to a decade after the war began, can be interpreted as a deliberate move to stem the controversy around this war that was rife at the time. After the terrorist attack on the GHQ in 2009, General Ashfaq Parvez Kayani built the Yadgar-e-Shuhada on its premises. The war had come home, and the response, a national televised commemoration broadcast across the nation, was a counterattack launched from the same location: the GHQ.

Prior to YeS, *Youm-e-Difah* (YeD)—Defense Day—was held on September 6 every year and was devoted to the commemoration of martyrs and the celebration of Pakistan's alleged victory over India in the 1965 war.[16] Although YeD is linked to the 1965 war, until 2009 it had been considered sufficient tribute for subsequent military casualties, largely incurred against its traditional enemy India—for example, at the Siachen Glacier[17] or in the Kargil war.[18] YeD was a national day, celebrated by the state as well as the military, and was also a national holiday in Pakistan for some time. The general tone of the nationally televised YeD ceremonies was celebratory, extolling the heroism of the soldiers of the entire Pakistani military (not just the army) in the 1965 war. Martyrs were remembered through songs, but the tone remained light, with sacrifice glorified and revered. And although the challenges and grief that accompany martyrdom were mentioned, they were not dwelt on. The show was smaller in scale than the subsequent YeS ceremonies, with a limited audience and often in a civilian location, and was attended by members of the military leadership, sometimes in civilian attire, and civilian leaders as senior as the prime minister or president.

The army leadership decided to not include its tribute to the martyrs of the war in northwest Pakistan within the folds of YeD, opting instead to commemorate it separately as the Youm-e-Shuhada, hence the declaration on April 30, 2010. The televised YeS ceremony was much larger in terms of size, audience, and resources employed than was the YeD. It focused almost exclusively on martyrdom, predominantly referencing those who had died on the western border with Afghanistan or in counterinsurgencies, and was attended by a large number of NoK, the families of dead soldiers.[19] The tone was more somber, and there was a strong focus on emotive testimonies or experience sharing from mothers, fathers, and other family members of dead soldiers. This was an army affair held at the GHQ premises, presided over by the chief of army staff (COAS) and the senior military leadership in full uniform. An address by the COAS was a traditional feature, and the ceremony was attended by a number of foreign dignitaries and civilian leadership. The president and prime minister were not invited.[20]

In 2015, the military decided to discontinue the national YeS ceremony, although it continues to be commemorated across army garrisons in Pakistan on April 30. The erstwhile YeD national event was shifted to the GHQ, and from there on, the army has held one nationally televised commemorative event, referred to as the YeD ceremony, annually on September 6. The YeD shows from 2015 onward are markedly different from the earlier ceremonies and are, in fact, YeS shows in format, content, and location. For this reason, I refer to these national events as YeD/S in the text that follows.

The YeD/S shows are managed by the Inter Services Public Relations (ISPR) department of the military, which was set up in 1949 as a unified public relations system for the Pakistan Armed Forces.[21] A large chunk of the technical production of these shows is outsourced to private production companies, but the script, including song lyrics and poems, is often handled directly by the ISPR.

In explaining the genesis of the YeS ceremony, the ISPR colonel in charge of producing the show said to me, "You can't build a brand overnight. You have to sell your narrative. It has to be comparable and contemporary." He went on to explain that YeS was set up to buttress the "morale of troops and families by providing a formal commemorative space" and to reclaim the "strategic concept of shahadat" by winning the "battle of narratives" between the Muslim militants and the Pakistani state. A separate day for the commemoration of martyrs of the war in northwest Pakistan was a proclamation by the military to mark a new phase of warfare for Pakistan: a shift from the more tradi-

FIGURE 1. *A billboard announcing YeD 2015 at Zero Point interchange in Islamabad. (Photo taken by author.)*

tional enemy (Hindu India) and conventional war to a new enemy (fellow Muslims) and an unconventional war, an assertion that was contested through the discourse on shahadat. The YeS was a stage to brand martyrdom anew that gave the military flexibility to shape the new enemy while keeping the old one (India) intact (as annual YeD ceremonies were also held on the side).

The ISPR major centrally involved in scripting and designing the show elaborated: "We [the organizers of the show] are talking about two things, purpose and feeling. The sentiment towards the nation-state and feelings towards those [families] who sacrificed their loved ones . . . you have to give [family members] space for expression of these feelings towards these [dead] relations and [space for] feelings that we [the nation] have for them [families]. This is how you convey that it [the sacrifice] was a purposeful thing." Another ISPR major recalls the testimony of a dead soldier's widow: "[It was] a *brilliant moment*, when she [the wife of a dead soldier] stood there with her three children, the youngest in her arms, and said she wanted her son to go into the army like his father. It touched a chord; it was a very emotionally charged moment. It is to create such moments that these commemorations are done." The widow so clearly described by the second major is an image—"She stood there with her three children, the youngest in her arms"—created for consumption by the nation. The nation as spectator and third vector is clearly acknowledged here. The sentiment, the grief, of the family member toward the dead loved one is central. The bodies of grieving family members are the conduit through which the military conveys its message of purpose and sacrifice to the nation. The appeal to the nation is made on affective terrains, relying on the deliberate "creat[ion]" of "emotionally charged" moments in which the family member's expression of loss "touches a chord" with the audience. A response that seems natural, as though drawn from the depth of their being, speaks to the appeal of these "brilliant moment[s]."

THE SCRIPT

One way to decipher the narrative of service and sacrifice to the nation is to look at the content of these spectacular performances. Scripts are important in their explicit content, for they make obvious the rhetoric that the state wants its subjects to imbibe. They also become a window into the state and its anxieties, despite the wish of the script writers to exert influence outward. Reiterated again and again in these scripts are the threads that the military deems important but also considers possibly fragile. They must therefore be reinforced to keep these bondages intact.

Nation-states actively promote national cultures and create narratives of the nation through a range of institutions involving the use of memory and history making.[22] These narratives rest heavily on kinship metaphors.[23] In his study of nationalist discourse in Italy in the nineteenth century, Alberto M. Banti suggests that such discourse draws on "deep images" for its intense emotional appeal. He says that these images deal with "primal facts" that are "elaborated through materials that come from a pre-existent discursive continuum." This makes them "easily recognizable" and "adaptive within new discursive contexts."[24] Banti identifies these images as kinship, love/honor/virtue, and sacrifice. The latter brings in "themes of suffering, mourning and death" and has the potential to transform "national belonging as a sacred experience."[25] This revered framework for understanding the nation helps explain and exalt the death of its martyrs. Suffering, mourning, and death are rendered meaningful and thus sufferable by the family that deals with the loss and by the soldier who prepares and trains for this sacrifice.

Pakistani narratives of the nation have been filtered through *deep images* of religion and kinship that are staunchly gendered.[26] These images feature heavily and predictably in the script of the YeD/S ceremonies.[27] The use of religion in these shows is reflective of a wider religious nationalist ideology, which has had constitutional backing since Pakistan's early years. The Pakistani military's use of religion and the idea of shahadat as a motivator for training, fighting, and dying for the nation are well established.[28] The word *shaheed* itself has a clear religious connotation, and religion comes up repeatedly and predictably in YeD/S scripts. Some shows begin with a reference to a verse from the Quran that declares the shaheed to be forever alive. More often than not, the nation-state is mentioned within the folds of faith. The COAS's speech almost always makes a reference to religious duty, and the claim that Pakistan is an ideology and not just a geographical state is often repeated. Videos, songs, and documentaries feature shots of mothers on prayer mats or soldiers praying on the battlefield. Poems and imagery refer to Islamic history and terms that are clearly connected to Islamic battle history, and Islamic texts in general are often invoked.

Riste (relationships), or kinship, is a recurring theme to which the script is tightly bound, and the shows bring this deep image to life through an intense focus on the families of the dead. This is evident from the opening sequence of the ceremony, in which a chosen group of next of kin (NoK) is paraded into the pavilion to be seated (while the rest of the audience stands in respect). This is followed by the testimonies of NoK, played on giant screens or relayed live onstage, or videos, songs, or poems dedicated to them. The final poignant sequence of the show depicts the families paying homage to the dead with flowers at the Yadgar-e-Shuhada monument.

The 2014 show started with a detailed relation-by-relation dedication of the show to the dead soldiers' family members, including fathers, mothers, wives, sons, and daughters. The lost are the fathers and sons; those who feel their absence most are the mothers, wives, and daughters. Although the testimonies of male family members are part of these events, the military clearly foregrounds the female figures—especially the mothers.[29] Twice in 2010 and again in 2014, the COAS's speech singled out female relatives and acknowledged their grief, while in nearly all shows, the tribute to the *azeem maan* (great mother) is underscored and draws the most emotive reaction. As the ISPR major explained to me, "A mother's investment and attachment is more. The man is physically composed, and it is easier to expect the man to say 'Go, my son [to death]'; it is harder for the mother to say this. Her sanction means more; her grief is more." The mother's grief is exalted and considered more extreme than that of others, and it becomes a powerful symbolic resource to be harnessed, invoked, and then managed to produce maximum effect, all in the service of militarism. She is to grieve and then, paradoxically, not grieve. The invocation "*Shaheedon ki maan roya nahi kartein*' [Mothers of martyrs don't cry]" is repeated often within the show. The mothers' testimonies are carefully balanced, and so alongside her inconsolable grief, her stoicism and willingness to sacrifice her most treasured relationship for her nation are also highlighted. She symbolizes the final moral authority, *maadar-e-watan* (the mother of the nation), who gives her blessing to the violence on the body of her loved one. Central to the commemorative ceremony, the mother's appearance is saved for the grand finale, and she is singled out as the affective relationship whose sanction is critical to making this sacrifice possible.

The widow is also routinely invited and is the second most emotive figure on stage. The ISPR major remarks on the dilemmas involved in inviting the wife: "A man has two relationships. One is that with the mother, and other is that of romantic love; romantic love is tricky because it is considered un-Islamic. Everyone has a mother, plus one may or may not have a romantic attachment with the wife; romantic love may or may not be part of the marriage." There are obvious tensions associated with the figure of the wife. The overreliance on the mother happens partly because the soldiers who die are often young and unmarried. The reference to the perceived un-Islamic connotations of romantic love also points to the need for a pure, asexual figure who folds more neatly into this narrative. Some wives no longer live with the family of the deceased, and some move on and get remarried; thus the demands of the narrative, that memory and suffering are kept alive, are better met by mothers. The wife is also a contentious figure, as there may be family discord because of dissatisfaction over how compensation has been divided between the heirs of the deceased. This does not mean that the wife does not appear onstage; she often does, especially if she is older and has children, but these challenges point to how her inclusion is peppered with considerations.

These tensions notwithstanding, the military clearly seeks female affirmation within this commemorative space. Nationalist imaginings within Pakistan, as in other South Asian states, remain heavily gendered, with women playing a central role as repositories of national honor as well as of cultural and religious traditions. The use of gender tropes suggests that the masculinized, militarized, and nationalized self cannot be imagined without reference to the feminine; hence the feminine is invoked to strengthen and underline the differences between men and women.[30] So the tears and helplessness of the mother and the wife are deliberately juxtaposed with the strength and resolve of the male soldier—a useful binary that can then be extended as a metaphor for the relationship between the military and the nation. The repeated reference to the feminine serves to create the complementarity in gender relationships that the militarist project seeks to reinforce; that is, masculine armies protect the honor of the vulnerable (feminine) nation that in turn produces soldiers. The military and the nation, just like male and female subjects, become intertwined: partners in the project of war. The masculine militarist project needs this suggestion of complementariness to survive, and hence gendered references to relations are continually made in these shows.

For the father, the son's death is constructed in these ceremonies as a loss of companionship. Fathers are also depicted as role models for sons, and sons of dead soldiers often voice their desire to join the military. For the military, this desire to enlist emboldened by the father's sacrifice and death is an important part of the script, voiced through the onstage testimonies of male children and brothers, as when a son came onstage wearing a mock army uniform in 2010. A popular dialogue in mothers' and fathers' testimonies is "If I had ten more sons, I would send them to the military." Fathers, and mothers even more so, are portrayed as having brought up their sons in ways that made this sacrifice possible, a deliberate rearing of the child to make him more selfless and more willing to risk his life. Painted as collusion from the beginning, the sacrifice is not just about passive acceptance of a glorious death but about gratitude and pride that the son is dead in the cause of the nation. Back home, in the villages from which these men are mostly drawn, the desire to offer another family member is often a direct reflection of the scarce options for making a living and the need to make up for the loss of income that the family had come to rely on. In recognition of this dependency, the military assures service in its ranks to a male member of the family as part of the compensation package. When family members make such an offer onstage, however, it is presented as a voluntary desire to serve the nation and sacrifice for it.

The *rista* (relationship) between the qaum and the military is a recurrent theme in these national commemorations. A slogan for the 2011 YeS ceremony, "One force, one family, one nation," captures the symbolic folding of relationships into a militarist frame. The emphasis on oneness serves to silence or hide from view voices that may not be in line with this narrative. More importantly, it does so under the shadow of metaphors of kinship: gendered familial relationships that inspire love and thus are deemed natural and rendered unquestionable. In 2013, a video poem titled *"Tum ye kaise kar lete ho"* (How do you do this?) presents a dialogue between the admiring nation and the warrior soldier. In an incredulous voice, the poem's narrator presents a series of images of a safe, carefree family life juxtaposed with scenes of dangerous and risky warfronts, asking the soldier again and again how he can *choose* to do what he does. The narrative then shifts beyond the intimate to a larger landscape in which the soldier figure is shown helping those stricken by national calamities such as floods and earthquakes. The question shifts to "How do you take on the troubles of the entire nation and make them your own?" The soldier then responds, giving two reasons: first, because his family's support gives him the strength to fight, and second, because the nation stands alongside him. He says, "I am not alone; the entire nation stands with me." Sacrifice is possible because both the family and the nation support him. The script also highlights a tension and, in so doing, speaks of an anxiety. Paradoxically, the very bonds of kinship that are invoked again and again in the YeD/S script are the bonds that need to be weakened, for he has to *choose* the nation above his family if he is to perform his duty and be willing to fight and die. This theme is also reflected in military training,[31] in which there is an invocation of relationships and then their negation, representing a choice made easier when the mother is replaced with the motherland, the family or home with the idea of the military or unit as home, and the son of the mother with the son of the nation.

THE CRAFT

I sit in the somewhat crowded office of the ISPR major. The YeD ceremony is only two days away, and a rehearsal is about to commence. Some of the people in the rooms are servicemen and servicewomen from the three branches of the armed forces who will be called onstage at different points in the ceremony. Others are civilians who are assisting with the show in various capacities, for example, as script writers or as technical producers of video documentaries. The air is light, and the conversation flows readily in response to my questions about how the military identifies families for participation in these events. This process of selection determines who is or is not picked for participation in these spectacles of state mourning and what is to be spoken and what will remain unspoken. I am told that to convey diversity in sacrifice for the nation, those who appear onstage and those whose testimonies are recorded as part of video packages are carefully screened. It is deemed essential that all types of bodies that die in the war on terror are represented, with special attention paid to identity markers such as class, ethnicity, branch of military force, and army regiment. The next step in the selection is to prepare those who are allowed onstage. The officers in charge of prepping the families who go onstage seem confident in their ability to shape the testimonies of family members and suggest that a fair amount of backstage instruction ensures that just the right message is delivered. A pleasant young army major, smartly dressed in civilian attire, tells me about the prepping process:

> It is a hard job because we pull at their scabs. The son died two years ago, and we want him to talk about it, relive it. We have to give the right dose, injection, because he can't break down completely. I prepped this *baba ji* (father), who used to cry, for two days. It is a delicate task, just the right emotion and some acting. It has to be a mix. We tell him his grief is not just his grief; his son is not just his son. He needs to think about grief beyond him. He has to share his grief so others can also grieve and know what it feels like.... He did a good job, spoke well, and the whole audience was crying, and he didn't cry, just a little bit. And then as he walked away, he made a thumbs-up sign at me.

His fellow officer, listening intently to us, interrupts and asks in an incredulous voice, "In front of everyone?" The young major smiles and responds, "No, it was when he was backstage, but it was a strange moment because [it showed that] he was acting. It's a mix of grief and two percent of acting. That's the way it is done. It's a performance that uses real emotions."

This was a surreal exchange, in which the very intense and personal emotions of the bereaved father became material for state scrutiny and crafting. Raw material, genuinely felt emotion, that had to be channeled such that it became just the "right dose" of feeling. The performance onstage could not appear crafted, and the illusion of authenticity had to remain, as evidenced by the concern when the major was asked if the man's thumbs-up sign was visible to the audience (or the camera). The testimony was made possible by a *manufacture of the authentic*, a calculated and carefully planned mixing of the felt and the constructed, or as the major put it, "just the right emotion and some acting."

These live testimonies onstage require continuous management. In another exchange backstage at the YeD ceremony in 2015, the military convener and the master of ceremonies (MC) discussed a testimony that was to be given onstage. The major asked the male MC teasingly, "Are you wearing mascara"? The MC broke into a smile. The major continued, saying, "I hope you checked if it was waterproof?" The convener replied, "I asked the same question when they were putting it on," and laughed loudly. The major then asked, "Are you going to ask any questions of the father [of a dead soldier, who is to appear onstage]?" The MC responded by saying, "I will see if it is needed; it is a live show, and I don't want to cause any problems." The major reassured him, "No, he [the father] is very strong. He is too good; don't worry. [*He pauses.*] You can decide if you want to make a prick or two."

The concern for the right image, a depiction of pain yet also of the unshrinking resolve of the family member of the dead soldier, is obvious in this exchange. It indicates a certain calculation on the part of the organizers as well as collusion between them and the families, who are "too good" and "very strong," something that was obviously determined in the preceding prepping session. *Prick* here refers to a drawing out of emotion in case the testimony of the father is unemotional. The intent here is not to simplistically paint the organizers as heartless or manipulative or the subjects as artificial but to simply foreground the fact that putting on this spectacular event unavoidably involves a surreal blend of the contrived and the authentic. And yet, even as the fake and authentic lie together, the ability to recognize the fake remains; the old man's thumbs-up sign speaks to that ability, a realization that this is a moment in which he must perform and not cry or break down. The script of the nation then becomes a crutch, a language that he can speak without breaking down, a language that will strengthen his ability to stand and not crumple, and a language that when spoken sometimes becomes devoid of emotion, although tears can seep through when a deeply intimate memory of the son is pricked by the MC, per the instruction. Raw affect is reformatted and reworked through the concerns not just of the military but also of the subjects. This reformatting and reworking still permits the realization that this is acting, the thumbs-up sign acknowledging a job well done, but the acting cannot be questioned because it rests on real emotion.

In discussing the script of the shows, one of the writers explains: "Our goal is to tell people we all feel pain." He scoffs, saying, "Earlier, we used to tell people we are made of stone, superheroes. When I get hit as a soldier I feel the same pain. . . . [In the case of] the mother of the shaheed, why should I tell people that she says she feels no sorrow at his grave?" His voice rises indignantly. "It's a lie. Does this happen? He had a self; he had something at stake." There is a sense of frustration on the part of scriptwriters regarding their search for a more believable script, one that does happen. The stoic mother can feel sorrow, and the stoic soldier is not "made of stone" either. So the video documentaries of soldiers' lives that are played at YeD/S highlight that they have a difficult choice to make between love for their family and love for their nation. The goal is no longer to show that these sacrifices are easy but instead to impress on the audience that they are very hard. This shift allows video reenactments[32] in the shows to focus on the life of the dead man beyond his identity as a soldier in ways that can be used to more effectively invoke affect. Over the years, the shows have become more video intensive, the videos technologically more superior, and the stories more developed and personal. In 2014, the reenactments and testimonies were no longer limited to one section of the show but were littered throughout; the change indicated not so much an increase in the number of stories but a blending in of these stories so that the figure of the martyr is omnipresent even as the themes become more diverse. The soldier is no longer depicted as a one-dimensional man in uniform storming into a building with a gun or saluting a flag, and the mother is not just sitting on a prayer mat or kissing her son's brow, although there are still many such scenes. Spliced into this typical imagery are newer, more mundane images showcasing the *ordinary* soldier and all his family members (not just the mother), the bonds of attachment, and images of happy family life. Family members speak of him in the video, and as the documentary ends, the MC reads out, in a tearful voice, the part of the script that welcomes family members onto the stage. At this point the camera's gaze captures the audience—already close to tears, with some already crying—and then the family members they saw immortalized on-screen a minute ago walk onstage. In earlier shows, the MC stood on a separate dais, with families coming in and speaking at another. Since 2012, however, the MC has stood alongside family members, often with an arm around them, ostensibly to give them support or lead them offstage in case they break down. In a comic twist, sometimes the relentless buildup to emotion can have unexpected results, and such moments can prove all too powerful. A major ruefully recounts how in the 2013 show the female MC started to cry with the mother: "The mother stopped crying, [but] she [the MC] was crying; she couldn't speak. This can complicate things."

The ability of affect to resonate and spread to other people is central to these spectacles of mourning. As the YeD/S program unfolds, with reenactments of the bravery of dead soldiers, recorded and onstage testimonies of mothers and other family members, and the choked voices and wet eyes of the MCs, the audience is often in tears. The camera captures these displays of emotion, shifting from the stage with remarkable and almost obsessive frequency. When the camera focuses on the audience, women and men are visibly moved, some shedding silent tears and others sobbing openly. What often marks these spectacles is the composure of the families despite their deep grief. This composure and stoicism are carefully constructed, part of a delicate oscillation between crippling grief and resolute commitment to further sacrifice. So subjects (families) resonate with emotions that simmer on the surface and spill over into tears, yet their speech never falters and their words never go off script, at least as far as the audience and nation are concerned. This composure is often at odds with the unbridled and ready display of tears in the audience, and the camera seeks out and displays shots of women, and sometimes men, sobbing and heaving with emotion. This is an exteriorization of the family's affect, in which the expression of emotion associated with the interiority of the subject is delegated to others, in this case the audience, resulting in a transfer of intimate feelings.[33] These affective flows between the families and the immediate audience are crucial to completing the spectacle for the nation, where the emotive audience acts as the channel of emotional discharge for the less emotive family. There is a need to project the devastation of loss and grief, but the families cannot serve that purpose because that would destabilize the script of willing sacrifice. The loss has to be highlighted and tears invoked to garner sympathy, however, and the audience fulfills this function. The immediate audience—representing the feminized, weak nation in need of protection from the stoic, more controlled, masculine family, representing the institution of the military—becomes locked together in an emotive relationship through the transmission and exteriorization of affect.

Political spectacles such as the YeD/S produce a one-way flow of communication using technology (mass media, for example) that mutes any response from those who participate by reducing them to mere spectators.[34] The ability of the spectacle to restrict avenues of independent political thought and foreclose resistance is in part enabled by its potential to allow spectators a sense of involvement. A way to understand this sense of involvement is to be alert to the fluidity that exists between the participant-spectator dyad in these ceremonies. If we position the qaum as the subject of the military, produced within militarist discourses, and further distill from this mass the semimilitarized families of the dead and the civilian spectators of the show, there are two sets of subjects that shift between participant and spectator roles in different but interrelated ways. In the context of semimilitarized families, we may need to reframe these processes as collusive affairs in which families *participate* by allowing their affective selves to become spectacles.[35] The second set of subjects, the spectators, can be further divided into two types: (1) the audience at the show and (2) the wider citizenry—the people watching on television. Those in the audience at the show, who are not strictly military and who mourn visibly, do not remain spectators but become participants, crying with the families and sharing their grief. The camera captures this for the benefit of the wider public. The audience thus adds another layer to the ranks of those who serve as conduits for the relationship between the military and the nation. Through this further layer, grief and sacrifice become potent tropes through which the military communicates with the wider citizenry. These ceremonies create an image of families as willing, compliant beings who offer up their sons to the military and an image of the audience as a nation that weeps and stands alongside these families and soldiers, which translates into standing alongside the military and its policies. The transmission of affective energy between grieving families and the audience allows these spectacles to speak to the watching nation about appropriate ways of responding to and showing support for the military.

The script, including the central characters of this performance (*what must be said and by whom*), remains an essential site for the deconstruction of these spectacular performances. But it is perhaps the crafting of these shows (*how it is to be said*) and the direction and technologies employed to convey the script that become crucial. These tactics involve delivering the right dose of grief through careful preparation of family members for testimonies onstage, showing video documentaries that emphasize the ordinariness of the soldier and families to further accentuate the extraordinariness of his sacrifice, and skillfully using the camera to draw in the audience as participants. All of this serves to lock the citizenry and military in an emotive relationship. These illusions made possible through a manufacture of the authentic, a skillful crafting of genuine pain, also involve a deliberate masking of other realities and experiences that unravel behind the main stage.

OF OTHER SPACES AND STAGES

Explicit content is often just half the story, and within this content there is much that remains hidden, visible only in its conspicuous absence. I contend that who is not to be allowed onstage, what is not to be said, and what is to be hidden from view is important if we are to understand more clearly what the state constructs.

Going Off Script

Officers acknowledge that when family members are onstage they can sometimes say things that are considered inappropriate. Examination of this inappropriateness reveals interesting insights into the anxieties of the military and into the voices and expressions that must be managed if the narrative of sacrifice is to remain stable.

Mothers and other family members are discouraged from making the death "too real" and from speaking of the body while onstage. Officers are very clear that depiction and talk of the dead must not become too vivid and that "she [the mother] should not talk about the dead body of her son. Some things are very gory; we don't want them to be said onstage." The body can be glorified in death only if it is seen as intact: whole, smiling, and at peace and not as a gruesome or bloodied image. This discomfort with the mutilated body is also apparent in the ambivalence the military shows toward those maimed in the war. These soldiers are known as War Wounded Persons (WWPs) in military parlance. WWPs made no appearance at YeS shows until 2012, and then they were only in the audience. Short documentaries were dedicated to them in 2013 and 2014, however. They disappeared from the stage in 2015 except for when male celebrities paid tribute to them toward the end. The shows thus give them space and then take it away; the camera rests on them during the ceremonies but not for too long. Their late inclusion and subsequent exclusion point to the fact that the disabled represent a cost of war that is inscribed on the body such that it makes the military anxious. The disabled hover in a space between the dead and the living; the valiant *ghazi* (warriors) and the glorious dead and refuse easy categorization and appropriation. In response to their growing number, the narrative has had to make space for them since 2012, but it does so in constrained and ambivalent ways.[36]

The testimonies of families can also potentially threaten the official transcripts of certain events. Sometimes family members may share sensitive information about the operation in which a soldier died. At other times, a family member may express rage against the enemy in an uncontrolled way. During their prepping session, officers will carefully filter testimonies for such details. The military is interested in controlling not just the pain of grief but also possible anger. This could be strategic, for in this case the enemy is liminal and confrontation with him has to be carefully managed, which is an acknowledgment that he may not have been totally discredited with the masses or within the military. Whatever the cause for controlling expressions of anger against the enemy, it is interesting that the depiction of a family member as angry causes discomfort. Perhaps the politics of anger, of rage, can threaten the politics of sorrow, because the image of a passive, grief-stricken family member does not sit comfortably with the unyielding, angry father who seeks revenge.

Any mention of monetary compensation for the army's dead is missing from the show, and families are discouraged from mentioning it. It is well known that compensation for military dead is greater than that received by members of other law enforcement agencies or that handed out by the state to civilian NoK after death or injury in terror incidents. Yet any mention of this topic is missing to the extent that all that is made visible to those watching the show is the ideological narrative, almost as though compensation did not exist. The military goes to great lengths to ensure that the realities of bitter property disputes and family estrangement are hidden from public view. The intent of the show is to build the military's image as savior and *muhafiz* (protector), and it cannot afford to be thought of as a well-compensated security establishment.[37]

The terrains on which families and the army officers prepping them find themselves at odds tell us something important about these relationships of power. What the military seeks to hide from the grand stage also reveals tensions and ripples within relationships (between the military and the families of the dead) that can seem untrammeled and invulnerable.

The NoK Enclosure

The vast NoK enclosure is marked by a number of signposts surrounding it. The marking and separation of each sitting enclosure in these ceremonies are typical of how the military attempts to categorize and organize space as a way of maintaining discipline and making crowd management easier. Yet this physical separation also serves as a metaphor for other differences, including those of location, ethnicity, and class, because the vast majority in this enclosure are from rural areas of Punjab. These differences bring into focus how collective narratives of the nation and of sacrifice mask the fact that the nation-state offers unequal representation to and demands unequal sacrifice (in terms of military service) from the members of its community, depending on who they are. The overrepresentation of Punjab is partly because of the Punjabi dominance of the military and partly because the audience at the GHQ ceremony is drawn largely from the immediate environs, the Rawalpindi division. To smooth over these distinctions, onstage reenactments and testimonies also show soldiers and families from villages and cities in KP, Sindh, Baluchistan, and Gilgit Baltistan. The number of casualties is higher in the soldier class, which is largely drawn from rural areas, and the NoK enclosure is dominated by people from villages: men in traditional white *shalwar kameez* (traditional dress consisting of a long shirt over loose trousers) and women with *chaddars* (large, often white, cotton cloth) on their heads. Although some people (usually parents of officers who have died) in the NoK enclosure are in western suits and some women are more fashionably dressed, the difference between enclosures is more pronounced because of the complete absence in the other enclosures of these rural men and women from lower socioeconomic backgrounds. It is a sign not only that the nation may demand unequal sacrifice from different classes but also that the only time rural men and women can be visible on the national stage is when they make this sacrifice.

Another difference between the NoK enclosure and the rest of them is that of mood. People in this enclosure remain uncertain, vigilant, and uneasy in this vast expanse of grandeur ostensibly set up in their honor. The NoK in this enclosure are relegated to audience status while their stories are played out in front of their eyes. The camera seeks them out when the re-enactments are done, when their testimonies are presented, and when the COAS mentions them. Thus, every time the script speaks for them and through them for the dead, the camera rests on this enclosure. For the qaum that watches, the presence of these families serves as an expression of their unwavering support for the military and makes these political spectacles complete.

As shown in the vignette at the beginning of this book, the persons whose lives and stories are told on the grand stage do not always relate to the rest of the audience. Yasmin, the mother whose son Nawaz had died in Wana, South Waziristan, and with whom I sat during the YeD ceremony, remained skeptical about the mother who came onstage and presented her other son to the army. Yasmin has refused to send her second and only surviving son to the army, although a secure place in her dead son's regiment had been offered to them. She distanced herself from that mother, saying, "I don't know who these women are," and she cried openly through much of the ceremony.

When I visited Yasmin's house a week later, she was not at home. Instead, I met her nineteen-year-old daughter, who had recently been married and was visiting her family. She had wanted to attend the YeD ceremony this year, but the invitation was for her mother and father only, and despite attempts to secure an invitation, she had not been able to go. "Mother told us about the show and how grand it was, but she remained upset by it, her heart felt *okha* (uneasy). She said there were many people; there were lots of other mothers, and they all cried. She was saying that they [the military] should just take this money [spent on the show] and distribute it amongst the people, so that someone could benefit. She said watching the parade just made her heart sad, and she missed Nawaz more." Nawaz's father, sitting close by and listening to our discussion, gently rebuked her, saying, "Yes, they spend a lot of money; they give us money for travel and also put us up in a fancy hotel and feed us, but if they gave us this money it would never be enough, even if they gave us a crore [ten million rupees] each it would never be enough. Who will remember them then (the dead)? We will forget otherwise." The daughter looked at me and attempted to further explain her father's remarks: "My father is a political man. He did his matric (ten-year school certification) when very few people in our village had done so. He thinks; he sees things differently. My mother is uneducated. She is emotional; she only feels."

The "uneducated" mother, who "only feels" and whose bonds of attachment and ability to express affect are deemed vital in these commemorations, says that the resources spent on these events should be distributed so that someone can benefit from it. She implies that no one really benefits from these grand shows, therefore rendering them pointless. She further suggests that her grief, expressed within nationalist frameworks and spaces, has grown and has not eased. This signifies a disconnect, in which the nation no longer figures in private scripts. The nation is also missing from the "political" father's comments, but remembering through meaning-making and memory is important in easing his grief.

That these families are militarized civilians produced by statist ideologies is one way to understand the complicity of families and their testimonies onstage. This explanation seems reductive, though, in view of the old man, whose thumbs-up sign signaled awareness of the act of performing as he spoke about something that overwhelmed him. It also proves to be an inadequate explanation of families' reactions during and after the ceremony. These testimonies are made possible not just by the internalization of nationalist and religious ideologies but by painful affect that, while harnessed by the military's disciplinary power, seeks its own balm, and not just the one that is so glibly and clumsily offered. Collusion with the militarism project works in subtle, layered ways and is not a result of appropriations and manipulations summoned by the language and text of the nation alone. It is a compliance made possible not because of a firm belief and faith in ideology but because people are desperate. It is marked by desire not to see, even as vision seeps through in the spaces in which the camera (or the gaze of the military) does not reach, and it is sometimes expressed as cynicism. The scripts offered by the nation then become the language used to stand, a crutch leaned on to face an intolerable reality that can be made bearable only if it fits within available cultural constructions of sacrifice and honor. When grief is deep enough, the nation becomes an afterthought.

Other moorings, more compelling than the nation, rise up in the fog and also make this compliance possible. These moorings are haunted by memories, the need to remember, and the fear of forgetting. At the YeD ceremony, Yasmin, Nawaz's mother, turned to me during a video about ghazis that showcased brave, well-trained soldiers, and said, "Look how fit they are, how they train, and all they have to do to be able to fight."

She said this ruefully yet with pride. I remembered the many conversations I had had with her in which she lamented how army training was very tough, how weak Nawaz had become, and how she had cried when she saw his condition the first time he returned from training. Nawaz's father had proudly pointed out his son's unit when they marched across the pavilion to the beat of the army drum, remarking on their distinct uniform and the feather in their green berets and telling me how his son used to wear it when he came home. These regimes of discipline—the symbols, colors, and music—were familiar to them. Sohaila, the mother of Imran, an eighteen-year-old soldier from Palwal who died after three months of service, was seated next to us and told me, "We come [for YeS] because they [the army] call us, look after us. We always do because he [her son] was fond of the army, its parade and uniform." These moorings are made stronger by the hauntingly familiar terrain, for this is what was familiar to their loved ones: the sounds of the army band, the uniform, and the parade. And so as parents, they attend, because it was their child's world.

These are feelings heightened by the glare of the bright lights in the public space of the nation. They are the feelings of people who finally have a chance to stand in that space, villagers or women who are suddenly allowed into the national narrative. A deep sense of obligation to honor the son's memory, fueled by deeply felt affect, leads them to cling to and be soothed by what is familiar, not so much to them but to the ears and eyes of their dead sons. Sounds, images, and associations saturated by affect calm them; communities of grief-stricken families thus sit within these grand settings in which there is talk of wars and enemies. This terrain is alien yet still achingly familiar through the language of a keenly felt loss.

MOURNING NO MORE

An investigation into these ceremonies reveals that the stage on which the dead are mourned by the nation-state is never just that. It slides into domains that are no longer about the dead. Within these ceremonies, the military uses the bodies of the dead and the grief of families to shape the "enemy," glorify and situate militarism and war as something to be celebrated, create illusions of equivalence and solidarity between civil and military dead, and provide a legitimate stage (literal and otherwise) for the military (the COAS) to address the nation and comment on affairs of governance.

The Elusive Enemy
The COAS's speeches in 2012 and 2013 alluded to the controversy around the war, and the shows reiterated the status of the dead as shaheed through familiar invocations from the Quran and from Pakistan's history and identity as an Islamic nation-state. But it was not until after the 2013 controversy around military martyrdoms that the military boldly turned the debate on its head, redefining the enemy as lying outside the folds of faith (an allegation that the TTP has made against the military). In 2014, there was a specific documentary film in the form of a poem about the enemy. The poem attacks the "Muslimness" of the new enemy, calling it a mask, a curtain behind which he hides and manipulates minds. The enemy is portrayed as backward, as using religion and culture to exploit and manipulate young minds. In 2015, a slight slippage in this narrative was seen in a video documentary profiling the enemy. Two of the three terrorists are shown as Muslims, of whom one is an Afghan national. The third is depicted as an unknown whose religion and nationality cannot be ascertained, hinting at the presence of a foreign (Indian) hand in this without stating it explicitly. The shift in the emphasis between internal Muslim enemies and external enemies reveals interesting tensions. It seems that the intensity of focus that can be on the internal enemy without losing sight of the perceived threat from the external enemy, India, is a concern for the military. The first three YeS programs did not mention the external enemy, but in 2013, more forcefully in 2014, and much more clearly in 2015, there was a resolution of this tension, with both enemies being conflated as one. The COAS's speech in 2015 also referred repeatedly to external threats without naming India. Ostensibly designed as a tribute to martyrs, this stage became a strategic site for how the nation is to think and rethink the enemy.

Celebrating War
Ghazis were given a special tribute in the YeD ceremony in 2015. The video package was a reenactment showing how conflict played out in Zarb-e Azab, an operation in North Waziristan declared by the Pakistani military in June 2014. The clip is slick, depicting the military as modern equipped with the latest weaponry and technology, the soldiers speaking English, and the enemy as a mix of Pakistani and foreign nationals. The tone here is markedly different from earlier reenactments, which bordered on being heavy and somewhat morose, if resolute, and in which tears and pride mingled. The mood was light, as though war was an almost enjoyable sport. In the video's first shot, the officer takes cover behind a large rock and declares, "Here we go. *Ab maaza aye ga*" (Now we will have fun)! In the final encounter, the enemy and the soldier throw down their weapons and engage in hand-to-hand combat, with the soldier emerging victorious. The last minute of the video breaks into a catchy song and shows troops gathered around the fire singing *"Humara Naam Ghazi Hai"* ("We Are Warriors"). The stage paying tribute to the dead is also one on which war and its accompanying violence and killing can be glorified, enjoyed, and even celebrated.

Sharing the Stage
The first three YeS ceremonies focused exclusively on the military martyr. Only in 2013 did the army decide to pull in other civilian law enforcement agencies, such as the Frontier Corps and the police, as well as journalists and politicians. In the 2014 show, the ordinary man was also shown as dying in terrorist attacks. The opening line of a reenactment in the show posits a sameness between the dead from the police and from the military. *Wardi ke rung mukhtalif ho saktein hain farz ke nahi* (The colors of the uniform can be different, but the colors of duty remain the same). A more inclusive event that acknowledged martyrdom for all members of the nation was an admission by the military that other lives were also being "sacrificed" in the war. This blurring of boundaries between the military and the civilian dead, however,

suggests a misleading equivalence, because the YeD/S shows hold the khaki-clad military martyr above others. The civilian dead are included in this terrain, where exaltation occurs according to militarized scripts and within parameters set by the military, but the focus remains on the military martyr. The inclusion of the civilian dead also serves to mask very real differences in the compensation accorded to them, including civilian law enforcement forces such as the police, and creates a false equivalence in the honor and tribute granted to them, even as it sets them up as an added, unintended consequence of the "real" war being fought by "real" soldiers from the military.[38]

The Policy Speech
An address by the COAS, considered the most powerful man in the country, is a traditional feature of this event. This is a space in which the COAS, having summoned media personnel, celebrities, the national government, and foreign dignitaries, speaks to the nation while standing under the literal shadow of the shuhada monument. The speeches at the first and second YeS shows were about martyrdom for religion and the state and the need for the nation to acknowledge this immense sacrifice and show support to the families. The COAS spoke of the nation and the military as one united entity, "a rista that can never end." These themes continued in subsequent speeches, but they read more like policy statements, and martyrdom and families were relegated to the beginning and end. The heart of the speeches was dedicated to governance issues such as elections, democracy, reassertion of Pakistan's sovereignty, and foreign policy, including Pakistan's relations with its neighbors. The text of the speeches was also instructive in how it referred to the war. The former escalated over the years, from soldiers dying because of terrorism to the nation going through difficult times, Pakistan being at war, and, finally, the country being in a state of total war, in which the citizenry and institutions had to collectively fight the enemy.

The military now seems confident that it has made sufficient headway in reclaiming the narrative of the shaheed so that those who died fighting other Muslims can now stand (or lie, as they are now six feet under) shoulder to shoulder with those who died fighting in wars with (Hindu) India. The major in the ISPR elaborates on this shift within the public and attributes it to the efforts of the ISPR in rebranding martyrdom: "Back in 2006 I was asked to take the dead body of a soldier home. It didn't have a head. . . . There was nobody except for the family and close relatives who wanted to come for the *janaza* (funeral). . . . I gave a motivational lecture, and some people rallied and came. On that day there was nobody to bury him, but I am sure today his grave is a shrine where people come and pray. That is how we have changed the narrative."

In 2015, the Pakistani military decided to merge the military-organized and highly affective YeS show with the earlier-instituted semimilitary YeD ceremony. What the merger achieved is the removal of even the illusion of civilian control over the war, the defense of Pakistan's borders, and Pakistan's relationship with its neighbors, all of which the YeD had hitherto portrayed. YeD shows from 2015 onward play out as slightly revised versions of the YeS format, complete with the GHQ venue, military uniforms, band, and parade. They are now purely military affairs, wherein the COAS makes a policy speech about democracy, governance, and foreign policy, while the civilian leadership and the citizenry watch and resonate carefully crafted affect.[39]

The *militarization* of civilian spaces is a maneuver by the military institution; this process is marked by the bringing of military discipline, control, and regulation into otherwise civilian, chaotic, and disorganized spaces in which a multitude of cacophonous narratives may strive for attention.[40] In YeD/S ceremonies, the maneuver is opposite, and unruly, emotional civilians are drawn into military spaces. The military incorporates civilians into these commemorative ceremonies, and these civilians participate in the reproduction of military power, an *apparent civilianization* of military events and spaces. Within these spaces, formidable but cold military strength is juxtaposed with appealing vulnerability, and militarized narratives seem less about calculated military policy or the desolation of war and more about warm, endearing, and heart-wrenching scripts for the watching nation. Here, on the hardest and most fortified of terrains—the General Headquarters of the Pakistan Army, which is the power nucleus of the country—habits of the heart are crafted.

The next chapter, in the hope of further understanding the relationship between the military and its subjects, shifts to a local terrain, a famed martial district that continues to act as a labor pool for the Pakistan Armed Forces.

CHAPTER 3

THE LAND OF THE VALIANT

IN HIS BOOK *Rusticus Loquitur, or the Old Light and the New in the Punjab Village,* Malcolm L. Darling narrates how, when on a tour of Punjab in 1929, he asked villagers why they had joined the British Indian Army.[1] He asked them to choose one of two options, each of which was simplistic but descriptive of how motivation for military service has traditionally been explained: *shauq* (interest) or *bhuq* (hunger). He reports that they said "bhuq" first and "shauq" later.

In 2015, as I met with person after person in villages in the Chakwal District in Punjab, a key recruitment area for the British Indian Army and the Pakistan Armed Forces, the response to my query about why people from the district enlist would circle around one word: *ghurbat* (poverty), followed by another phrase: *pakki naukri* (secure government service). Claims of a warrior past and of defending national honor and religion rarely came up first in these discussions, although they would come up later and were rarely missing. Three features of this comparison over time are important. The first is that not much has changed—the reasons for enlistment are largely economic, as before. Second, over the years enlistment has come to be seen as a profession—a long-term, systematic, often generational investment that may mean the difference between a life of penury and a more settled existence with the security of social welfare. Third, although my interlocutors nearly always articulated nationalistic or religious drivers, they were mentioned much later in these conversations.

In order to better understand the physical spaces and the persons who stand ready to serve and sacrifice in the Pakistan Armed Forces, I investigate the Chakwal District in this chapter by tracing patterns of relationships established during colonial times that are replayed and transformed in modern-day Pakistan.[2] The conditions that motivate people from this area to continue to invest in the military are often cited as economic desperation brought on by the constraints of geography and deepened by historical anchoring in the idea of so-called martial races. Insofar as these conditions act as foundations for the present context, there are distinct shifts that this chapter attempts to capture. These shifts lie in both the mechanics of these relationships (the actors between whom they are conducted) and how they are represented. The parameters of the relationships continue to rest on welfare and economics, yet their protagonists have morphed, and there is a weaving in of newer themes of the nation and of religion. Recruitment within the military is now obfuscated by the discourses of the nation-state that portray military service as noble and selfless. Popular rhetoric around military employment remains firmly hinged on service, welfare, and national honor and does not tilt into bhuq and ghurbat. This rhetoric is managed by a host of local paternalistic and watchful military apparatuses and by the subjects themselves, who strive to inscribe service and sacrifice for the nation on their imaginations, their bodies, and the landscape of the district.

GHOSTS OF THE PAST

Discussing the militarization of Chakwal District (previously part of Jhelum District) without glancing at history would render the story incomplete. This is not a symbolic, perfunctory nod to the past but a necessity, because the contours of the present relationship between the district and the institution of the military are tied into structural colonial antecedents.

The racist recruitment doctrine of the martial race that led to the specialization of certain districts in Punjab[3] as the labor pool for the

British Indian Army was set in motion after the Revolt of 1857.[4] Muslim soldiers from the Salt Range (the hilly part of western Punjab where Chakwal is located) had proved useful in military campaigns against the Sikhs in 1848–1849 and further proved their loyalty to the Raj during the 1857 uprising against the British. Many demonstrated their willingness to enlist because they had suffered economic hardship during Sikh rule in Punjab. For the British, whose divide-and-rule policy meant that regiments and companies were subdivided according to religion, class, and locality so they could be used against each other if a rebellion broke out, these Muslims were an effective counter to the Sikhs in the British Indian Army.[5] In the third quarter of the nineteenth century, military thinking went through another shift. The British Indian Army ceased to be conceived of as just an internal policing mechanism and began to be organized as a protective force against an attack expected from the northwest, namely Russia. The earlier divide-and-rule policy took a back seat, and recruiting available and willing fighters became the foremost concern.[6] This led to even more intensive class-specific recruitment, with intake restricted to certain races and districts. By the end of the nineteenth century, this policy was no longer a preference but a full-blown recruitment doctrine that would remain in place for the next fifty years. Various handbooks for the British Indian Army were produced during the last decades of the Raj, describing the men from these regions as possessing bravery, loyalty, and masculinity.[7] The doctrine was tweaked over time to include newer castes due to the vagaries of demands during the two world wars. Six territorial recruitment depots were set up in 1891 in the areas in which the martial races (Pathans, Punjabi Muslims, Hindu and Sikh Jats, Dogras, and the Hindu castes east of the Jumna River) were concentrated. Of these, four were in Punjab.[8] The Rawalpindi depot was reserved for recruiting Punjabi Muslims and was ideally suited for drawing men from the Salt Range, namely the districts of Jhelum, Attock, and Rawalpindi. These localized recruiting patterns also enabled the army to have close contact with the classes and districts from which it was recruiting.

Regarding the recruits themselves, in keeping with the martial race doctrine, some (mostly proponents of the martial race theory) have suggested that for certain of the so-called martial races, a readiness to pursue a vocation in arms has reflected a cultural propensity to be militarized. Although *cultural propensity* may be an essentialist term, there may be some twisted truth to it. Muslim tribes such as the Gakkars and Awans of the Salt Range were traditionally part of armies even before British rule, and this area is located at the strategic northwestern gateway to India from Central Asia that has seen an interminable onslaught of invasions.[9] Some of these tribes perceived military service as evidence of their high social status, an escape from manual labor, which they considered beneath them. Historians agree, however, that by and large what drove this region to military service as a source of livelihood was the physically broken, rain-fed terrain that made the results of agricultural activities unpredictable and led to low yields.[10] High recruitment from Punjab during colonial time is also said to be attributable to the development of colonial capitalism, which intensified the backwardness of these *barani* (rain-fed) areas.[11] The British, by legalizing the private right to absolute land ownership, deliberately created a landowning class, who they could then bargain with.[12] This economic reorganization resulted in the increased vulnerability of the peasantry and the concentration of land in the hands of a loyal class of landowners.[13] The remarkable ability of the newly created elite to meet the massive manpower demands of the war machinery in World War I is evidence of how effective the wheels of colonial capitalism were in pushing sections of Punjab's rural population toward the army.[14] Five districts of Rawalpindi division, including Jhelum (parts of which constitute today's Chakwal District), were among the eight most heavily recruited districts in Punjab, with 33 percent of the total male population of Jhelum enlisted by the end of World War I.[15]

Beyond official rhetoric, the British authorities accepted the mercenary nature of the army that served the colonial state. The British Indian Army served the British "when all is said and done, for the monthly wage, the other pecuniary wages and the pension."[16] Termed "advantageous reciprocity," the peasantry of Punjab that enlisted was rewarded by their close interaction with the British.[17] As a result, pre-partition Punjab developed as a "garrison state" that benefited enormously from British patronage in terms of pay, pensions, and land allocation.[18]

In some annals of history, Punjab is represented as the traitorous province that helped the British gain control of the subcontinent after the sepoy revolt of 1857 and then ensure its reign by virtue of being the recruitment base for the British Indian Army. Of course, this *advantageous reciprocity* between colonizer and colonized existed naturally, and it would be foolish to suggest otherwise, but a reading of this history needs to be more carefully examined through an analysis of class.[19] There were gradations among recipients in benefits earned as well as differences in how much was staked for those earnings. At one end of the spectrum, we have the ordinary tiller who was recruited. At the other end, we have notables such as Sikandar Hayat Khan in Attock and Malik Sardar Khan in Rawapindi who were appointed as recruiting officers during WWI. These "local collaborators" were rewarded for their loyalty to the Raj for enlisting men from their areas.[20] Those who stood to benefit more were primarily the local landowning intermediaries, the deliberately fortified feudal class, and *pirs* (Sufi spiritual guides), who were generously rewarded with land grants and, later, political status.[21] The creation of militarized districts in Punjab was possible because of the creation and protection of a class of landowners willing to exploit their mutually advantageous partnership with the British, with the cost paid by Punjab's rural population as a whole. Punjab's loyalty to the colonial military machinery should not be seen in the "context of modernization"; a better parallel would be "feudalism."[22] The relationship between the peasant-soldier and the army was marked by a starker imbalance of power because of the local intermediaries who served as middlemen, leaving the peasants with much less bargaining power.

It was nonetheless a symbiotic relationship that allowed benefits such as pay, pensions, status, and land allocation to trickle down to the peasants.[23] Loyalty to the colonizer on the part of troops was an essential part of this relationship. Land distribution as incentive for military service also served as a mechanism to ensure continued loyalty. Soldiers were eligible for land grants after completion of twenty-one years of service, and grants were conditional on continued loyalty of the soldier to the colonial state.[24] Correspondence between *sipahis* and their families during World War I shows that soldiers were appreciative of the government, because they knew that being "faithful to the salt of the *Sirkar*" (the government) would yield material benefits for them and their families. In one such letter, a Sikh soldier asks his wife not to worry: "Do not be anxious. If I die, you will profit greatly. For the Government will give you a pension. Why should you worry? If I live, then Government will give us still more."[25] The incentives or rewards offered to the soldier were couched in a language of welfare and assistance, handouts by a benevolent state that was protective of its loyal subjects who had served in its military. The military was the *maa baap* (mother-father, or all in all)[26]—a paternalistic entity that gives generously and in return expects loyalty and gratefulness, as opposed to a professional institution that must provide for its soldiers in return for services rendered.

The integration of the functions of the military and the civil authorities through the emergence of the District Soldiers Boards (DSBs) was an important feature that enabled the successful mobilization of men during World War I. DSBs were set up by the colonial state to offset rising discontent among demobilized troops because of allegedly unfulfilled promises of land grants after the war.[27] Economic adversity as a result of wartime controls, inadequate monsoon rains at the end of the war, and deepening political unrest as a result of growing nationalist movements in the rest of the country all aroused intense trepidation in the British state that the loyalty of the martial districts could be affected. It was vital for the British that the recruitment bases remained pacified and inoculated against subversion or disaffection. To ensure continued loyalty, the DSBs were introduced at the district level, as this was considered a place at which the soldier's loyalty could be won or lost. Over the years these welfare organizations for war veterans developed into local institutions that safeguarded the interests of the military and those who served in it.[28]

Over time, these districts became specialized zones for recruitment,

FIGURE 2. *A commemorative plaque placed in Chakwal by the British government in India. (Photo taken by author.)*

in which livelihood was reduced to one major activity: military service. In addition to economic desperation, "the cultural effect of military specialization in the barani areas reproduced self-valorization of its population as a military class," and military service assumed a "'natural' order, becoming intertwined with the regularities and habits of rural life" (emphasis in original).[29] Mustapha Kamal Pasha suggests that these barani areas became locked in a codependent relationship with the colonial state in which the state relied on these areas to ensure its survival and in which these areas, as suppliers of military labor, relied on the state to survive. Another effect of the specialization of these areas as a labor market for the military lay in exactly how the paternalistic state asserted itself by uniting its military and civil functions and ruling through a militarized bureaucracy, that is, in the emergence of the DSBs. These institutional mechanisms brought the caring *sarkar* down to the local level in ways that blurred the lines between the civil and the military. The tone of these relationships between the colonial state and its subjects had profound consequences for the relationship that emerged between soldiers and the military institution in the postcolonial state of Pakistan.

RECRUITMENT IN THE POST-COLONY

At the time of partition, Punjabi preponderance stood at 80 percent in the military[30] and 55 percent in the bureaucracy.[31] Colonial economic structures remained intact, and newer exploitative groups, such as the indigenous bourgeoisie, were added, in the guise of industrial development, to the feudal baggage that Pakistan inherited.[32] This alliance further strengthened during the Cold War, when Pakistan chose to become a client state of the United States.[33] In its early years, Pakistan was led by a Punjabi-dominated, pro-West, anticommunist group of politicians and bureaucrats, with military leaders actively involved in and eventually leading this trajectory.[34] It should come as little surprise that the first budget to be announced pledged a massive amount (over 65 percent) of the central government's total revenue to the Pakistan Armed Forces, a trend that has continued with little variation, to the detriment of the country's social, industrial, and economic development.[35]

The Pakistan Army is a volunteer force, as per Article 39 (Participation of People in Armed Forces) of the 1973 constitution. The composition of the Pakistan Army is largely Punjabi, with Pashtuns in second place; this ethnic domination is reflective of the British Army's martial races policies. Recruitment patterns after partition remained largely localized for a considerable time in key districts in Punjab (Chakwal, Jhelum, Attock, Rawalpindi, and some surrounding areas) along with martial districts from Khyber Pakhtunkhwa (KP), although the spread within Punjab and KP did expand.[36] Until 2001, 71 percent of the Pakistan Army's manpower came from Punjab.[37]

The Pakistan Army Act of 1952 states that compulsory conscription can be introduced, although the army has never needed to do so. This is unlike the route many postcolonial states have taken, in which nationalist governments have emphasized representativeness and citizenship through mandatory military service. One simple reason for this may be that the army receives more applications each year than it needs to fill its ranks.[38] In response to the question of why people from martial districts enlist, the army officers I interviewed almost unequivocally mentioned widespread unemployment, rain-fed terrain, and the exposure of the area to military service over several decades. There seemed to be no mystery to solve here, an open understanding that it was sheer economic desperation and a lack of other viable, secure forms of employment that drove people to the long lines at the recruitment and selection centers in these districts. These factors have ensured a steady stream of potential recruits who want to join, believing that this is their best possible shot at pakki naukri based on their historical advantage of generational service to the military.

Reluctance to introduce conscription or expand army recruitment to other areas has also been attributed to a deliberate intent on the part of the postcolonial military-bureaucratic oligarchy to continue with the Punjabi-dominated profile of the military. This "hangover of the martial race theory" is ascribed to a number of factors, the most significant of which is the obvious strategic benefit to the Punjabi-dominated ruling class that Pakistan inherited.[39] Another reason cited is tactical advantage; in Pakistan's early years the practice allowed the army to ensure that various ethnonationalist insurgencies in Baluchistan, Sindh, and KP could be handled without conflict of interest.[40] Of course, the fact that many of these nationalist struggles are rooted partly in anger against unfair treatment, including inadequate representation in military recruitment, by the Punjabi-dominated establishment at the center suggests that this tactical logic is somewhat counterproductive.[41]

SUSTAINING THE (OLD) MARTIAL

The Armed Forces of Pakistan are one of the largest employers of underemployed labor in Pakistan. The pay, pension, and welfare schemes (education, health, and housing facilities) offered by the military to its officers and enlisted personnel continue to be by far the most comprehensive provided by any large public-sector employer in Pakistan.[42] These services extend not just to men in service but also to their families and to ex-soldiers and their families. Using the same recruitment pool for almost all of the first fifty years of its postcolonial existence has enabled the military to establish enduring roots in thousands of villages in Punjab, especially in the Salt Range. Pay and pensions form the bulk of many village incomes, and military service represents a bulwark against destitution, providing stability and social security. Within martial districts there is also considerable valence and prestige associated with military service, especially at the local district and village levels. The military's domination of the labor market in these districts should therefore come as no surprise.

In addition to pay and pensions, two other types of benefits are particularly important to highlight, as they cause the most discontent in the classes not recruited for military service. The first is the urban and rural landholdings given to ex-servicemen, both soldiers and officers. The second are the benefits accrued from the military's extensive industrial holdings that serve retired soldiers and their families. One of these is the Fauji Foundation, discussed here because of its strong presence within districts.[43] In 1954, the British Military Post-War Reconstruction Fund, intended for soldiers who had fought in World War II, was invested by the Pakistani military in commercial ventures with the aim of using its profits to support ex-servicemen. Renamed the Fauji Foundation in 1967, it has become the largest military-owned business conglomerate with commercial and welfare wings. It offers health, educational, and vocational services to families of ex-servicemen, including the families of those killed or disabled in war, and assists them in finding jobs, mostly with its numerous businesses, including cereal companies, farms, and factories producing cement, petroleum, and fertilizers, to name a few.[44]

Two other institutions—District Armed Services Boards (DASBs) and Army Selection and Recruitment offices and centers within districts—serve as facilitative bodies for district populations. Their visible presence in districts and their extensive network allows the institution of the military to establish deep roots in local spaces. Across the nation, there are twenty-seven Pakistan Army Selection and Recruitment offices and centers, which open for recruitment twice a year. There are ten in Punjab, five in Sindh, five in Baluchistan, four in KP, two in Azad Jammu and Kashmir (AJK), and one in Gilgit Baltistan (GB).[45]

After partition, the DSBs set up in martial areas were renamed District Armed Services Boards (DASBs). As the membership of the military expanded to other districts and provinces, the number of boards was increased. There are now twenty-six in Punjab, thirteen in KP, eight in Sindh, two in Baluchistan, three in GB, and ten in AJK, for a total of sixty-two DASBs across the country.[46] The district commissioner heads the district board, but the board's functions are run by the secretary of the board, an ex-military officer. A further body of welfare officers, ex-NCOs, and JCOs act as honorary welfare officers (WOs) at the DASB level to ensure that facilitation reaches every village in the district. The WOs maintain records of ex-servicemen in the area and assist regiment centers in verifying information needed to provide welfare to ex-servicemen. They help families prepare documentation for claiming pensions, benevolent funds, and other compensation as well as arbitrate disputes between family members about compensation and pensions. They also facilitate the reemployment of ex-servicemen in the public sector by military-affiliated groups such as the Fauji Foundation and by private companies. An annual general meeting organized by the DASB and presided over by the district commissioner brings together WOs and heads of district departments such as education, health, and forestry. This forum allows WOs to put forward suggestions for the development of their area.[47] The DASBs are important local mechanisms that use civil machinery for the benefit of those who serve in the army as well as their dependents. These organizations form a bridge between the civil and military machinery, ostensibly serving as an arm of the civil machinery but acting fairly independently by virtue of the nature of their services and their direct links to the GHQ, regimental centers, and units. The DASBs continue to carry out their earlier functions, acting as localized doorstep welfare systems that ex-servicemen and their dependents can count on and make claims to.

The Pakistan Armed Forces is modeled along modern meritocratic lines, with opportunities for upward mobility in terms of class and socioeconomic status.[48] Anatol Lieven suggests that the military in Pakistan is exceptional in being the only state institution that is not plagued by traditional kinship loyalties, patronage politics, or ethnic or religious divisions. He proposes that over the years the relationship between the military and its soldiers has come to be based on ideas of collective defense, much like a kinship group. The Pakistani military meets two essential criteria of kinship groups: (1) the ability to look after and protect the interests of the group and (2) affective investment in the group through ideas of honor and prestige.[49] The institution of the military can demand this loyalty because of the unparalleled economic benefits it offers, not as payment for service but as paternalistic welfare assistance garbed in robes of honor and collective solidarity. Entry into military service is a desire for membership in an institution that protects you from the vicissitudes of life that are your fate in a state perceived as predatory and as failing to fulfill its promises on social justice and welfare. Ironically, the reasons for the military's immunity to kinship demands lie in its ability to extract a large share of resources from the Pakistani state, often to the detriment of other institutions of the state. This ability enables it to function as a kinship group itself, extracting patronage from the state and distributing it to its own members.

CULTIVATING THE (NEW) MARTIAL

In the late 1990s, the Pakistani military made concerted efforts to move away from recruitment in martial areas and toward a more nationally representative force. Tracing this trajectory of the army's recruitment policies lays bare for inspection the politics that drives them and the processes involved in cultivating new districts for service.

Recruitment policies for the soldier class of the Pakistan Army can be divided into three broad phases. The first phase, immediately after partition, was most clearly marked by the martial race hangover as British-trained native officers, who came from the martial regions, continued British policies. The districts' long association with the military meant that inductees from these areas were halfway to being soldiers already.[50] They were willing *volunteers* who met the immediate demands of the Pakistani military as it struggled to fill the insufficient force it had inherited after partition.[51] The army's regiments were mostly pure, meaning that their soldiers and officers were of broadly the same ethnic origin, because most of their members were drawn from the same localized recruiting pools created by the British. The three large infantry regiments—Punjab, Frontier Force, and Baluch—were comprised mostly of Punjabis, with Pashtuns in second. After the 1965 war, the smaller East Bengal Regiment, formed after partition, was upgraded, and there was some increase in induction from East Pakistan.

After 1971, the clamor against Punjabi domination of the military increased, intensifying further in 1973 when Prime Minister Zulfiqar Ali Bhutto called in the Pakistani military to settle the insurgency in Baluchistan. This marks the beginning of the second phase, featuring some movement toward the encouragement of induction from Sindh and Baluchistan.[52] The predominant groups represented remained Punjabi and Pashtun, albeit from a wider net in Punjab. The Sindh Infantry Regiment was raised by General Zia in 1980 partly to offset the popularity of Zulfiqar Ali Bhutto. The opportunity for recruitment into the army was used to win support in areas that were resentful of a Punjabi-dominated military. Around this time, regiments stopped being pure. This move was largely due to lessons learned from the Bangladesh debacle, when pure Bengali units mutinied against West Pakistan. The shift toward more ethnically mixed regiments was sluggish, and although men from these provinces were encouraged to apply, no serious quotas were set. Recruitment happened largely via mobilization teams working through local schools and mosques rather than through local institutional apparatuses such as the recruitment centers scattered strategically across Punjab, although some centers were set up in these provinces. The number of Sindhis and Baluchis did increase, but that also included sons of Punjabi ex-servicemen who had settled on land given to them by the army in Sindh and Baluchistan.[53]

The third phase, which started in the late 1990s, saw the Pakistani military move away from geographic and ethnic localization toward a more nationally integrated force.[54] Since then, the Pakistan Army has claimed to follow a specific policy of broadening its recruitment base, and it put forward a recruitment plan to not just encourage but ensure recruitment from Sindh and Baluchistan as well as increase minority recruitment.[55] District quotas for induction for the soldier class are based on male population figures from the 1998 census.[56] Induction numbers are derived from yearly rates of *wastage*, a term used by the GHQ to refer to soldiers lost due to death, injury, desertion, or retirement. The Personnel Administration (PA) Directorate at the GHQ claims that whereas provincial quotas are fixed, district quotas can be shifted if district targets are not met. A fall in recruitment from Punjab, from 63.86 percent in 1991 to 43.33 percent in 2005, was accompanied by a corresponding rise from all other areas of Pakistan. Furthermore, in 2005, central Punjab had a higher recruitment rate (7,500) than did northern Punjab (5,000), where the martial districts are located.[57]

Opening up recruitment does not immediately translate into long lines at the army's door. The soldier class has traditionally been rural, and in many of the newer provinces educational qualifications were not sufficient to meet the selection criteria. Furthermore, military discipline and service—which came so easily to those in Punjab—seemed alien in these newer terrains, and many young men were hesitant to enlist. For those that did join, the dropout rate remained high. Over the years, recruitment from less-represented areas has increased only gradually. This expansion has been made possible by relaxing criteria, easing accessibility issues by adding more recruitment and selection centers, and sending recruitment teams to districts less amenable to military service. The military has also invested in efforts to reach out to these areas, largely through long-term measures such as cadet schools and colleges, hospitals, regiment centers, and military cantonments. In this way, they hope to establish a visible presence and build trust with local populations. Unlike the British, the military in these provinces does not rely only on local feudal leadership—some of which may actually lean toward support of the ethnonationalist struggles that the state actively suppresses. Instead, it relies on its own considerable resources and network of auxiliary organizations to slowly increase military valence within the area. This is not to suggest that economic backwardness is not an important motivating factor. As a colonel from the Army Selection and Recruitment Center, Rawalpindi, remarked, "The situation in some of these areas [backward parts of Baluchistan] is dire, and I have seen soldiers cry when they receive their first pay, as they have never seen so much money."

The move toward a nationally integrated army is ostensibly an acknowledgment that it no longer serves the military to draw from only one or two provinces. While this acknowledgment might be couched in the language of national integration and the right to serve, it also translates into extending military patronage to other parts of Pakistan, to districts and provinces that did not benefit from the job opportunities and extensive welfare system that the military offers its employees. This extension of patronage to a wider group garners more support and loyalty for the institution and also addresses the criticism that the military is Punjabi dominated. Continued success in developing areas amenable to military service depends on a blend of providing economic incentives and embedding a positive image of the military. Material incentives on their own are not sufficient inducements; motivation to enlist is also filtered through the crafting of paternalistic ties between these districts and the institution of the military, which builds a presence through investment in infrastructure and services. Over the years this develops into a relationship of patronage that can be hard to dislodge, which the colonel from the Army Selection and Recruitment Center likened to a *chaska*, an addiction that is hard to let go of once tasted. Ensuring loyalty from these nonmartial classes may turn out not be such a huge obstacle, as paternalistic bonds and relationships continue to strengthen over time. But expanding the recruitment pool to the rest of the country poses a challenge for the military in terms of how it will meet the costlier demands for welfare and surveillance in areas that are no longer geographically concentrated.

LIVING IN THE "LAND OF THE VALIANT"

General Zia-ul Haq, who came to power in Pakistan's second military coup, upgraded Chakwal to district status in 1985 by combining parts of Jhelum District with a *tehsil* (administrative subdivision of a district) from Attock District. Chakwal District, lying in the northern parts of Punjab, forms part of the Salt Range and the Potohar Plateau, which are characterized by uneven terrain, large deposits of rock salt in the soil, and uncertain rainfall. The Salt Range is situated between the valleys of the Indus and Jhelum Rivers. Its terrain, covered with scrub forest in the southwest and featuring plains interrupted by dry rock in the north and northeast, has been described as "a confused medley of hillock and hollow."[58] This district is in a barani area, and 96 percent of agricultural demand for water is met by rainwater.[59] As a result, there is limited land for cultivation, and it is agriculturally insecure even in areas in which agricultural activities are carried out. Agricultural land holdings are typically small, and the district's primary reliance is on service in the armed forces (army, air force, or navy) and civilian law enforcement, including the police. The Pakistan Army is the largest employer among these, followed by the air force. Other sectors that provide some employment in the district are mining, transport, and poultry. A growing employment trend has been migration as unskilled labor to the Gulf States and Saudi Arabia. Chakwal's rural population is among the highest in Punjab, with over 81 percent of its people residing in rural settings. Its population has grown from 1,083,725, according to the 1998 census, to 1,495,982 today.[60] It has a relatively high adult literacy rate of over 73 percent, among the highest in Punjab.[61] Chakwal has seventy-one Basic Health Units (BHUs), nine Rural Health Centres (RHCs), eight dispensaries, and six government hospitals.[62]

North Punjab[63] includes four of the region's traditional military recruitment areas: Chakwal, Rawalpindi, Jhelum, and Attock. It has the fewest registered factories and the fewest adults who report daily labor as their primary occupation. It has the highest number of concrete houses, the highest figure for remittances as a proportion of total household income, the largest proportion of houses reporting migrant labor,

FIGURE 3. *A signboard marking the entrance to Chakwal city. (Photo taken by author.)*

and the greatest percentage of the working-age population employed by government.[64] The number of those who have completed matric (the basic educational criterion for entrance into the armed forces) is also the highest. Households in North Punjab are integrated into the national and international labor market, and as a result the North fares better than other regions in Punjab despite low industrialization and its inherent dependence on rain-fed agriculture.[65] It can well be argued that these statistics partly reflect the cumulative impact of years of acting as a recruitment base for the armed forces. It also highlights the district's willingness to search outside its borders for employment as well as an inability to find secure local employment, a socialization that has been honed over years of service in the military.

Chakwal has two National Assembly and four provincial assembly seats and is considered a pro-Pakistan Muslim League–Nawaz area. Chakwal's political landscape is complex, and it is claimed that the hold of the local Shia feudal landlords has lessened over time. This is due in part to the rise of the Sunni middle class, aided by remittances coming from abroad, the rising influence of religious-political Sunni parties, and a new political elite with military roots.[66] General Majeed Malik, Ret., who served in World War II under the British Indian Army, controlled one of the National Assembly seats through five general elections starting in 1985, defeating Sardar Ghulam Abbas, a key Shia political rival and an important landlord. In 2002, graduation from university became a mandatory educational qualification for National Assembly members, and Malik retired from active politics. His nephew, Major Rao Tahir, Ret., has won the same seat in subsequent elections, though, except in 2007, when a power-sharing agreement led to the retired general backing another politician.[67]

Because of its large military class, a sizeable portion of the district's development has been linked to senior military officers who have carried out development work in their own villages during their service or after retirement. Some of these projects have been private efforts only partly subsidized by the military, such as the setting up of schools, colleges, and hospitals. Others have been district development projects, funds for which have come from provincial and district governments. Military generals have facilitated the construction of roads or the supply of gas to their villages and often also to villages along the way. This development work is not carried out by ex-army officers acting as elected officials but by former or serving senior military officers who use their influence over the civil machinery.[68] Although it may not be accurate to suggest that the demand to establish Chakwal District materialized only as a result of military patronage, it is a fact that the district was approved by General Zia, with active lobbying from a retired general from the area, Majeed Malik, at a time when the governor of Punjab was also a general—General Ghulam Jillani, Ret.

The Fauji Foundation's welfare projects in Chakwal include hospitals, dispensaries, vocational and technical training centers, and schools and colleges. The foundation estimates its beneficiary population within the district to be close to 709,176. In 2013 and 2014, as many as 67,857 of these beneficiaries accessed health projects run by the Fauji Foundation. As of March 2015, close to 3,000 ex-servicemen and their next of kin were employed in the Fauji Foundation's various projects in the district.[69]

Chakwal has its own Category A[70] DASB, which was set up in 1988, three years after the district was formed. It facilitates pensioners in the district, including mothers and widows, and has a total of sixty-eight WOs for Chakwal's more than seventy union councils (administrative subdivision of a tehsil). An additional office in Talagang Tehsil, an administrative unit of Chakwal District, handles the higher number of pensioners in that area. The Selection Recruitment Office (SRO) in Chakwal was established in 2013 because the Jhelum office was having a hard time maintaining discipline and handling the large number of applications received from both Jhelum and Chakwal Districts.

The Fauji Foundation's programs, DASBs, and SRO in Chakwal serve as local, accessible mini versions of the military institution, especially for the extended military family—the dependents of the soldier class—in these local spaces. These are friendly reminders that the institution is invested in the district and will continue to provide it with patronage. To some extent this is the same purpose served by DSBs in colonial times, yet relationships have shifted.

LOCAL RECRUITMENT POLITICS

Intake from Chakwal is 4 percent of the national total, a ratio assigned based on the National Integration Policy announced by the adjutant general of the Pakistan military in 2001. This ratio was calculated from male population projections from the 1998 census.[71]

The data in table 1 was provided by the PA Directorate at the GHQ and shows that Chakwal's contribution ranged from 3 percent to 5.6 percent of the total intake over the ten-year period from 2004 to 2013. There are two intakes every year, one in October/November—a more popular season, as it coincides with the results of the matriculation exams (the ten-year school certification, which is the minimum

TABLE 1. *Pakistan Army Induction Figures, 2004–2013.*

Year	Applications registered	Actual inductions	Inductions from Chakwal
2004	178,974	33,152	1,330
2005	153,917	37,355	1,587
2006	113,632	41,343	1,903
2007	80,765	30,665	1,719
2008	77,246	38,238	2,093
2009	117,678	56,243	2,494
2010	139,518	53,804	2,099
2011	143,940	27,133	861
2012	166,530	37,529	1,248
2013	146,320	21,041	650

Source: Personnel Administration (PA) Directorate, GHQ.

qualification for entry)—and one in April/May, for which applicant numbers are lower, because many aspiring candidates work as farm labor during the reaping season that falls during these months. Police service inductions around the same time also contribute to lower turnout during this intake. Although cognizant of this, the major in charge of the SRO at Chakwal feels no great trepidation regarding target numbers, because according to him, an average of 7,000 to 9,000 apply each year, of which the total intake will be between 650 and 2,494 (the lowest and highest intake figures for Chakwal in 2013 and 2009, respectively, during the ten-year period). The intake numbers peaked in 2007 and 2008, with 5.6 percent and 5.5 percent of the total, while there was a corresponding decrease in the number of applicants nationwide. As noted earlier, district quotas can be adjusted within provinces, which suggests that Chakwal's willingness to line up outside the recruitment center serves as a backup in case the need for recruits is not met elsewhere. On the whole, however, there has been a steady decline in selected recruits from Chakwal, with only 650 men (3 percent of the total) chosen in 2013. The recruitment process is a stepwise multiple-hurdle model, with applicants screened out at each stage, which includes a medical examination and a battery of physical, intelligence, and personality tests. An official notification in the city's newspapers announces the commencement of induction; this notification is accompanied by banners announcing the opening dates. A two-to-three-week registration process follows, in which the hundreds of applicants who line up every day are screened for basic eligibility criteria such as education, domicile, and, if applicable, their father's military discharge papers. A special column allows the person applying to state whether he is the next of kin of a *shaheed* (martyr). Approximately 60 percent make it to the next stage—a physical examination.

Large posters on the veranda where these boys wait before going in for the physical exam display various physical deformities that would make them ineligible. Boys can be rejected at this stage due to their height or chest measurements falling below standards or for having knock-knee, flat feet, poor muscle development, color blindness, a depressed chest, spot baldness, or leukoderma. This last ailment is a skin disorder with no apparent manifestation other than a discoloring of the skin. The major in charge of the SRO at Chakwal informed me with a shrug of his shoulders, "The men need to look smart; a person with leukoderma is disfigured, so if I have so much choice, why not? I can pick the best of the best." According to the army physician in charge of the physical exam, the rejection rate at this stage is almost 50 percent, because many of these boys are undernourished and have been exposed to hard manual labor in the fields during their developmental years.

The twelve applicants that I interviewed during an intake at the Chakwal SRO offer a glimpse of how the district and its aspiring recruits view enlistment. Most were from families with male members who had served in the military. There was a mix of sentiments. Many seemed determined to get in, and some were applying for the second or third time (the military allows them to reapply provided they are under twenty three). Others were there to placate anxious parents who wanted them to apply and try at least once to get into the army. This rang true based on my experience in these villages, because it was rare to meet a male who met the army's minimum educational criteria and who had not at some point applied to the armed forces. Pressure often comes from parents, particularly fathers who have served in the military, and it seems the older generation is more invested in continuing with the area's specialization in this type of labor. As one young man wryly put it, "In our village, when a child is born, the village *maulvi* [local cleric] gives *azan* in one ear [a ritual that involves the Islamic call to prayer being whispered in the ear of the newborn, marking the child as Muslim], and in the other the mother and father whisper, 'Son, grow up and become a *fauji* [military man].'"

Akmal is a thin eighteen-year-old boy who was slightly nonplussed by my presence in a bustling male-only recruitment office. A far cry from the somewhat scruffy young men I had seen in the villages I had been visiting, he has slicked-back hair, and his beige *shalwar kameez* (traditional dress consisting of a long shirt over loose trousers) is crisply ironed. He has been here since eight o'clock in the morning, and the midday heat of the May sun is making him perspire profusely as he stands in line waiting to be called out for his medical exam. He informs me that he has come from Choa Saidaan Shah, Tehsil, in Chakwal District and that his paternal uncle and a cousin had served in the army before him.

> Me: How many of you applied from your class?
> Akmal: We were sixty, out of which thirty passed, and about twenty-one of us have applied.
> Me: Why do people from this area apply?
> Akmal: We want a bright future, and we also want to serve the country. If something happens to us, then our families, brothers, and sisters will benefit. Whether we serve or die, we get a pension, medical coverage. If we talk about civilians, they are not serving the nation in the same way we do. They are thinking of their own selves, like you doing your research; you are thinking about yourself.
> Me: Those in the *fauj* [military] don't think about their own selves?
> Akmal: No, the fauji is not thinking about himself; he is handing himself over to the fauj, he is serving his country, and he is serving his family.

Oddly reminiscent of the letter cited earlier from the Sikh soldier in the British Indian Army, Akmal says that the military is a benevolent institution that you can risk your life for because it looks after the family, and dying and living can mean the same thing in some ways. Yet what Akmal suggests is also different: the applicant now also looks on the army as a "bright" career path, a path of sacrifice that is superior to the selfish civilian way of life. He creates a dichotomy between civilian and army ways.

These relationships are set within the same paternalistic frames as in colonial times, when the sarkar was looked on as a benevolent caregiver who would look after the sipahi. But they also stand apart from one another in two ways. First, in colonial times, loyalties and bonds with tribal kinship groups remained strong despite enlistment in the military, because enlistment itself was bound up with membership in these kinship groups. The Pakistani military is not a foreign force that needs local intermediaries, and moreover, years of sustained contact with these districts through institutional apparatuses that have direct local outreach have to a large extent made this intermediary redundant. Earlier military recruitment at the village level was looked on as a kinship privilege. A family or *biraderi* (extended clan) member who was ex-army personnel would encourage younger men in his clan to show up on recruitment day at the recruitment center or would accompany them directly to the regiment center to which he himself was attached and in which he could ensure entry. Mobile teams would also visit village schools and mosques, and potential recruits would be encouraged to visit the nearest recruitment center for qualifying tests and such. With the announcement of stringent district quotas and with the centralization of selection at the GHQ level, the recruitment process has become more streamlined. As a result, the role of local influential people (including ex-military officers and soldiers) has declined. Despite this, pressure from civilian feudal landowners and politicians is a common feature in military recruitment and the settlement of disputes around military compensation. This is hardly surprising in the national context, in which patronage politics is part and parcel of daily bureaucratic functioning. What is more significant is how pressure is regarded by military officers in charge of recruitment. When pressure and influence were considered stressful and also impacted decision making to some extent, these local influential persons were mentioned as encumbrances, not facilitators. These groups no longer act as intermediaries as they did in the time of British rule. Their position seems to have shifted from being an important, previously respected link in the chain, needed to ensure the ongoing supply of men, to a nuisance that creates obstacles in the smooth performance of functions. As the recruitment systems have become more formalized and criteria driven, the *sifarish* (nonofficial recommendation) that comes from ex-servicemen—both the officer class and JCOs who have access to the senior officers with whom they have served—still holds weight.[72] The institution is increasingly insulated from civilian pressure but is vulnerable to pressures from within. As suggested earlier, the military acts as a kinship group, in which favors and patronage are given to its members in a perpetuating fashion. It provides patronage and protection directly to its constituents and increasingly regards local politicians and influentials as encumbrances.

Second, unlike in colonial times when loyalty was tied to the sarkar, in the former colony this bond is with the institution of the military, which can at times be locked in a power struggle with the government. In Pakistan, with its history of three distinct military coups and of military interference in politics and civilian affairs even during times when power rests with the civilian establishment, the sarkar is no longer perceived as an uncomplicated singular category. Instead, the fauj and the *hakumat* (government) are often viewed as two distinct entities. The contention this situation causes is highlighted through an analysis of the discussions about the opening of an exclusive SRO in Chakwal. This move was welcomed by the district at large, because it saves applicants the expense of repeated visits to the SRO in Jhelum. There was some competition, though, between the district's civil administration and local military representatives over who would take credit for bringing the recruitment office to the district. This speaks to the dynamic in the district, in which facilitation of recruitment from the district is a way to score points with the population, an indication of the district's strong valence toward military recruitment. The competition also clearly points to how the sarkar is no longer seen as a mono-

FIGURE 4. *The* Yadgar-e-Shuhada *(Martyrs' Memorial) in Chakwal City. (Photo taken by author.)*

lithic category in present-day Chakwal, where the military establishment is seen as distinct from and sometimes in competition with the civil administration. This is more pronounced among the military class in the district: soldiers, ex-soldiers, and families. They refer to *hakumati* (governmental) policies versus fauji (military) policies and to hakumati modes of working (defined as incompetent or often corrupt) and military discipline (defined as efficient and fair) as distinct and sometimes incompatible.

Over the years, with continued direct and indirect military rule and the continued accessibility of systematic welfare schemes through local military institutions integrated with bureaucratic machinery, the association between the military and the soldier class has shifted. It is now a direct relationship, with the military as a group standing apart from the government, often without the presence of the traditional local feudal leadership. The soldier in Chakwal enters into a social contract with the military, and it is to this entity that his loyalty is tied, sometimes over and above loyalty to the civilian government, which is often viewed in pejorative terms.

INSCRIBING SERVICE AND SACRIFICE

A hundred and fifty years and more of steady specialization as military labor have produced a district that pronounces itself the embodiment of all that is martial. The entrance to Chakwal City, the main city in Chakwal District, is marked by a dark wooden structure made of thick planks displaying its martial legacy in large shiny silver letters: "Well Come [sic] to Chakwal City, The Land of the Valiant." It is a district that has served both the colonial state and the national state, and it has sacrificed the blood of its loved ones for both. The sacrifices are visible in the graveyards that dot the rural countryside marked by the national flag, and on tombstones with regimental plaques and colors and white stone edifices left by the British sarkar that state the number of men who went from a particular village to the world wars as well as the number of those who did not return. Independence Day celebrations and other national commemorative events in Chakwal celebrate the district's martial identity and honor the sacrifice and service of the district's men in the various armed forces. Parents of martyrs will often be invited to these events, and local school children will be asked to prepare speeches or stage plays on the same themes. Vernacular literature, some written by former military servicemen in Chakwal, also pays homage to the district's military service. Service is visible in the new *Yadgar-e-Shuhada* (Martyrs' Memorial) monument on Chakwal's main thoroughfare, in an old fighter plane installed by civil society in a public park with support from the district government, and in references made to military service and sacrifice on national days and during trade and cultural events in the district.

As a district of the martial belt, Chakwal continues to fashion its imagining around its martial traditions, even as newer narratives of

FIGURE 5. *A poster installed for* Chakwal Mega Family Festival, *April 2015. (Photo taken by author.)*

identity creep in. These narratives intersect and sometimes conflict with each other, and structures of power in communities compete for new articulations of identity. Examples include an increasingly urbanized village life, exposure to consumer culture and lifestyles that make military discipline less appealing, claims from rival militant religious groups that may be in contention with the state, and competing employment opportunities as migrant unskilled labor in the Gulf States and Saudi Arabia. Steady remittances from abroad have translated into upward mobility for a rising middle class. The shifts in fortunes of these families are more pronounced because the improvement in lifestyle happens faster than the investment in service. This change is also conspicuous because migrant work in the Gulf and in Saudi Arabia involves manual labor and so was initially regarded as demeaning. Hence, those willing to venture abroad were from the poorer, nonlandholding classes. Despite these trends, the military's continued ability to draw long lines at the recruitment centers suggests that the valence around military service in Chakwal continues.

The gradual unlocking of the relationship between the district and the military institution, as the military reduces quotas from these districts and turns to the new national integration policy, has given rise to anxiety and resentment among the district's residents. This is especially true of its rural base, which continues to depend heavily on employment in the military for its livelihood. As a retired havildar bemoaned to me, "Our area has been in service for a long time. War is our livelihood. The army has brought prosperity; it has brought in a regular monthly income. . . . Now people don't get service in the army. . . . The army is taking from everywhere now; Chakwal is no longer that important." In a similar vein, another retired officer from the Pakistan Air Force, frustrated by his son's inability to enter military service, recounts:

> One of the problems now is caste, this Sindhi, Balouchi, Pathan, and Punjabi. Our people [from Chakwal] face a number of difficulties because of this. A Sindhi gets in, he is primary [educated up to class five]; a Punjabi goes [to the recruitment center], he is FA or even BA [high school or graduate degree], but the Sindhi gets in because there is a vacancy in the Sindh quota. The poor Punjabi is left holding the degree in his hand; his space has been taken up by this uneducated boy. . . . The policy is okay—it is everybody's right to serve—but they should set vacancies looking at areas' needs and resources.

Residents of Chakwal clearly feel resentment about what is perceived as unfair treatment of Punjabis. They see themselves as more suited to serve based on higher literacy rates, a track record of having served in the military, and lower rates of industrialization and other employment opportunities in their area. A retired subedar is of the view that people from Chakwal see military service as their "*muraba* and *saanat*" (land and industry), and they feel justified in staking the first claim to it over and above other parts of Punjab and Pakistan that possess irrigated land or developed industrial zones. Dissatisfaction is also expressed at the centralization of the recruitment process. The recruitment system demands that after selection, names are sent to the GHQ, which then finalizes entrants. According to the PA Directorate at the GHQ, this allows them to fine-tune lists based on their current induction requirements and to keep a strict check on unfair recruitment practices at the district level. For the district, this translates into a reduction in their ability to use their local patronage systems—local influentials and ex-army servicemen—who before this centralization were in a better position to influence the final selection. By and large, the district perceives that these final lists are not always based on merit but are influenced by those who have better contacts in the military itself, something that is out of reach for many. Some are still able to utilize loopholes, such as direct intake at the regimental level, which they access through servicemen in their area. Army regiment centers are also mandated to take in recruits for the army soldier class, a parallel system of induction through which regimental centers can recruit independently. According to the army recruitment officer in the district, this preoccupation with sifarish, or unfair use of contacts, is reflective of the district's response to reduced quotas. He suggests that many feel they are being cheated out of what they believe is their birthright, an entitlement to military service.

In response to this loosening of ties, the district holds on to its martial contribution tenaciously, unwilling to let go. The district residents feel a sense of frustration at their paternalistic master yet are loath to confront it. This anxiety and resentment expresses itself through an assertion of the district's martial history, which residents hope will remind the military institution of the district's contributions and sacrifices. The white marble memorial called Yadgar-e-Shuhada was installed in the city's thoroughfare by the district government in 2015 to show support for the armed forces and its contributions to the war in northwest Pakistan. In the third week of December 2014, the Chakwal District government inaugurated the Allied Bank Park. The park is centrally located in Chakwal and is a short distance away from the now defunct railway station built during colonial times. It displays a decommissioned air force plane donated by the Pakistan Air Force as an acknowledgement of Chakwal's *askari khidmaat* (military services). A retired squadron leader and a Pakistan Air Force chief technician from a

FIGURE 6. *The* Allied Bank Park *in Chakwal. (Photo taken by author.)*

nearby village (who, along with a number of retired army servicemen, runs a welfare and development foundation) initiated this idea. On their initiative, a request was made to the Air Headquarters in Islamabad. The district government was initially not as forthcoming with funds, but after some local media lobbying, it supported the installation and donated money for it.

The inauguration ceremony was endorsed by the local civil machinery, politicians, the business community, and the ex-military elite in the area, and it was covered extensively in the local media. The headline inscribed on the banner for the event read, "For the People of Chakwal, the Land of Martyrs and Warriors." The banner was decorated with pictures of senior officers from Chakwal, including Sepoy Khudadad Khan, a resident of Chakwal who was the first Indian Army recipient of the Victoria Cross during World War I. The retired squadron leader explains the importance of this monument.

> We have served the country; we call this a martial area, but there is no sign that marks it. In the time of the British, they asked the soldier, "What do you want?" They said, "We want a cannon," so they installed a cannon in their village. . . .[73] This [plane] is not a decoration piece only; there is a cause behind it. Chakwal needs to be recognized. If a person enters the city, he should know that this is the area that loves the armed forces, the one that is called martial. . . . It is not a martial area by name only, but we have sacrificed and are doing so every day, and this should be visible. . . . We have graveyards full of shaheed; we have their families [and] their parents, who instead of pain feel pride. So this pride is reflected through these things.

It is important to note here that this was a civilian affair, an initiative of ex-servicemen in the area, the media, and the district government. There was no representative from the Air Headquarters, whose role was simply to respond to a request and dispatch the plane. I do not take away from the fact that the plane was dispatched to Chakwal, a district that the armed forces recognizes as having been overrepresented in the past. Neither do I neglect the fact that the request letter to the air force highlighted the askari khidmaat of the district. My emphasis here is instead on the military institution's role as a passive facilitator. The desire to visibly inscribe loyalty to and affiliation with the Armed Forces on the district comes from the district itself, or, more precisely, from its large ex-military population.

Generative and productive mechanisms of power whereby the district "produces domains of objects and rituals of truth" are apparent in these moves.[74] Subjects themselves strive to make their martial status visible in the district; this inscription is made more visible because of rising anxieties about reduced intake quotas from a district no longer considered martial under the new military recruitment policy. These domains and rituals are ambivalent productions, not in the resolve to create or ritualize but in their substance, as they mention the nation-state and its martial past in an almost rhetorical way. Although discourses of the nation-state and memories and myths about a martial past and tradition are abundantly voiced and echo through this terrain, they are just hollow sounds that endlessly repeat themselves. So although the district may build monument upon monument, decorate grave upon grave, and fly the flag of Pakistan higher and higher over the graves of its dead, what drives these men to continue to invest in the military are the desire to escape ghurbat and to obtain pakki naukri. Systematic and generous welfare services for troops and their families are what legitimize the military's claims on the bodies of men. In this local terrain, narratives of service and sacrifice become a bargaining chip for continued membership and claim making in the modern kinship group that is the Pakistani military.

These historically feudal societies turn toward their modern benefactor, the Pakistani military, and fight for their right to serve up their young men in return for continued patronage and favors. Once recruited, soldier-subjects in the making must sustain this coveted status by submitting to military training—exhaustive regimes of discipline that meticulously create distance from former objects of affection and ways of living and mark the trainees as different, not only from others but also from themselves. The next chapter tells their story.

CHAPTER 4

MANUFACTURING SOLDIERS

> You take a civilian; you cannot afford to waste a single minute. He is absolutely raw material; he doesn't know how to talk or walk. He is basically a wild animal in a *shalwar kameez*. I wish you could see the recruit when he comes to us. You should see his body language. You only have twenty-three weeks, and you have to make him into a proper fighting soldier. . . . [He] must be converted into someone who is physically fit, almost hyperfit. He must be mentally robust. It is only twenty-three weeks of training, and there is no time to spare. It's like putting the boy through a *bhatti* (furnace)—he goes through these hardships so that the fear inside finishes. He must be professionally trained in battle tactics, firing weapons, and admin, and he must be a motivated soldier. By this, I mean esprit de corps,[1] to feel a sense of pride in *my* unit, *my* platoon, *my* regiment. If a man learns to fight for his unit, he will fight for his country, because we fight for our home and what we love. Second, there is the religious point of view; it is a sacred profession.
>
> —Colonel, infantry regiment training center, Abbottabad

THERE ARE two competing visions of the modern nation-state soldier: (1) that of a professional, distanced from civilian life, formed through meticulous training and discipline and (2) that of an armed peasant or worker.[2] British imaginings of the Indian soldier in the service of the British Indian Army operated between these two poles. The *sipahi* was an "occidental soldier," subject to military bureaucracy, laws, and discipline, and yet at the same time he was still "recognizably Indian," a "pseudo-historical" subject, an accident of the ever-changing definitions of the mythical martial race.[3] In the first vision, he is no longer a civilian or a primitive, which is a dramatic shift from his earlier being, whereas in the second vision he is essentially unchanged, just armed and better trained in violence. The Pakistani military's dependence on what the British Raj regarded as martial areas for troops lasted until as late as 2001, where it continued to rely on an expanded pool of districts within Punjab and Khyber Pakhtunkhwa (KP) as its primary recruiting ground. Many officers and soldiers I interviewed suggested that men from the martial regions of Punjab and KP had a greater willingness and ability to serve because of their extended exposure to the military lifestyle. This made it easier for boys coming from families and districts in which the ethos of the army was not so alien to adapt to the demands of military discipline. Despite this, as the earlier passage shows, what happens in the military training institution is looked upon as a complete metamorphosis of the being subjected to it. The imaginings of the British Indian Army continue to haunt the modern Pakistani *jawan* (young man).[4] A dual articulation of his subjectivity positions him as socialized into martialness and already half a *fauji* (military man)[5] yet also the uncouth primitive who has to be trained into an occidental soldier.

The figure of the jawan, the subaltern soldier of the Pakistan Army, is interrogated within this chapter from two perspectives. First, I look at how the military institution sees its soldier class; what aspirations, desires, and apprehensions it carries; and what kind of soldier it wishes to create. Second, I investigate how the soldier lives and experiences this molding, the experiences he brings to these rituals of transformation, and the ways he copes within these regimes of discipline. The descriptions that emerge from juxtaposing these perspectives bring into sharp relief the split visions around the soldier-subject: the instinctual given of the martial race versus the necessity of the monotonous, steady inculcation that is soldier training; the image of the honed diamond that emerges after training versus that of the mindless automaton he is reduced to; and the soldier figure who follows orders in battle much like a machine versus the soldier who is paralyzed in battle and has to be cajoled like a child or taunted and humiliated to fight.

The fluidity of these depictions was apparent in the inability of my interlocutors to present a settled image of the soldier—the picture they presented was incoherent and unstable. A sense of incompleteness haunted my conversations with soldiers. For as I sat with these men, talking with them about their lives, hopes, and anxieties, I was conscious that while they said much, there was much that remained unspoken. This inhibition sprung not so much from the confines of our gender or class differences or an awareness of the watchful gaze of the military—although I am sure that too must have played a part—but instead from self-censorship; from carefully cultivated habits of the heart, mind, and body; and a resignation to the inability of knowing and the impossibility of accessing the self. These were halted, silent conversations, even when words flowed freely.

OVERSTATING THE AUTOMATON

To prepare men for war and killing requires meticulous regulation of space, activity, and time. The infantry training center in Abbottabad is an artificial world, separated from the familiar, bounded by walls, and guarded by sentries. The mechanics of disciplinary power that are deployed to create "docile bodies," as detailed by Michel Foucault in his seminal work *Discipline and Punish: Birth of the Prison*, are on predictable display here.[6] Fundamentals of training involve depersonalization, constant surveillance and absence of privacy, rigid time tables, enforcement of dress codes, arbitrariness of chores, tediousness of physical training, and strict compliance with military rules and punishment regimes.[7] Space becomes a medium of control managed through the "principle of enclosure," in which bodies become confined within boundaries, and by "partitioning," in which they are distributed and placed within allocated physical locations. Each recruit is allocated a space at a given point in time, and each place is allocated its recruit. Activity is controlled through the use of strict "timetables" (that aim to regulate and "establish rhythms"), the "temporal elaboration of acts" (as in marching), a focus on the most efficient correlation of body and gestures (such as the correct posture for walking or running), "body-object articulation" (learning the most efficient and aesthetic way to fire or hold a weapon), and "exhaustive use" (regulating time so that idleness is not possible).[8] Within the center, each unit of time is accounted for. There is no time to spare and no spare time! These mechanisms produce bodies that respond to commands that "trigger off the required behavior," commands that are precise so that obedience becomes almost an automatic action, a "prearranged code" set in motion as though from within.[9] A retired infantry general explained it this way: "This training makes you mechanical. It tunes your reflexes. . . . You don't have to think at that time about what to do, but your reflexes have been automated; it becomes your second nature. . . . You start to think in black and white, your grey finishes." Within these institutions of mass manufacture, each individual is marked in ways that make him forever visible, locatable, and detectable. This visibility paradoxically also renders each soldier invisible, so that "when they finish training, you can't tell them apart," a general who was ex-director of military training at GHQ informed me.

This exhaustive and often tedious detail—in which there is a purpose for every act, gesture, or movement—may seem baffling to the external observer, but as I interviewed the instructors at the training center, it became obvious that the schedule was meticulously planned and organized. The colonel in this chapter's opening quote suggests that the boys who arrive at the training center on the first day are uncouth primitives whose lives have so far been restricted to the village. They are an unruly lot, coming from different locations, experiences, and perceptions of military service, and their uniqueness is a challenge to be overcome. They are boys that need to pruned and made into predictable, classifiable beings. The technologies of rule employed by the military institution that enable the shift from the civilian to the martial are marked by urgency and claim to turn the "wild animal" into a "proper fighting soldier." There is a honing of the rustic, unrefined body that transforms him from an object of ridicule ("You should see his body language") into a person worthy of respect who serves a "sacred profession." His mind is put to the test so he can think in militarized ways, in terms of tactics, in which everything has a name and everything is a battle. His heart becomes one that does not fear, that is sculpted by love and loyalty to new objects of attachment built on primordial essences such as religion, land, and home. Training aims to change all three: body, mind, and heart. He looks different ("hyperfit"); he thinks differently ("mentally robust . . . [and] professionally trained"); and he feels different ("motivated soldier").

For most soldiers I spoke to, the training period—the stage marking their transition from civilians to soldiers—was the most formative period of their lives. Many were able to describe in great detail the various disciplinary mechanisms they were exposed to and why. A sense of entering a new world, isolated and removed from the familiar, was highlighted by many as they spoke of their memories of the training period. Many distinctly articulated a sense of things shifting and a sense of transformation. Everything was done according to a timetable; a regulated time was set aside even for recreation—time for fun bookended by the afternoon drill and the call to dinner. There was a feeling of urgency, of always being in a state of preparedness for the next slot in the schedule; their lives were predictable but rushed. Each slot in the day was a test in which they had to prove themselves worthy. They expressed feelings of mastery, of pride at having survived harsh army training. It was a change affecting all aspects of their being—body, mind, and heart. The things that shifted included tangibles such as physical fitness and a newly acquired love of discipline as well as more nebulous realms such as a cool-headedness that, in their minds, set them apart from the emotionality and animallike nature of those in their villages. This change was experienced as superiority, or a specialness, as becoming more than they would have had they stayed in the village. This was linked to but not wholly because of increased financial prowess, a rise in stature coming from the ability to command a stable and secure income. The demands of military training initially experienced as cumbersome and limiting became part of the self, and the unruliness and lack of order in the village became irksome and inferior.

Yet the much-coveted transition was rarely presented as smooth and welcome. Describing the training experience, a *subedar*[10]—an instructor at the training center—informed me that "the *zehen* (mind) shifts slowly; it takes two to three weeks to make the zehen. The first week is the hardest, and most want to run away." Many soldiers spoke of the initial few weeks as being extremely painful and bewildering. Some expressed a sense of being watched, of being constantly monitored and never free of the gaze of superiors or peers. There was a heightened awareness of the self, a need to hide certain kinds of emotion, especially those associated with weakness. Thus homesickness had to be hidden and bottled up, to be released only in bathrooms, where there was some sense of privacy, or when the lights went out at 10:00 p.m. Thirty-three-year-old Havildar[11] Nasir recounts his early training: "I did not mind the hardships or the punishments, but when I returned to my barracks in the evening I would miss home. I would burst into tears; I would go to the bathroom and cry my heart out and then return dry-eyed to the room. All of us were like that at the beginning." Punishments were a regular feature of these training institutions, proof itself that the body, mind, and heart resisted this subjection, at least initially. Punishment, or the threat of it, was never far away, and it was often a humiliating test of mental and physical endurance. These were harsh verbal invectives or corporal punishments, such as sit-ups or being made to stand upside down, often in public, in full view of the other boys. There was also solitary confinement, reserved for more severe offenses. These boys accepted grueling bodily discipline and their ability to face punishment as signs of endurance, pride, and masculinity. The physical pain accompanying the punishment was seen as improving the body, much like, as Foucault suggested, corrective or coercive measures come to be looked on as productive.[12]

The mind and the heart found it harder to conform. Many spoke about the challenges of settling in. For them, the first few weeks were about a secret desire to run away, while for others this desire was not secret and led to action. This action had to be carefully weighed against the reaction of family members, censure and ridicule from the village, retaliation from the military, and, most of all, pragmatic considerations of material needs. I asked Havildar Nasir, who joined the service at the age of seventeen, if he had ever tried to run away. Nasir responded,

> I thought if I returned home my family would ridicule me; they would say, "You ran away from service, couldn't survive it." I even thought of doing something, running away from life itself . . . . My family was very happy when I got in (the army), but my zehen was not able to accept this. A friend I spoke to said there are many benefits in the army. It was true, but in the army you feel very odd at the beginning. We were free before this. . . . I said this is

not the army; this is like a prison, and you have to live in this prison for eighteen years or twenty years.... My heart was restless, and one day I picked up my box and ran.... When I returned [home], there was much arguing and fighting in my house. People started finding out that I was home.... One morning my father woke me up; my bag had already been packed. He came all the way to drop me at Mardan [the city where the army training center was located]. I was seventeen and a half then, just a *bacha* (child).

Nasir, a havildar with over sixteen years of experience, looks back on his initiation into the army as forced and coercive. His experience brings home quite starkly the economic drivers and the accompanying pressure from the families of these young men that bear heavily on a soldier's decision to serve in the military. He speaks of the army as a "prison," a metaphor that echoes how many soldiers describe their experience as being *paband* (restricted). Officers and the soldier class alike suggest three interconnected factors that determine recruits' ability to stay in training. Most commonly mentioned is the financial condition of the family they left behind. Those from decidedly poorer families are more likely to stay, because for them the discomfort associated with homesickness and enforced discipline is acceptable compared to the uncertainty and the hard life of work in the fields that awaited them back home. It seems that poverty and the famed martial resilience to training go hand in hand. The second reason is the geographical location from which recruits come and their consequent familiarity with the military, especially if they had family members who previously served in the military. The third reason cited is the recruit's ability to rise above the pangs of separation from loved ones. Those who managed to flee were referred to as *bhagoras*, meaning those who run away from hardship. This is a pejorative term, but the disparagement of the village is not derived from the shame of buckling under pressure and shying away from the hardship of military service or service to the nation-state. Instead, these people are censured as *bewakoof* (fools) and considered shortsighted, because they throw away their chance to socially and financially better themselves and their families. The decision to so recklessly throw away this chance of *pakki naukri* (secure employment associated with government service) is equated with madness, an act without reason. These men viewed themselves in a similar way, especially when comparing themselves to their contemporaries who had decided to stay and were receiving pensions.

Shades of discontent also appear in the narratives of those who stayed. Forty-year old Havildar Sohail, about to retire after twenty-two years of service, refers to his upcoming retirement, saying, "In six months I will be *azad* (free)." There is a realization that fitting into the army, becoming a fauji, means giving up the right to question or think, leading to others regarding them as automatons, incapable of independent action and thought. Sipahi Omar, who was forty years old at the time of our interview and who left the army after six years of service, described the experience of mindlessly following orders as *"musalsal zehni koft"* (continuous mental irritation), a paradox in itself, for the zehen of the fauji is apparently no longer meant to be capable of reacting independently. Omar goes on to describe how the jawan views the discipline to which he is exposed, an account somewhat at odds with the automaton supposedly produced after the rigor of army discipline: "The person who is a fauji, especially one who is a *sipahi*—he doesn't need to use his brain. The reason for this is that even if he has to do something like dig a hole, he will do it on the orders of his superior; otherwise he doesn't do it. If he sits, he must sit in a particular way, although in his home he is a completely responsible man." After leaving the army, Omar came back home against the wishes of his family and to the ridicule of his peers. We sit in the courtyard of the office of his small catering company, which provides tents and chairs for village weddings and parties. Initially hesitant because he said he left military service many moons ago, he warms up to the subject and explains how the soldier copes with training, saying, "At home I am a responsible adult. . . . I know what I need to do—dig a hole, plant a tree, work, get clothes and shoes for my child. But when I go there [to the army unit] I become *masoom (*innocent), like I know nothing. This is because if I take initiative there and dig a hole, they will ask me, 'Why did you do this?'" When he looks at me, his facial expressions betray a benign exasperation, as though explaining the irritating habits of a loved one "So, in the *fauj* (military), a person cannot have *apni marzi* (free will). If I do anything, they will ask me, 'Why did you do this; who ordered you to do this?' So I just stopped using my brain, and I waited for orders." The soldier-subject follows orders, yet he recognizes what this demands of him: a willingness to give up thinking. He *becomes* the *innocent*, a child, when he is in the barracks and ceases to be a *responsible* [thinking] *adult*. Although I do not suggest that this becoming is a choice, for choice here is limited severely by the external pressures that have propelled his current position, it certainly reflects a conscious *switching* to suit the demands of the situation.

Foucault builds a daunting picture of the ability of modern institutions to use technologies of power to produce subjects that respond not to an exterior or negative influencer but to an internal productive one, in which subjectivities are but the product of these power relations.[13] This seems to preclude the possibility of finding in the subaltern a worldview that might resist or even think through the conditions of the subaltern's formation[14] or the impossibility of taking "an oppositional relation to power that is, admittedly, implicated in the very power one opposes."[15] The practices of soldiers bear testament to the "enormous significance of those modern microphysical methods of order" that Foucault outlines, because they are certainly formidable in their ability to appropriate every gesture, movement, and habit. Soldiers' self-descriptions of how they lived and experienced these disciplinary techniques, however, suggest that the "coherence of these technologies" to make us into automatons may be overstated, for these self-descriptions proclaim soldiers' awareness of the mechanisms they were exposed to and the repercussions those mechanisms had.[16] So what does this *awareness* of the processes of subjection imply? Inasmuch as this could be partly a temporal effect—a gradual understanding over time, as many of my interlocutors were men whose training took place between five and twenty-two years ago—I hold that our interpretations must consider the full range of soldiers' narratives that speak to their experiences, even if they are retrospective.

It may be useful here to allude to the concept of *enframing*, a term used by Timothy Mitchell. He alerts us that "new modes of power, by their permanence, their apparent origin outside local life, their intangibility . . . [appear] as something non particular and unchanging—as a framework that enframes actual occurrences." Power seems to be inevitable, unchangeable, and "*external* to practice" (emphasis in original).[17] The difficulties that soldiers experienced as they transitioned into soldier-subjects were acceptable to them. They felt that they *had* to enter military service to secure livelihood; they *had* to be toughened up for the kind of harsh service the military demanded; and they *had* to mindlessly follow orders for military systems to work. There was an acceptance of *inevitability*. It was also a transition they valued, for it held its own rewards: status, greater financial stability, and a heightened sense of masculinity. The subjects of militarism view the world as enframed, and because of their inability to see it any other way, they are limited in their capacity to demystify it completely. And yet, as is obvious from their earlier narratives, they have a pronounced ability to *see* what these mechanisms do to them. Their appreciation of the transition does not preclude an awareness of a sense of loss, a consciousness that this transition was coercive and that they *played* the subject. This enframing *limits* but does not altogether take away the subject's capacity to be aware of how he is himself imbricated in disciplinary mechanisms of power. This is a seeing through that neither impedes subjects' willingness to be molded nor creates any overt subversive action. Instead it implicates subjects as conscious beings in a process, in which they continue to acquiesce despite the failure of these disciplinary mechanisms to make them complete automatons.

KINSHIP AND NEW FAMILIES

If modern militaries and standing armies are about regulated acts of violence, then it can be argued that the manufacture of soldiers for these acts is closely tied to the management of emotion. While explaining to me the principles of military training, the retired infantry general acknowledged their centrality: "Emotions need to be streamlined and channeled. All of us have the same basic emotions, but to convert them (civilians) into standing armies they (emotions) need to be channeled; they don't *just* go away."

Amplifications of hate are central to military strategies.[18] After partition, the version of Pakistani selfhood constructed by the state relied on the physical and cultural othering of the Hindu.[19] This included the dehumanization of the Hindu enemy and the steady inculcation of an attitude of bravado and superiority over him.[20] Yet, in his discussion of patriotism, Benedict Anderson does well to remind us that the roots of nationalism lie not only in racism, fear, and hatred of the other but also in love. Nation-states inspire "profoundly self-sacrificing love" because the nation "is assimilated to skin-color, gender, parentage, birth-era—all those things that one cannot help" and that demand "disinterested love and solidarity."[21] The turn toward crowd theories and group dynamics in soldiers' training in Britain and the United States during World War II suggests that love and not just hate enables violence in war. These theories are based on the premise that potent group identification displaces self-love onto the group, which reduces the fear of death and diminishes inhibition regarding violent acts.[22] The deliberate development of affective relationships with fellow soldiers, who signify families, and group leaders, who stand in for father figures, can be a means to prepare men for killing in that love for fellow comrades can become an enabler for the killing and aggression demanded of combatants in war.[23] Within the Pakistani military, notions of *ghairat* (honor) and *izzat* (prestige) are deeply embedded in rural environs from which the military draws its workforce. These notions, traditionally associated with female members and with the *biraderi* (extended clan), are extended in training to everything that is military, and it is said that affection for the regiment and determination to uphold its honor is what locks soldiers together like a family.[24]

The YeD/S imagery presents two images that the institution of the military uses to construct its soldier figure. One is the brave warrior who takes to war like a sport, while the other is the self-sacrificing heroic man. The prototypical soldier in the West also stands somewhere between the "bloodthirsty militant" and the "reluctant warrior," insofar as the latter "places [the] highest value not on killing but on dying—dying for others, to protect them, sacrificing himself so others might live."[25] Training in the Pakistani military uses a mix of both images, but I focus on the self-sacrificing soldier, because it is this image that military discourse and soldier narratives invoke more often. Explaining this away as political rhetoric that deflects from the devastating reality of combat would be too simplistic. The emphasis on sacrifice is reflective of how the creation of the desire to serve and die lies at the heart of military training and is achieved through affective regulation involving not hate but the production of love.

Training instructors at the center in Abbottabad repeatedly spoke of the need to handle the homesickness of boys who were too attached to their families. Female family members back home, especially mothers and grandmothers, were singled out by instructors as stubborn objects of attachment. Despite the different reasons given for recruits absconding, the dominant view at the center was that those who wished to run away were not tough enough for army discipline and had failed to live up to the ideal of the soldier. They were often referred to pejoratively as *ladle* (spoilt) or *beghairat* (without honor) by the instructors at the training center, made weak by too much female love and attention. "[The runaway is] a child who has never left his home or his village. He has only eaten *roti* made by his mother's hands . . . , so when he comes here he can't cope. There was a recruit last year whose father brought him back after he ran away; he said he hadn't slept without his *dadi* (grandmother) in all his life." The longing for familiarity and home is made all the more intense by the fact that the training center functions as a self-contained world, physically separated from the rest of the city. Glimpses of the previous world are strictly regulated, and the clean, whitewashed, and efficient inside stands distinct from the dusty, unpredictable, and chaotic environment outside. The retired infantry general suggests that isolation is deliberate, because "they need to be away from the city, from other people, (so) they feel like an entity, and then the esprit de corps develops." The intent is to exacerbate homesickness by severing contact with familiar objects of love, jolting the individual into a sharp awareness of his new and unfamiliar surroundings. The bonds with the family arouse sadness so overwhelming that it is an almost infantile separation anxiety, threatening the ability to stay. The bonds are temporarily severed so they can then be reimagined through newer bonds, which is perhaps possible only if the shock and isolation are severe enough. The earlier bonds of attachment have to be weakened and the boys toughened up, not through the renunciation of love and attachment but by channeling love in other directions, to the new family—the army—with the superior officer as the father and the fellow soldiers as brothers.

This deliberate investment in developing ideas of love (camaraderie and esprit de corps) relies heavily on kinship metaphors. The military institution uses these metaphors and the love they invoke on two levels: first, the larger landscape, with the homeland as mother, the nation as family, and the soldiers as sons of the soil; second, within the institution itself, with its units, officers, and soldiers as one family. The unit is referred as the new home, and the army as the new *maa baap*, a benevolent benefactor that loves you, grooms you, and looks after you with an all-important caveat—the right to then ask you to kill or die for it. "Your fight is here. . . . You four boys in this trench, each one of you is more important to each other than your real brother. Because tomorrow if a shell lands, your blood will all be in one pool, and if one of you is injured and the other is not, he is the one who will help you and take you out, not your father." The injunction here from a commanding officer to his troops extols the virtues of camaraderie with fellow jawans as vital for survival. It asks for a replacement of earlier blood relations with new attachments also forged in blood. This reimagining of familial attachments through the concerns of the state not only involves a metaphorical reference to primordial givens, which is an intrinsic part of this manufacture of love, but also demands a replacement. This allows a more potent response of love, loyalty, and attachment to emerge.

The tightening of bonds with fellow soldiers in the unit can mean a corresponding distancing from the family and village back home. This distancing occurs because of the way the new self, a self that respects routine and discipline, is experienced. It is a different way of being that sets one apart from the emotionality and unruliness of village folk back home. This distancing is not an accidental by-product of the transformation into the soldier figure but is actively cultivated. It may be instructive to explore why this is considered necessary, why these newer bonds of attachment are tied to a loosening of bonds at home. I revert here to the discussion in chapter 2, in which a tension was highlighted in the discussion of the script for the YeD/S events.[26] The very bonds of kinship between soldiers and their families that are so vital for transmitting the military's message of purpose and sacrifice to the nation need to be destabilized at the training center if the soldier is to perform his duty to the nation and be willing to fight and die. Thus a delicate balancing act is required. These bonds, so critical for the military after death of the soldier, can be a threat to the soldier's ability to stay in service and fight while he lives. In the YeD/S scripts, the weakening of bonds has to be handled sensitively, as the entire show revolves around an invocation of relationships. The shift is presented as a choice that represents a willing sacrifice. Within the confines of the training center, however, there is no longer an allusion to choice but an inculcation, a steady drilling, and the price of not conforming or failing to rechannel these objects of love can be quite high. The consequences for those who run away and are returned by their family or come back on their own can range from solitary confinement to court martial and civilian prison, depending on the severity and frequency of the offense.

For many of the soldiers I interviewed, the development of these new attachments reflects a pragmatic channeling, one that ostensibly serves the interests of earlier bonds of affection (since continued service assures income for the family) and also harnesses deliberately heightened homesickness. The soldier flits between the two worlds of attachments, the civilian and the martial, the old and the new—the demands often pulling him in different directions even as both set of attachments lead or push him in one direction: military service.

Insofar as pride and attachment to the unit came through in my conversations with the soldiers, it was when they spoke of their brothers-in-arms that they allowed themselves to smile. The camaraderie that the army sets out to inculcate was often expressed as personal friendship and shared experiences. The soldiers turn to each other as fellow travelers on the same journey, sometimes unable or unwilling to find similar camaraderie and attachment back home. Their new selves perhaps relate less to those with whom they shared earlier bonds and relationships, and there is comfort and ease in living with people who have been molded the same way and speak the same language. This is best captured by a joke shared with me by a subedar: "Some faujis arrived in hell, yet they seemed happy. Others around them were intrigued and asked them why they were happy. They said, 'We are together; we have created the same atmosphere here as the unit.'" There are two implications here: first, that army life is comparable to hell and second, and more significant, that bonds with friends enable you to make hell your home.

STATES OF SUSPENSION

Havildar Nisar, a thirty-three-year-old soldier, is on leave, home for six days. He is a tall man dressed in the usual village garb, a light-colored shalwar kameez. His face is unshaven, and he is heavily tanned. He looks like any other villager as he enters the room. The only thing that gives him away as a serving soldier is his posture, erect and alert. He has been deployed in combat areas on and off for the last seven years. He speaks of a sense of constant unease: "I don't think we stay normal. We may look normal. We are disturbed and don't feel a sense of peace. There is an odd sense of unease. I can't explain it." It haunts him both at home and when he is back in his unit. "My heart is not easy in the city with my family, and it is not easy when I get back. Over time, when for so many years we have seen the same thing, we don't stay normal. We are disturbed; [we] forget things. Sometimes I am faced with the realization that, my friend [addressing himself], I wasn't like that, this forgetting of things. We don't know what this feeling is." His inability to give a name or explain how he feels irks him. He repeats it again, searching for a better way to explain his predicament. He refers to seeing things that make him different from normal people, things that he can't unsee, and then in the same sentence alludes to how he forgets things and how this forgetting is associated with a sense of loss of the self ("I wasn't like that").

What Nisar also repeats is a sense of feeling different than normal. This is not just collateral debris from exposure to the horrors of war. Instead, this feeling mirrors the deliberate setting apart through military training of the soldier-subject from the primitive peasantry, the traditional source of most of Pakistan's soldier class, and from stubborn female objects of attachment. Training involves a fair amount of cajoling, insults, and humiliation that revolve around not being man enough or, worse still, being called a woman. This distancing rests on the prototypical separation from the cocoon of the feminine as young boys move into manhood. In the South Asian context, the separation of the boy from the feminine world and his removal to a more masculine one is a rite of passage that accompanies the transition into adulthood. This involves an almost physical shift, such as when the boy moves from the women's bath to the men's collective or *hammam* (public bath).[27] This distance also translates into a qualitative difference from the feminine and becomes a source of a permanent anxiety and crisis that can be resolved only by moving further and further from all that is regarded as feminine. The sense of being male is invariably expressed through a negation of the feminine, wherein a *real* man is "not a woman."[28] In my conversations with army men, faujis were defined as nonfeminine, noncivilian, and nonprimitive, subjectivities that emerged from a deliberate effort by trainees to create distance from the contaminating effect of the primitive, feminine civilian. There is strong anxiety of evaluation by and possible humiliation in front of other men (fellow soldiers and superiors), as the masculine militarist subject is informed through the approving or shaming gaze of other men.

To understand how this distancing is made possible, it may be useful to discuss the mastery and manipulation of fear and shame. In preparing the soldier for battle, instructors deliberately aim to sequence and break down each battle tactic and maneuver in such a way that when the soldier steps into the line of fire, he effortlessly performs the next of a series of coordinated moves that he has been practicing day in and day out as a combatant-in-waiting. The infantry general explains to me that this means "that individual bravery or chivalry is not needed. It happens—it has to happen like that—because you have been drilled like that. . . . You just have to follow the steps." The goal here is to ensure that fear becomes secondary and the automaton takes over. Yet it seems that all does not always go smoothly in battle. Fear is managed better in some soldiers and is trickier to master in others; shame and consequences loom large. The general goes on to elucidate further:

> The one who shows fear is lost; he has lost his honor and his reputation, and he will be taken to task. His promotion may be blocked. It's the same concept at home. You try many ways to fix your child—many times he does things that you cover for him. Because you fear that you [the regiment] will be shamed if people find out. . . . The senior officer might try and encourage him, so he may say "Get up, child, it's okay; *shabash shabash* [verbal encouragement implying in this context 'come, come']." If he still doesn't move, then the commander will become harsh. He will push him, kick him, and drag him, and he will ask two other people to take the weapon from him. He will be verbally abused, and they will shame him by calling him a coward, a woman.

Fear is real and common on the battlefield and needs to be disciplined and *fixed*. In describing the aforementioned scene, the general also mimicked the soldier's catatonic, embryonic posture—his body curled and arms folded in, an infantile immobility—and the soldier's dreaded return to the primitive and feminine. Fear is an unwanted, aberrant emotion, and it must be hidden from others, if possible, because visibility will bring shame. Drawing on earlier familiar tropes of family, the first attempt will be to cover for the person, but if that is not possible, there are repercussions, and the punishment will depend on rank. At first, the senior will try and cajole him like a child, but this can slide into violence, and physical torture and verbal insults invoking ghairat may ensue.

The soldiers I interviewed during the course of my fieldwork used a double language to speak of fear. It was a perplexing discussion; nobody denied experiencing fear, and many said it was a natural emotion, yet they spoke about it as a thing of the past, something that they had once felt but could no longer relate to. Instead, some spoke of being prevented from concentrating on the job at hand or even made to desert the battlefield because of worries about home. There seemed to be an unspoken understanding that a soldier's inability to perform was due to his inability to break the bonds with home and to his excessive worry about the situation there and that imminent injury or death on the battlefield were not to be feared.

There were dents in this armor of silence for those posted in areas in which combat operations were going on. In halting conversations about experiences on the battlefront, fear was sometimes mentioned as something they felt the first time they saw the dead bodies of their comrades or even of the enemy. Forced proximity to the dead bodies of the enemy or their comrades was something that many had experienced, and the memories of those experiences stayed with them. Memories were vivid, laced with sounds, smells, and sights, and they were expressed as though they had happened the day before. They were defining moments when the soldiers had seen death firsthand and realized that they too could die. Some described it as a feeling of terror, others as a deep, unsettling emotion, and still others simply as a time they could not forget, one that kept coming back to them. There was an unspoken rule not to share or discuss feelings back home or with other colleagues, apart from describing facts such as numbers, locations, and times. There was deep shame around the idea of being found out as fearful, a deep fear of fear itself, and a need to dissociate and not accept the helplessness experienced in the moment.

Soldiers had to find creative ways of expressing fear, because it was not permissible in its own right. Fear and possibly guilt for having survived could be expressed and made more acceptable as another emotion, such as grief for a fellow comrade who had died. Many spoke about how they would wail without shame for their friends who had died in battle. Havildar Nisar, who had lost two comrades from his unit in quick succession, was particularly articulate, bordering on macabre, as he spoke of this. He described the sequence of events that led up to their deaths, the injuries his colleagues had sustained, how many minutes it took for them to die, what they said, and how they looked. He had kept pictures of their mutilated dead bodies on his phone and said he looked at them from time to time so he could cry and not forget them. This seemed a less shameful release, permitted because it was not for the self and was camouflaged as deep grief for brothers-in-arms that could be openly expressed with tears.

Many soldiers I spoke to experienced their time in battle as if in a dissociative state, as having an ability to act without feeling or sensation. Joanna Bourke describes this as "separation from the self—including the moral self in battle" and goes on to suggest depersonalization as a way to justify acts of killing and violence during combat.[29] This includes experiencing oneself during battle as alien from the real self, a temporary cessation of the being. For many, this sense of alienation followed them home. Ijaz, a thirty-two-year-old Special Services Group (SSG) commando,[30] describes the challenges soldiering brings to his relationship with his family and his ability to participate in life outside the military.

> Ijaz: Your domestic life gets a little disturbed. My wife, my sister, my mother—I do not feel it, but they do, that I have become hard. [*Pauses*.] I don't feel. [*Lowers voice*.] It is true we change; for example, laughing and joking we can't do easily; I don't know why. Maybe it's because when I do that a little [laugh or joke] then my other zehen returns [and says], "No, don't do this so much; this is enough."
>
> Me: What do you mean by "other zehen"?
>
> Ijaz: Some things happen together in life, in practical life. Some people feel at the right time. For example, when someone dies they will feel for a few days, [and] then they will move on, perk up, and forget and come back to life and start enjoying it. I think as an army soldier, that instant happiness or sadness that people feel, we don't feel that. The reason we can't do that . . . [is] we have seen so much that our zehen is working on both sides. So today we are enjoying ourselves, and at the same time another disc is playing in our zehen that it was so hard to pick up that person whose body had been half blown away; earlier we did that and now we do this, so both these are playing in our heads. Just like a normal man enjoys something fully, we cannot do so.

This feeling of dissociation, of living in two parallel worlds, of a splitting of the self, came through in conversations with other soldiers as well. In describing the experience of Iraq War veterans, Kenneth T.

Macleish suggests something similar, in which "the labor of not feeling, the self-conscious mastery of affect, emotion, and physical pain" that soldiers carry as the weight of seeing (and doing) the horrors of war peppers soldiers' narratives. This labor does not banish feeling but requires a continuous doing, a cost of having to "actively ignore" the feelings that arise in reaction to their experiences. "This is an anesthetic that never quite takes hold and never fully wears off, and you remain perpetually aware, even if only at that proprioceptive level where feeling fades off into a tingly fog, of the feelings that you aren't feeling, which lie buried between brief punctuations of consciousness."[31]

These excerpts are from soldiers who have been involved on the battlefront for some time. These were interlocutors who were not only able to articulate this but seemed almost desperate to. Their sense of dissociation from others around them and, in many ways, from their own selves is certainly more marked, and it would be unwise to attribute this strong dissociative quality to all soldiers in the military. Their stories are more dramatic, colored with blood, death, and sharp contrasts between what they saw in war and their lives back home. Yet what I presented in the earlier sections speaks to similar strains, albeit less pronounced, found in the way most soldiers describe their relationships with their families and their need to switch back to village life when they go home on leave. Most soldiers describe a sense of emotional distancing, a silencing from others who were once the same but who can no longer understand or relate to what soldiering is about. The home, family, and village represent people and places that they loved but that were different, caught in patterns of thinking and ways of doing that seem alien to the new self. This is an othering not just of the enemy but of relations and acquaintances and of the self. The difference so carefully sought and crafted through the meticulous organization of space, time, and movement exacts a less tangible toll, a sense of dissociation.

In the introduction to this chapter, I referred to the incompleteness that haunted my discussions with the soldiers I spoke to, a sense of fragmentation that seemed to intensify rather than dissipate. This feeling was more pronounced with soldiers I spent more time with or those I sensed were more open or willing to talk. Thus, I do not attribute this inhibition to less rapport or deliberate censorship. Rather, I experienced it as the appearance of a self that felt split, fragmented, and incomplete, a self that was uncomfortable with appearing but that still wanted to engage. I argue that this splitting and fragmentation is a result of the experiences of the knowing automaton: the deliberate creation of distance from former objects of affection and ways of living and repeated regulation and control of sadness, fear, and shame. This regulation becomes so internalized that parts of the self become inaccessible. Yet here too, as the earlier conversations illustrate, there was an awareness of what had been lost.

CHAKWAL'S RETIRED SOLDIERS

An account of the soldier's experiences would be incomplete without a look at what happens to the soldier figure once he returns to his village (he must return because the military demands his service for a defined period of time only). Charting this reentry is important also because the dynamics of reentry serve as further evidence of the transmutation that he undergoes in order to be a soldier.

Retired soldiers return to the village after eighteen to thirty-two years of service, depending on how high they were allowed to climb in the army's hierarchy. These soldiers are interesting figures, although I did not seek them out. Rather, they kept being referred to me as possible interlocutors, or, more typically, they found me because they felt I should speak with them. As college professor Shamil puts it sarcastically, "There are as many subedars in Chakwal as there are used shopping bags." The reference to shopping bags here is a not-so-attractive image of bags that no longer have utility and that are strewn across streets and fields, a common sight in overcrowded cities such as Chakwal.

The retired soldier is typically envied as someone who was lucky enough to get into military service and managed to leave in one piece, someone who has received his commutation and will continue to receive a pension for the rest of his life. Because of his steady income, over the years he may have accumulated a number of material comforts, such as a television set, a washing machine, a refrigerator, a computer, and other household goods that set his house apart from others. He may have installed a plaque outside his home displaying his military rank and retired status. He may also have used his military contacts to get his brothers or cousins into service or financially helped his father and brothers to acquire more land or modern machinery for farming and thus secure a more comfortable financial situation. Upon retirement, he may decide to invest his accumulated savings and the commutation he receives at the end of service in a business venture. He will be a welcome member of village committees, and generally people will regard him as trusted, disciplined, and reliable.

This is only one side of the story, applicable to those who rise higher up the army hierarchy to the rank of subedar (JCO) or those who came from relatively less impoverished backgrounds to begin with. The less fortunate ones (and the much larger proportion), who retire after eighteen to twenty years of service, may find themselves too young to retire from work. The younger retired fauji may continue his employment through army-supported mechanisms (the local DASB or the Fauji Foundation), which will facilitate his entry into other jobs. His army background, exposure, training, and contacts are an asset, and he will rarely stay in the village but will continue related service elsewhere. He will also act as a reservist for some time to come, occasionally called back to his unit for refreshers.

The older soldier figure, who remains in the village and about whom the shopping-bag remark was made, walks a fine line between being ridiculed and revered. He is respected and admired, as mentioned earlier, but he is also the butt of many jokes made by civilians, unruly villagers whom he so carefully established distance from and superiority over. Professor Shamil explains this to me.

> His mental makeup is different. He can't easily readjust, but he has skills in administration, paperwork. If he adjusts he can lead; those who cannot become redundant. There is a joke that there was a person in our village who wrote to the GHQ and said, "Please don't make any person from our village a subedar, for when they come back they don't listen to anyone." There are those that are soluble and those that are insoluble, who stay away from people, who can't mix with normal people.

This insolubility is attributed to the mind's inability to readapt, or as Havildar Sohail suggests, his "*fauji zehen* (army mind) persists and doesn't go away." Sipahi Omar explains this: "It is a restrictive institution, and the person inside it also becomes restricted [and] can't function outside," because following orders day in and day out "finishes [his] brain." The insoluble fauji is viewed as rigid and uncompromising in his ways, a stickler for detail, a simpleton who cannot understand the *real* ways of the world. He is fit only for taking orders and living in the confined space of the barracks, in the self-contained world so deliberately created for him. He is a target for schemers, and I was told many tales of how such and such subedar lost all his commutation money in a business venture that didn't pan out or was cheated of his money because he was too simple. This was often told with a chuckle and a wink; it seemed the village perversely enjoyed the idea that the superior fauji was brought down a notch or two.

To some extent, the retired faujis I interviewed saw themselves the same way. Many were acutely conscious of their limitations and their insolubility and tended to view these as the defining and irrevocable influences of fauji life, a life that was simpler and easy to predict. It seemed that their ability to switch had diminished over the years, or perhaps they did not want to switch anymore. They found themselves unprepared for the civilian world, which was referred to in pejorative terms—as crooked, disrespectful, and unreliable. Being a retired fauji was an asset; it granted them status. But they were aware that it also made them somewhat vulnerable to covert ridicule. The many retired subedars, havildars, and sipahis I met in the village were easy to tell apart from their neighbors by their manner of dress, posture, and even language, as many could converse in fluent Urdu as well as in their native Punjabi dialect. The difference that had been so carefully created seemed difficult to shake, which was also the experience of their wives and children, some of whom had spent time with them in various units. They were nostalgic about their past—the friends, experiences, and environments that were so different from those of the present. And whereas earlier there had been a continuous balancing as soldiers flitted between the civilian and martial worlds, the flitting now was between past and present. Ironically, now that they were finally free and back in the civilian world, they continued to live stubbornly in the martial world, because as Sipahi Omar said, "The poor man, he stands still because he cannot do anything else; the fauji is only good for the fauj."

The narratives shared with me of soldiers' lived experiences are varied, for this living traverses a multiplicity of characters and moods in myriad physical placements. The seminaked seventeen-year-old puffs up his chest and throws out his shoulders as the measuring tape is put around him in the district recruitment center. The hesitant new recruit's tears and homesickness hang like smoke in the bathrooms of the regiment training center. The shortsighted fool flees the mold and the *pakki naukri*, running back to the familiar village. The soldier encounters sights and feelings in combat that can't be processed even within the interiority of self. The retired simpleton returns after service and floats about the village, forever changed and distinct. These varied glimpses of the soldier figure are separated by time and represent what the soldier experiences at different points of service. The next chapter continues the stories of the soldiers of Chakwal, who have been marked in ways more permanent than the ways that the body, mind, and heart were during soldier training. These are the sons, given to the military—a new family, a new mother—who come back to the village—the old family—in coffins.

CHAPTER 5

GRIEF AND ITS AFTERMATH

When I cry, then I ask
You were a child looked after by God

My child, I would wake
I would wake up at dawn to grind wheat
You would be lying asleep
And I would grind the wheat
Then I would leave,
Sometimes for Karsal, sometimes for [Rawal]pindi[1]
Sometimes I would leave you in the room inside
Sometimes I would throw you on the cot outside
You were a child looked after by God

When dusk approached
I would feed the cattle
Or pick peanuts from the field
Or I would cut sugarcane
When I returned in the evening
Only then would I feed you
the little milk I had

You should have died then
I would have forgotten you by now
Why did you not die then?
When I cry, then I ask
Why did you not die then?
—From a vaen by Sajjida, Palwal, December 2014

SAJJIDA AND I were strolling back from the *barsi* (death anniversary) gathering of another *shaheed* (martyr) from the village when she turned toward the cemetery, opened the side gate, and walked in. I didn't comment on the detour, because Sajjida's house lay across the field in another direction. She made her way to her son's grave, sat down on some stones nearby, and resumed talking. Sajjida's husband had died young and left her with six children to look after. She had farmed her small landholding and also worked as a laborer in other people's fields for much of her life. All four of her sons had applied to join the army, and two had managed to get in. She had lost her second-youngest son six months ago to the conflict between the army and the militants in Wana.[2] The grave was surrounded on all four sides by three-foot-high walls that had been painted and decorated with ornate wrought iron railings. The grave itself was still uncemented, because according to tradition, a *pakki qabr* (cemented grave) isn't to be made until one year after burial. A large Pakistani flag waved atop the grave, and there was a cupboard in the enclosure containing the Quran. The *vaen* (a Punjabi mourning ritual) quoted at the beginning of the chapter was spontaneous; she broke into it as we sat by the grave. I heard her say again and again, her voice deep and raspy, that she wished her son had died when he was a child, when death would have been less painful to her, albeit less meaningful. The tone of the vaen was bitter, the choice of words reflecting a deep rejection of the narrative of meaningful death and demonstrating the need for release from pain. This was a lament filled with reproach and torment. Unlike the grief spectacles organized on the national stage, the story of Sajjida's grief and loss unraveled in the local space of the village.

Through an ethnographic exploration of military death and its reception in rural Chakwal, this chapter highlights the complicated ways in which powerful grief undergirds the relationship between the military and the families of dead soldiers. Rituals surrounding the deaths of soldiers signify a balancing between split worlds. This theme ran through the last chapter, in which I discussed the battle for possession of the soldier's body, mind, and heart, and continues in this chapter, in which the battle is now for the body and its ghost. The military continues to claim the soldier in his death; he is handed over in constrained and modulated ways. Control is of the essence and is founded on arrangements that manage information and emotion, create connections with family members in gendered ways, and form coalitions with local religious leaders. The military sets death in the service of the nation apart from *aam* (regular) death, and they achieve this through the spectacular and performative nature of the funeral, setting out procedures and rules for each step. Within these enactments of grief, women come to signify a necessary, emblematic, cathartic force, making untimely violent death both acceptable and at the same time a point of concern. The anxiety this causes is dealt with by seeing the woman as irrational and primitive.

The grief caused by the death of a soldier can be assigned three temporal phases, marked by how the private moment shifts into the public space, moves in sync with the demands of enforced military discipline, and yet retains its interiority. The first phase is the news of death and the points at which the body arrives at the house, is reclaimed shortly after by the military, and is buried in the village graveyard with full military honors. The second phase begins after the trucks leave and military attention fades to some extent. The third phase, in which grief goes beyond the local and expands to the nation, was covered earlier in the book. These phases are lenses that allow for a study of how raw grief for a dead son is transformed into willing sacrifice for the nation. No linear progression is implied here, because in real life and real time the grief goes back and forth between personal and public.

PHONE CALLS, COFFINS, AND SPECTACULAR PARADES

In rural Punjab, grief and mourning is heavily gendered, with women and men playing contrasting and complementary roles. Men get on with the business of grief, taking care of details such as arranging the funeral, and although they too will break down and weep, these are isolated incidents that are tolerated for short periods. Women are allowed more extravagant displays of vocal grief featuring loud wailing, beating of the body, and abandonment to the throes of pain, in which they almost refuse to accept the separation of death. They are expected to hold on to the corpse, which, regardless of gender, is placed in the inner (female) sanctum of the house before burial. The wailing will be loudest when the moment of separation actually happens and the coffin is taken out of the house to the mosque or a nearby field for the funeral prayer. In addition to members of the family and the *biraderi* (extended clan) from near and far, neighbors and professional female weepers will descend on the household. The weepers will undertake vaen, a Punjabi mourning ritual involving weeping and wailing, in which the deceased is remembered in a dramatic elegy that can convey pain, loss, and anger at the parting. This is addressed to the deceased, and the women will recount the loss to the family and the fate of those left bereft.[3] Women typically will not accompany the body to the mosque for the funeral prayer or to the graveyard for burial.

The rituals of military death and mourning differ from the practices just described, an echo perhaps of the many disconnects that mark the soldier during his life. Families recount the first phase of grief as beginning with the news reaching them, often as a phone call, which is sometimes official and sometimes from a friend who was with their son. If the news is unconfirmed, then the wait for the next phone call is terrible. Even when the news is from an official source, though, the crippling wait continues, as the dead body can take up to a week to arrive. For the military, the normalcy of death—its very expectedness and their preparedness for it—is in sharp contrast to the intimate permanent rupture that the family experiences. Control over information is deemed vital by the military at this point, because this moment sets the tone for the relationship that emerges between it and the family. The military is concerned that the news reaches the NoK through the *right* source and in the *right* way, before the family is informed by media reports or friends. The military's administrative machinery rolls out preordained standard operating procedures that detail who will inform, who will be informed, how many will go to the funeral, which units will be mobilized, how the body will be transferred, to whom money for funeral expenditures will be given, and so forth. The body arrives with an NCO, JCO, or officer (a captain, major, or colonel), depending on the soldier's rank. It is placed inside the house of the deceased, and a soldier is assigned to guard it. If the funeral is to be held on the same day, twenty or thirty soldiers will accompany the body. If it arrives at night and the weather permits burial to be delayed, more soldiers arrive for the funeral the next day.

The military's preoccupation with appropriate grief is evident at this point in their call to the family to not cry or mourn. *Matam* (mourning) for the shaheed is disallowed; instead, it is a time to rejoice. This is repeated not just by military officials but also by the village cleric and villagers as they console the family. Vaen is discouraged, especially once the military has arrived. Martyrdom has to be treated differently, as a religious trope that folds into the demands of military funeral rites. Displays of grief are controlled, and emotions are held in check. The village cleric informed me that

> in an *aam janaza* (regular funeral), the public reacts and responds in a different way. Grief and sorrow are expressed here [at a military funeral] but differently. It is true that the sadness of separation is also there in the case of a shaheed, but it ebbs away under the flow of emotions. . . . At a funeral of a shaheed, we naturally have to sometimes give an [additional] sermon for five to ten minutes . . . for those who have lost a dear one. He should let go of this grief and shock and instead express joy that he is the father of the shaheed. There is absolutely no mourning for the shaheed. This is a moment of pride.

Military officials accompanying the body fill in male members of the family about the requirements of the military funeral. The refrain to not cry is directed more toward women, with men called on and expected by the military to ensure that women's affect stays within prescribed limits. A consequence of the differentiation between the roles of men and women at this time is that men experience this affective regulation as less intrusive, because as I spoke to the families in villages, it was the women who spoke more often and more freely about the many ways in which the military disciplined and controlled this moment. Despite the refrain to women to not cry, or perhaps because of it, when women spoke of the news and the funeral, they spoke in the idiom of tears and crying. Ayesha, whose nineteen-year-old son had died after eighteen months in service, is one of many who attested to the policing of affect by men, in this case her husband. She explained that "they did not take me to the graveyard. Women normally don't go, but when someone is a shaheed, women will go along to watch the parade. His [the dead son's] father did not take me. He said to me, 'A woman can bear less, for she is weak.' He said to me, 'You say *namaz* (funeral prayer), [but] the shaheed has a high status; you can't cry for this death.'" She stopped and then added, perhaps to further explain to me why her husband didn't think it was wise to take her, "I looked at the flag on the coffin, and I felt *okha* (uneasy). I still feel that way when I see the flag."

Another way that affect is managed is through controlling physical access to the body when it is handed over before burial. Women often discuss whether family members were able to see the dead body and whether they were permitted to touch it. Sometimes they were allowed to touch the face. Other times, when the body was too mutilated, the coffin was sealed, and mothers would remember the helplessness of not being allowed to hold their sons one last time. For some women it signified an inability to be private in that last moment of parting, a longing and regret they lived with. For others it became a moment of defiance, a taking back of the son given to the military before he was reclaimed one last time to be buried forever. Parveen, whose son had died in the Kargil war, recalled the night before the funeral when she pried open the glass on top of the coffin while the soldier guarding it slept. "I folded back the cloth that covered him. There was a crisscross of bandages on his body.... I didn't open the coffin; I had just removed the glass. There was a lock on the coffin. I took off the glass to look at him." She added defiantly, "To look at the face of *my* child."

Women are singled out for recompense by the military as per military compensation policies, and money exchanges hands right from the beginning. Kausar, a widow, recalls the first few hours after her husband's body was placed in the home: "They [the military] don't stop us from crying. They know they can't, even if they say so. They do say, though, 'Stay away, sister. Have *sabr* (patience). Don't cry so; he is alive.' But nobody listens at that moment." Kausar suggests that the military navigates cautiously through the rawness of the emotion unleashed in such a moment. She says, "Who can listen to anyone at that moment? They put their hands on our heads and say, 'Listen, sister, mother, don't cry. Your brother, your son, is alive; he has left you with so much.' But nobody is listening." The military allows women to cry, recognizing that it has little control at this juncture, yet its desire to stem the grief is evident when it tries to discipline them with religious platitudes ("Your son is alive") and by referring to the compensation that the mother and widow will receive ("He has left you with so much"). Compensation becomes a clumsily applied balm, and the patriarchal institution steps in to support "helpless" women who are to be taken care of now that their sons or husbands are no more.

Military funerals are fondly remembered events, a part of village history, and are retold with great gusto by the village that serves as audience for these spectacles. The colors, inflections, and moods in these descriptions change and shift according to the narrator and his or her proximity to the deceased family—the closer the relation, the more morose and intimate the recollections. People recall it as being a grand event, citing the *sohni* (beautiful) or *zabardast* (spectacular) parade, the impressive gun salute, and the large numbers of people coming from afar to watch. Video recordings by families of these tightly choreographed ceremonies depict a mix of ritualized imagery and snapshots of raw, uncontrolled pain.

The first shot of the recording of the funeral for Aslam, a soldier from the village, is of a dead body shrouded in white. It is not a serene body. The face is mutilated, with black sutures around the mouth, possibly to stop it from bleeding. The white shroud has two distinct bloodstains. The eye area is discolored, swollen, and bruised. The shot captures the body from all sides, dragging over the disfigurement. The lingering gaze of the camera is in direct opposition to how military protocol demands that the body remain covered. This persistence in recording the mangled body that the army wishes to veil, the desire to repossess the dead, defies the narrative of the glorious body, dead in service. It is a body of someone not at peace, possibly in much pain when he died. There is no sound at this point. The body is inside a coffin, but the lid has been opened halfway. Once the lid is closed, the body is lost to sight, with only a small portion of the face showing through the glass section. As if this distancing were not enough, a flag is draped over the coffin.

The second shot is of an all-male crowd of villagers carrying the *charpai* (traditional woven bed) with the coffin through the uneven dusty terrain of Palwal village. In the background is the sound of bitter weeping, possibly from a woman standing close to the person filming. There is no order to this crowd of mourners, at least to the onlooker. It seems that there is a central group holding the coffin aloft, with others swirling around it. There is the sound of men chanting a verse from the Quran, a dull morose sound, rhythmic and repetitive. The coffin's progress is not even; it stops, apparently for no reason, and then starts again. It almost meanders through the field, giving the impression of a lack of purpose, as though the group doesn't know where it is going or is in no hurry to arrive there. The men in the front, or at least some of them, are visibly distressed even as they chant along. Some wipe tears from their eyes. Women follow at the back, separated from the main crowd. Hesitant and scattered yet very much there, these women have come to see the *janaza* (funeral), unlike the men, who have come to read the *namaz-e-janaza* (funeral prayer) and be part of the funeral procession. Many women are perched on rooftops that dot the landscape, their more colorful clothes providing relief from the rather gloomy, drab, and colorless procession that moves forward, seemingly going nowhere.

At one point the camera swerves, and we acknowledge a new presence: two men, strolling along wearing combat camouflage, the Pakistan Army's battle dress uniform. The two officers have come to attend the funeral. Some soldiers can also be spotted in the more traditional khaki uniform. They stand out as different, out of place, on the fringes of the crowd. They look deferential and almost hesitant, their downcast eyes and posture totally at odds with what is to follow. Another swerve of the camera and we see three army vehicles: one a large truck and the others a Toyota Hilux and a small bus. There is no metaled road here, just dusty, unmarked terrain, so the presence of these vehicles stands out. There is no video of the namaz-e-janaza itself. I was told that the videographer stopped filming in order to join the namaz congregation himself.

After the earlier chanting, the silence that follows the namaz-e-janaza is almost deafening. Cocks can be heard crowing in the background. The body has been handed over to the military after the janaza. Around the newly dug open grave, the villagers are seated as in an auditorium, watching and waiting. Four soldiers now carry the charpai to the graveyard from the large field where the namaz-e-janaza was read. Gone is the studied nonchalance; these smartly dressed men are charged with purpose as they march in unison past the tombstones, through a corridor of soldiers, and toward the open grave. A few villagers are in sight. As the coffin moves forward through the corridor, soldiers salute by changing the position of their guns. The coffin is carried ceremoniously. Each step is measured, in marked contrast to how it was carried in a burdensome manner earlier, as though the men carrying it were without purpose, were grief-stricken almost to the point of impotence. But here there is purpose, order, and meaning.

The charpai is placed on the ground. The men carrying it march away, and four other men walk up to untie the flag draped over the coffin, which is folded ceremoniously and put aside. The coffin is now carried to the grave, with two men on each side, and lowered into it. Villagers and family members join in the process, and as the coffin is lowered, the camera captures it descending. There is the sound of someone sobbing—a continuous, monotonous crying. Someone says, "*Mere bache!*" (My child). But these are inconsolable, disjointed sounds, almost an aside. No one takes much notice, and no one joins in. There is a brief shot of a man sitting next to the open grave, emitting the steady crying sound. Then there is a flash of color: a woman at the grave, maybe the mother or maybe a sister, but the camera doesn't linger on her. Unlike on the national stage, women are peripheral to the image here.

The soldier in charge shouts "*Doje admi peeche ho jayein!*" (Unnecessary men should retreat), and order reigns once more. The momentary chaotic lapse when the coffin was being lowered passes, and the gravesite becomes visible again. Halfway through the filling of the grave, the soldier holding the national flag walks up and affixes it to the head of the grave as earth is poured in. The next image we see is of a mound of earth covered by rose petals. Three wreaths prepared by the military are now laid on the grave, one each by the regimental and unit commanders and one by the soldier's father. The wreaths are identical, but their bearers differ, as does their grief, which may last longer for some than for others. The men are brought up one by one to lay their wreaths, each accompanied by two marching soldiers. Their movements are exaggerated, their arms swaying like well-modulated pendulums and feet stomping in unison as they turn from one side to the other. Another soldier then marches up and moves the wreath to the side so the next one can be placed. There is a man for each job; each step is automated and ordained, following in a seamless fashion. The master of ceremonies calls the father to step forward and take the flag and cap from the officer in charge. The father, a drooping old man clad in a beige *chaddar* (loose cotton wrap) and white *pagri* (traditional Punjabi headdress), steps out of the mass of spectators and shuffles to where an army officer waits. He stops a few yards away at a designated point, clearly having been coached. Holding the flag and cap, the officer and a soldier march forward and hand them to the father. The officer touches the father's arms as though to support him. The officer then moves back abruptly, turns smartly on his heels, and marches back. The father continues to stand there uncertainly, and then a younger man, maybe his nephew, walks up, takes the flag from him, and leads him back. It looks as though the father has broken down and is sobbing. Before the camera moves back to the grave, the same officer is seen embracing the father, an acknowledgment of the uncontrollable grief that takes place outside the prescribed ceremony.

The ceremony goes on, because the chain of events cannot be broken. The guard commander, a JCO, now takes the microphone and recites two verses from the Quran:

> And say not of those who are slain in the way of Allah, "They are dead."
> Nay, they are alive, though you perceive [it] not.
> —Quran, 2:154

Think not of those who are slain in Allah's way as dead. Nay, they live, finding their sustenance in the presence of their Lord.

—Quran, 3:169

The guard commander starts to give a brief sketch of the soldier, who has now been buried. He hesitates while he searches for the soldier's name and details and then starts again. His name, his village, his unit, his joining date, and where he died are the most significant things mentioned in this representation. That he played cricket on the very field where the village read his janaza today, that on his last leave home he lied to his unit officer and stayed an extra night so he could watch the *kabadi* (traditional wrestling) match taking place on the same field, and that he was pale faced and ashen when his family went to say goodbye to him as he left for Waziristan with his unit are unimportant details in this rendition of his life. The JCO announces the *azazi salami* (ceremonial salute): "All are requested to stand in respect. Those of you in uniform and those wearing a pagri will now salute this loved son." The call is clearly to men only and addresses all men in the gathering, even as it addresses army men and civilians separately. Women continue to just sit and watch.

Two rows of six soldiers standing a few yards away alongside the grave come into view as the guard commander asks them to change their positions from attention to at ease. The guns go up and down in sharp, coordinated moves. Their synchronized movements are impressive as they shift their weapons from *neechay fung* (the ground arm position) to *bazoo fung* (the sling arm position) and then to the front of the body with both hands in *salam fung* (the salute position). This is followed by a perfectly coordinated gun salute. A soldier standing by the grave plays the "Last Post"[4] on a bugle horn, a direct remnant of the British Army. The song is a mournful note played to signify the final farewell. It symbolizes the end of the day, that the soldier's duty is done and he can now rest in peace. This is followed by an invitation to a local *maulvi* (cleric) to come and say an additional *dua* (prayer). The spectacle needs closure to seal the sacrifice within the folds of faith, and this too needs to be managed so it is just the right length. Hence, the cleric is instructed by the military beforehand. The camera shuts off at this point.

The rites accompanying the death of a soldier, from the point the family is notified, to the time the coffin arrives, to the moment the last truck leaves, are a zigzagged patchwork of deeply private moments of pain interspersed with ritualistic, regulated grief performed for effect. Despite strict regulations, there are many moments when this discipline is defied and pain threatens to take over, such as when a mother opens the coffin to touch her son, or the camera and memory lingers over the mutilation of the body, or a father sobs as the coffin is lowered and the son is lost forever.

The management of the family and their affect during this period is heavily gendered in a series of conflicting moves. The masculine military manages the external business of dying, much as the men do in a traditional Punjabi household during a regular funeral. Thus the men in the family are rendered passive during military funerals. They are reduced to the helpless feminine, merely receiving instructions from the military. The father weeping helplessly at the side of the grave or breaking down during the ceremonial handing over of the cap and flag juxtaposed with the composed and stoic military reflect other emasculations.

The way women grieve is a point of concern for the military. A brigadier from the military directorate, which organizes funerals, explains this preoccupation.

> The soldier's family, especially the mother and wife, are very *jazbati* (emotional). The soldier has gone through training; he is more educated and less emotional. Grief affects the *zehen* and can demoralize and stop future generations [from joining the army]. We don't want to distress them [the family] further, so sometimes it is best that they do not see or touch. We want to save them from pain and distress.

The military attributes strong, uncontrollable emotions to the family, especially the women. It constructs women's affect as primitive and irrational because it recognizes that unconstrained grief can be demoralizing for others. The need for management of women's emotions is couched as benevolent concern for their own good and also emanates from a desire not to upset the valence that military service has in these terrains. Sara Ahmed, in delineating the gendered politics of emotions, has suggested that the subordination of emotions "beneath the faculties of reason and thought" serves to "subordinate the feminine and the body." Women "less able to transcend the body through thought, will and judgement" are regarded by the military as too jazbati to be able to navigate this painful moment.[5]

A denouncement of the feminine ways of grieving not only regulates affect counterproductive to militarism but also gives male members an opportunity to *become* male again. The military calls on men to grieve differently than women by involving them in managing women's grief and in paying tribute during the funeral, which acknowledges only males in the public space, in keeping with village tradition. Men are allowed a role as spectators, and their presence is acknowledged. And men (not women) are called on to salute the shaheed at the funeral. Women and their grief must be watched and controlled, yet this grief must also be visible and emphasized to allow the emergence, so crucial to the militarism project, of distinctions between the gendered bodies of stoic men and those of helpless women.[6] By setting themselves apart from women and controlling them, the men in the family grieve differently and thus delineate their own manliness and hardiness. Through this control they regain their masculinity, which has been threatened by their own overwhelming grief and the military's takeover of death and its rites. These moves gender how mourning is carried out in the village, where men rally around a military that calls on them to be men and separate themselves from the feminine, the weak, the primitive. The concerns of the military mean that traditional gender roles are appropriated and reimagined, just as they were when the soldier went through similar ministering in his military training.

The family is silent during funerals, unlike at the national ceremonies, where they often appear onstage and speak. On the national stage, set up on military terrain, the military's control is supreme, and the body of the martyr and the grief of his family can be appropriated to the military's best advantage. In national ceremonies, the mother and father *civilianize* the military space by bringing emotion and pathos. In the local setting, the civilian space must be *militarized* to bring order and regulate unbridled grief. The local stage demands a different, more intimate management, for it is a raw moment in which the mutilated body is ever present and the grief fresh. At this time, the father and mother would be unreliable conduits through which to portray the compliant, self-sacrificing subject. The military machinery pays careful attention to the affective content of these incidents. The encounter here between the military and its subjects is in a space that is not entirely predictable, so the tenor of the relationship must be set in deliberate, precise ways. The masculine military manages the external business of dying and permits the excesses of the naive feminine, personified here by the family and village, whose permanent and devastating rupture is controlled according to the military for their own good. Theirs is a negotiated stance that will discipline affect and yet tolerate affective overflow and deviance through benevolent management.

AFTER THE TRUCKS LEAVE

I turn now from these dramatic and spectacular events to the ceaselessly mundane life of the village and its residents. The picture I sketch in this section is based on recollections by the families and friends of dead soldiers and on reminders, or hauntings, of these young men, visible in the homes and public space of the village. For the former, I obtained differential access to a range of gendered characters based on their willingness to engage with me. The latter is an exercise in *hauntology*, a neologism suggested by Jacques Derrida that acknowledges the ghosts that are ever present in the now.[7] These ghosts appear in the speech of the living and are made visible through tangible physical mementos and memorials in locations in which they once existed. They also manifest in affective spaces in which memories conjure faces, bodies, and objects that no longer exist yet make their absence felt.

Reminders of the villages' sacrifices for the nation and the lives loved and lost are visible across the physical landscape and in the privacy of people's homes. Palwal's landscape is overrun with images of the state and representations of the dead, both physical and concrete; they linger in space and hang in the air. A billboard displaying pictures of the martyrs of Palwal adorns the entrance to the village. Initially, the faces of the men on the billboard were just a blur to me, indistinct and inseparable from one another, not just because of the symmetry imposed by the photographer's shots and the army uniforms they wore but also because of their expressions: solemn, determined, and uncommunicative. As my fieldwork progressed and I spent more time with their families, I saw pictures of their premilitary lives, read their diaries, and heard their childhood stories. Then their faces started to look different. Just as the billboard changed for me with time, so did the substance of the stories that emerged from the families and villagers.

The predominant narrative, one that burst out almost before I started to inquire, revolved around the ideas of willing service and selfless sacrifice. Like the faces on the board, these narratives blurred and merged into one another so that there were not five different lives and five different stories but one monolithic version of what happened to all these men. I heard similar scripts of service and sacrifice for the nation repeated to me again and again as I was welcomed into the homes of dead soldiers. One after another, mothers, fathers, wives, brothers, and sisters spoke about the inevitability of death, how it was preordained as God's will. There was constant reference to the sacredness of this death, a sense of pride that the son of the family or the village will live on and be remembered, unlike many others whose lives and graves go unmarked. Dying for the nation was considered synonymous with dying for Islam, thus the dead soldier was a shaheed, to be accorded the highest place in heaven. The lost son had been special from the beginning, different from others, brave and loving. Some had expressed a desire to sacrifice their life and attain *shahadat* (martyrdom in the name of Islam). Men would dominate the conversation, but because I was a woman, the mother, sister, or wife of the dead soldier would sit in. Families would share the date he died, where he had been serving, how they heard the news, who had come to tell them, and how the funeral had happened. In a village space in which most people cannot accurately recall their own age and in which time and space seemed suspended, there was an almost uncanny remembrance of the son's death, sometimes down to the day, the unit he was in, and his military enrollment number. For many of these women, tears lingered very near the surface and would spill over from time to time. The men would talk of grief but only briefly. Many moved quickly on to other topics, brushing aside conversations about the son. They would instead ask for support in making their demands to the military for greater recruitment quotas for the area, for a *pakki* (metalled) road, or for a medical dispensary in Palwal.

It was obvious that the families were accustomed to inquiries and scrutiny of their lives, and their scripts were ready and, for the most part, uncannily similar in substance to the YeD/S programs that the military produces every year. Yet they also seemed different in a more nebulous way. These conversations seemed charged with affect that bristled on the surface, and even as family members spoke of shahadat, the grief and sense of loss in the room was palpable. The pride they expressed seemed like a veneer that shimmered over the conversation but never quite settled down. For obvious reasons, the dead haunted the conversation, but the physical space of the house was also infused with their presence. Houses were often marked with the name of the martyr and his father on a plaque at the gate. A framed picture of the dead son in his army uniform (*recruitry ki photo*—a photograph taken on military graduation day) or a larger-than-life poster left over from the barsi held the previous year would also be placed in these rooms. These homes were affective spaces suffused with many references to the dead in objects and pictures. The presence of the dead was sometimes most marked by their absence from spaces that had earlier resonated with their presence, such as the doorway the son used to walk through when he came home on leave or the courtyard where he would sit on the charpai and eat peanuts. In one of these initial encounters, a mother kept staring at a fixed spot on the floor; she then told me her son used to put his army boots there when he came home on leave. There were no boots there today, yet as she spoke of her son, her eyes stared fixedly

FIGURE 7. *Graves of* shuhada *in Chakwal. (Photos taken by author.)*

at that space. These spaces were also haunted in more concrete ways, because many of these houses had been renovated using compensation money received from the military, so the brick and mortar bore testament to the loss endured.

Palwal, like most of the district's villages, holds on to its military roots in an intimate way that emerges from affect associated with soldiers who have physically lived, walked, studied, played, and prayed in these spaces. The graves of military dead stand distinct in the village graveyard, each conspicuously marked by a large Pakistani flag. The graves of the shaheed are surrounded by *chardevaris* (four boundary walls), which provide space for close family to eventually be buried alongside the shaheed. Although the practice of embellishing the graves of *shuhada* existed prior to the war on terror, adornment has become even more pronounced since the dead started coming in from the war in northwest Pakistan. The more recent graves are remarkably similar in style in terms of colors and tombstone engraving, with plants and ornate iron grills. The military has no role in their upkeep; these graves are maintained at personal expense. Questions about the appropriateness of adorning the shaheed's grave, the fact that the grave occupies a larger plot, and a certain rivalry about whose grave is the best looked after are themes that emerged as villagers and family members spoke about them.

Sometimes other members of the village begrudged the extra space taken up by the grave, and on two occasions there were altercations about how much space could be taken up. In one incident, the status of military death as shahadat was questioned in the context of the current war against Muslims. In the other, doubt was expressed about whether a death had been due to war injury or because of illness. Nobody was willing to talk too much about the tensions surrounding either of these cases. This reluctance speaks to the discomfort at disturbing the revered status of the shaheed and, through that, the honor of Palwal. The dynamic mentioned earlier in which the district inscribes service and sacrifice on its physical landscape partly to claim entitlement to military service is operational in this context. Yet on these very local terrains, the ornate graves and the Pakistani flags also serve to forever mark the village as a space haunted by those who were once present on the terrain and are no more. Unlike grand national monuments directed toward the citizenry at large, these are memorials that also turn inward, reminders to those who sacrificed.

Every year, Aslam's family celebrates the anniversary of his death in a ceremony held on the village field, complete with tents, carpets, and chairs. The local graveyard is adorned with rows of Pakistani flags, and motivational war songs blare over the public address system throughout the morning. A particular favorite is *"Eh wataan ke sajeele jawano"* ("The Handsome Young Men of the Country"), a melody that became iconic during the 1965 war with India and has since become associated with military commemoration of shaheeds. The local government school lets out early, allowing the boys to attend and sing *naats* (poetry) for Prophet Muhammad (a Barelvi[8] hallmark) and make patriotic speeches. A local cleric delivers a special sermon after afternoon prayer. Many aspects of the village ceremony mirror national commemorations, yet it is an altogether more intimate affair, because many of those who attend and speak at this ceremony knew the dead soldier personally. It is a male-only event, with the women attending a more private ceremony at Aslam's house, where they read the Quran. Food is served at both venues.

At around 11:00 a.m., young boys emerge from the school at the back. Most are between seven and sixteen years of age, identical dots in their blue shirts and grey trousers. As I watched, they grew larger and became more distinct. Some were quite small, others much older; some walked briskly, while others chattered, giggled, and loitered. A few recognized me as their English teacher and waved at me. I waved back hesitantly, as I knew I was already conspicuous. A woman sitting behind me who had accompanied me from the women's event shouted, "Don't talk! Walk in line!" Even as she said it, a man, probably a teacher, came into view and they started to fall in line, into columns of three waiting to enter the tented area. It was a surreal moment. Row upon row of young boys, not yet men, wait to be called, to join the (commemoration of the) nation's dead, a disciplining done by the village, men and women, young boys lining up against the backdrop of the Pakistani flags waving at the back.

Dramas and debates in schools often have a nationalistic theme, which is reflective of the larger national scenario. In Palwal this theme usually revolves around martyrdom. The private school in Palwal, hidden away within its narrow alleyways, often puts on short plays for its prize distribution ceremony. The year I was in Palwal, the theme was martyrdom once again. The children performed a skit in which five of them stood onstage holding pictures of the village shuhada and singing a patriotic song. On the side, four children were dressed up in costume as the family. The young girl representing the mother sat crying silently and holding an army uniform in her hand. The boy dressed up as the father was sitting and writing. He would look up from time to time to stare into space as though he was thinking. The younger brother was depicted playing with a ball, and the sister was consoling the mother. These are gendered depictions of who moves on, who continues to hold on, and who is more modern and educated and can think and grieve appropriately. Yet it was obvious that they all grieved. It was a sad song, even as the children sang it with spirit and energy.

To a great extent, the encounters presented here provide a glimpse of the militarized civilian in Palwal, militarized because of the similarity between how sacrifice for the nation-state is depicted by the military and how it is depicted by the dead soldier's family and the community. These depictions rotate around scripted themes: pride in the act of sacrifice for the motherland, belief in eternal life for the dead, and a plea for ongoing war so the sacrifice does not go waste. It is clear that Palwal chooses to remember and eulogize its dead with scripts very similar to those seen at national military commemorations. Within the local space, we can read these reproductions of the state along the lines of the Foucauldian analysis of power, as reiterations of power in which the subject is implicated.[9] These reproductions are clear evidence of state power working in a more dispersed way, with the state narrative finding its way to groups beyond its immediate gaze, in which subjects themselves are producers of statist discourses[10] and affective responses strengthen rather than dismantle the dominant social order.[11] Yet, even though the subjects did not always go off script in the verbal realm, this narrative was not all that was conveyed in these encounters. Grief was certainly palpable, and the physical spaces, the material objects, and the affective residues that lingered in them—what Yael Navaro-Yashin calls "affective geographies"—spoke of an afterlife of affect that defied easy or simple closure.[12] These were residues that refused to be painted over with pride alone and were visible in the pictures of the men placed at the village entrance, the plaque on the gate, the forsaken doorway through which the son used to walk back into their lives, and the empty space in which the boots once sat.

GRIEVING ALL WRONG

Imran had joined the army when he was a little over seventeen and had died in operations in Swat within his first three months of active duty. The father's drooping, sorrowful figure walking back and forth to his son's grave and sitting by it for long periods is a common sight in the village. The social studies teacher in the government school in Palwal, a young man, reflected on the grief of Imran's father: "I have noticed him; he has taken it to heart. He has not thought about it from the other angle [of shahadat]. If he thinks from this angle, that shahadat has its own position, reputation, then he might have got some relief. He is not thinking from this angle; he is only thinking from one angle: that his son is no more." The schoolteacher suggests that Imran's father finds it difficult to follow the path that will allow him to move on and come to terms with his son's unexpected and violent death. It is a story of grief that refuses to follow script, despite instruction. This and other similar stories are expressed even as the parallel script of shahadat remains intact, flowing along unhindered and unchecked, like the tears. In these villages, grief caused by military death shifts between the private and public realms and between familiar and unfamiliar scripts and practices of death, mixing yet insoluble, like two different colored dyes swirling around each other.

Sajjida, whose son's death was more recent, performed vaen for her son twice during my interviews with her. The first time she did so I was at her house. As she spoke to me, she asked her sister for a picture of her son. Her sister handed her two photos, one taken at the end of his training period—his recruitry ki photo—and another at his wedding, six months before his death. Other family members were there, women who sat around her and let her sing and cry as she rocked back and forth, the pictures in her hand. The vaen was slow, mournful, and melodic, and she asked for death for herself so she could be with him and not feel pain. The other women did not try to comfort her but joined her from time to time in chorus or in sobbing. In Sajjida's second vaen, discussed at the beginning of this chapter, she wished her son had died in childhood and not in battle. Like Imran's father, it seemed that she too was unable to find solace in the narrative of shahadat and sacrifice that the military and her religion offered her, defying it almost against her will through crying, a practice that the military tries to discipline. As she said, "I can't help it [crying]. You can lock someone up in a steel cage, but she still can't help it. As for my son, it is fate; even if I try, it [his death] will happen. I tell myself it was his fate, this shaheedi. Even then my tears don't stop."

Three deaths happened in the village within a year. As the dead bodies and military trucks rolled in, there was a growing sense of fear in the families that had sons posted in combat areas. The schoolteacher said to me,

> Families were under pressure, as the situation was dangerous, yet they couldn't ask them [sons in the military] to leave. The financial condition of the home is such that they cannot leave, so they wanted them to continue. So they tried to encourage them by saying, "Yes, times are difficult, but you have to do this no matter what." But they [families] were burdened. . . . There was another boy in the village, around the same age; he left the army and came home. His family told him to come back, . . . as they are slightly better off.

A thread that surfaced as families spoke about the loss of their sons was regret. They felt regret that he went into service, regret that they didn't insist that he desert when operations started, and regret tinged with guilt that they couldn't save him when he expressed a desire to leave. Some spoke about it in a wistful tone, some in anger, and some in deep grief. Yasmin, Nawaz' mother, recalls the tension and indecisiveness surrounding the last time her son went back to his unit, which was stationed in a combat zone. "The last time he went back he was very unhappy and restless. We had decided that we would not send him back. We didn't want him to go, [and] he didn't want to go. . . . People around us told us to not make this mistake; they said to us, 'Let him go; he will return.'" Nawaz's father agreed to speak to me after I had been coming to his house for over six months. An hour or so into the conversation, as he began to speak of his son's deployment in Wana, the conversation became more emotional; he was visibly distressed as he talked about his last few encounters with his son. He would stop, start again, and then stop; his eyes would become wet, and his voice would break. The following exchange was particularly emotive, and he seemed to shiver as he recalled the last time he spoke to his son: "If he hadn't gone into service he would not have become a shaheed. He called me. He told me that there was a boy from his unit who had died. He said to me, 'Abu [father], the shaheed boy was lying in my lap.' He [Nawaz] was agitated. He said to me, 'Father, get me out of here. I can't concentrate; things are very bad. I could become a shaheed too.' There was a short pause as he struggled to speak, his voice barely audible. "I had told my older brother take him to Saudi, but he didn't. He (Nawaz) went into the army because of the [financial] situation in the house."

Unlike Nawaz, Sajjida's son never expressed a desire to come home, but she struggled with not having done enough to stop him.

> Sajjida: My son, the one who is shaheed, I tried to stop him [from going back to his unit]. I said to him, "My son, the goats and cows have to be looked after. I have to work outside the home. I am alone; your father is dead, and now you also want to go. You can do so much here to help me."
> Me: You wanted to stop him because . . .
> Sajjida: I wanted to stop him for my *sukh* (comfort). You sit here, and I sit here. Who knows how we will die? What will be the means through which death will reach us—fever or vomit?
> Me: Or in war?
> Sajjida [*sharply*]: I don't know anything about war. I just wanted him to retire and come home, and that's why I got him married.

In the families' narratives, thoughts of *What if the son had left (or deserted) the military?* found their way into conversations, although they continued to refer to him using the honorific "shaheed." For many, military service is linked to family aspirations for financial security. The push to enlist has always been expressed as being about *ghurbat* (poverty) and *bhuq* (hunger). Military service is a gamble, a risk taken with the knowledge that it will result in the hardship of separation and a life away from the familiar. It can also extract a heavier toll, and when the odds turn against these families, a terrible price is extracted. Service in the military and the subsequent death of a beloved son cannot then be reduced to what it is—an aspiration for a better life—because that brings up intense guilt. The regret families feel for having *allowed* the death to happen is immense, and the difficult burden of guilt creates a lingering anxiety.

Closure for this stubborn afterlife of affect is not easy to achieve through the narrative of *shahadat*, or sacrifice for the nation. Affective residues and excesses, a mixture of regret and guilt, infuse families' narratives and are visible in the many ways in which mothers, fathers, and wives in villages continue to grieve "inappropriately," hinting at dissonance in these subjects of militarism. Inasmuch as these subjects seem to move within and only within the webs of disciplinary power that speak of this sacrifice, as is evident in military funeral rites and the practices after, in their affective displays they sometimes stand outside them. There are many moments when the hegemonic scripts of willing sacrifice for the nation fall short, and yet subjects continue to read from them. What follows is an investigation into this obstinacy, this desire to continue reading, by looking at the emotional and affective involvements invoked in these practices and rituals of death and at the kind of political subjects that perform, watch, and emerge from these performances of grief.

COMPLIANCE AT THE HEART OF AMBIVALENCE

To suggest that variances in the script of willing sacrifice during and beyond the dramatic burial represent a dichotomy between public and private narratives would be inaccurate. Although these slippages are more pronounced in the private realm, they seem to sit alongside military scripts, allowing for a lacing together of both critical and statist narratives. Villagers fluctuate between fetishizing the military and betraying a *knowing*, a *seeing through*, that they express through affect even as they actively perform during these moments and endorse the desired scripts of shahadat for the nation. Nawaz's father, who had earlier expressed regret that he did not have the resources to take his son out of the army after his deployment to a combat zone, explained this compulsion to me.

> As I walked back from the funeral, I received a call from the colonel of his unit. I said to him [that] if I had ten sons, I would give them to the country.... You say this because we exist because of this country, and [only] if the army exists then we have this country. *Kehna parta hai* (You have to say this) to the colonel [because] your *jazba* (passion) rises as the army gives you *izzat* (prestige) and *rutba* (status) and buries you with *azaz* (ceremony).

He seems to acknowledge that what is said in these moments is sometimes rhetorical, as subjects feel compelled to say something they may not mean because it is expected and because of the heady mix of honor, status, and ceremony that goes with military death. Mothers and fathers willingly and unconditionally offering up their other sons to the military in commemorative ceremonies is another example of the compulsion to say things that the heart may not desire. Back home in the village, Yasmin and Nawaz are grateful that the military has offered employment to another son but will only send him if the position is within a department that does not deploy to a combat area.

Peter Sloterdijk puts forward the notion that the dominant mode of functioning of ideology is cynical; the cynical subject is conscious of the distance between the ideological mask and his social reality, and yet he continues to cling to it.[13] Slavoj Žižek expands this further when he says, "Ideology is, strictly speaking, only a system which makes a claim to the truth—that is, which is not simply a lie but a lie experienced as truth, a lie which pretends to be taken seriously."[14] In her study of Syria under an authoritarian regime, Lisa Wedeen speaks of the "shared condition of unbelief," in which Syrians acted "as if" they revered the regime.[15] In the context of the Turkish state, Yael Navaro-Yashin speaks of "automatons" who, despite their consciousness of the notion of the state as an abstraction, continue to reproduce the state in practice.[16] Wedeen calls this the politics of "as if," whereas Navaro-Yashin names the condition "cynicism."[17]

As the villagers in Chakwal themselves reiterate, it is a mask they have to put on, and it's one they know they put on. They say, "*Karna parta hai, kehna parta hai*" ("You have to do this; you have to say this"), clearly signifying an awareness that wearing this mask is a symptom, but they are still compelled to do it. Navaro-Yashin attempts to explain this compulsion through the notion of "mundane cynicism," or a "pragmatic recycling of statism in daily life." She suggests that "for these cynics, the line between carrying or deconstructing the symptom is thin: it is the mark between livelihood and death; the symptom is a tool for survival."[18] If the symptom consists of endorsing military funeral rites and mouthing the rhetoric of the shaheed, then carrying the symptom allows a secure livelihood and social position. In this case, it is clearly about economics and material benefits. This would be one way to explain the military's obvious and extraordinary hold on these populations: their fear of the military apparatus and the repercussions of making their dissonance known. They wish to benefit from the compensation that is handed out at this point and safeguard the possibility of future recruitment into the military. But this description of the compulsion that makes adherence to the mask so necessary only half explains the story. In these villages, it is also about grief and the strong emotions it generates as well as a need to make meaning out of what has been lost forever so that the loss can be justified. I complicate the compulsion to hold on to the mask through Slavoj Žižek's reading of Lacanian psychoanalysis. Žižek posits a resolution to the dilemma posed by the seeing and knowing automaton: "Ideology is not a dreamlike illusion that we build to escape insupportable reality; in its basic dimension it is a fantasy-construction which serves as a support for our 'reality' itself: an 'illusion' which structures our effective, real social relations and thereby masks some unsupportable, real, impossible kernel. . . . The function of ideology is not to offer us a point of escape from our reality but to offer us the social reality itself as an escape from some traumatic, real kernel" (quotation marks in original).[19]

Here, ideology—the belief in the narrative of sacrifice for the nation's military—operates not to help families evade or deal with social reality—the death of a loved one—but to build a social reality (death seen as meaningful) to escape from some traumatic real kernel (their own implication in the death). In this case, the traumatic real kernel consists of guilt and regret, thoughts of *what if*, and more pragmatic concerns about how to accept the compensation money that is to be received. This real kernel is what makes the discarding of the mask unthinkable. Affect-laden moments, which are marked by tension, unease, and contestation and hold the potential for subversion, paradoxically become the very junctures that permit a return to hegemonic power. Affective residues create an anxiety that is soothed not by challenge but by reiteration of military narratives. There is a strong desire to make peace with the permanent rupture of death, a peace that is uneasy and unsettled and must be constantly reclaimed in the interest of social status and position and, more importantly, for the affective interiority of the subject.

I bring two further elaborations of this notion of ideology as "fantasy . . . an escape from some traumatic, real kernel"—not that the army used the son as cannon fodder but that family members themselves are implicated in that fact—both of which revolve around affect. Affect makes these fantasies possible and becomes its substance, and it is affect that makes these fantasies forever tremulous, never at ease, and in need of constant reaffirmation. The phrase *karna parta hai* (you *have* to do this) is spoken in the present tense; it suggests a constant doing, a perpetual fixing of meaning that seems to slip and that fails to stay in balance. There is compliance at the heart of ambivalence that refuses to settle. The rituals of remembering in local terrains try to suture through this ambivalence, which could potentially challenge the relationship between the military institution and the district and thus unsettle the district's dominant source of secure livelihood and bring in its wake unsettling affect about those *willingly* sent and lost in harm's way. This narrative is guarded not only by the military but also by the families and the village, expressed as reverence and love for the transcendental figure of the shaheed. There is a veiling of narratives in which grieving went awry that are seldom spoken of and yet understood. These are open secrets that everybody keeps.

The military institution hooks onto the grief and regret, claims it, and ritualizes it so that no other narrative can stake a counterclaim. For the families, collusion with the military implies that they wear a mask that does not stand for duplicity but signifies a veiling, a mask that is never at ease, because it nags and aches. In these rural spaces, allegiance to the script of sacrifice for the nation is linked to the need to keep grief, regret, and guilt at bay. Militaristic scripts of service and sacrifice are grasped tightly because they function as salves, a repurposing and meaning making that serves as protection from external and internal censure. Palwal keeps its dead alive in order to make sense of these ruptures and soothe hauntings of lives loved and permanently lost.

The next of kin stand ambivalent about the project of militarism and the use of their blood to serve a construct that they may not believe in or want to sacrifice for. Yet they accept this violence inflicted on them and on the bodies of those they love. They say "*Khena parta hai*" ("You *have* to say it") and behave as though they do believe. They say it because they know the military is watching. They say it because without this frame the son's death would be futile and the grief too great to make sense of. They say it because they *need* to say it to avoid the guilt and the realization that maybe the risk taken was too great and because they must accept the money and benefits offered, as it was for material needs that the tribute to the nation was risked in the first place.

The next chapter continues with the stories of those who die in wars and brings to the fore an associated aspect of military death—compensation and reparation offered and received against loss and damage endured for the nation.

CHAPTER 6

THE VALUE OF LOSS

THE MONETIZED ASPECT of military death is an imperceptible narrative that exists alongside the more visible stories of loss, pride, and sacrifice. The complicated ways in which material tribute is offered as reparation for losses that are essentially irreparable—because death is final and the loss of limbs or faculties permanent—becomes acceptable and even claimed aggressively by those who receive this compensation are also part of these stories of sacrifice. Ayesha, who lost her nineteen-year-old son in South Waziristan, expressed her pain and in the same breath juxtaposed it with the futility of the recompense offered for it. "My heart explodes [in pain] when I think of him. Money has no value *agar puttar nahio labda* [if you can't find your son]," Ayesha explained. "If he had not become a *naukar* [gone to serve in the military], he would not be a *shaheed* and would be alive today." Ayesha vocalizes the inability to find her son with *puttar nahio labda*, signaling a continuous searching. Much like the way the earlier phrase *kur nu purtu hai* (you *have* to do this) is spoken in the present tense, this phrase also signals a constant doing, a relentless burden of grief and regret that is not assuaged by what is offered in its place.

Material compensation offered by the Pakistani military is constructed as irrelevant and any mention of it is absent in the spectacles of commemoration and mourning despite it being an almost foundational weave in the tapestry that is military service. How and why is this invisibility desired, deployed, and maintained are important questions to answer to better unpack these economies as they yield insight into the desires and anxieties of the military institution and of those who receive compensation. The focus in this chapter shifts to the transaction, the paternalistic contract that serves as the bedrock of the relationship between the military and its subjects, and to the functions and limits of these regimes of compensation in case of death of the solider.

The reason for most compensation regimes offered by the state is to address losses incurred by its citizens for which it takes responsibility. Strategically, compensation regimes serve to present and uphold the image of a benevolent state that assumes responsibility for the safety and protection of its citizens. They acknowledge the state's inability to fulfill this responsibility and allow reparation for losses incurred as a result. Compensatory regimes for security personnel such as the police and the military, for whom death and disability are calculated risks of employment, are additionally driven by such practical concerns as sustaining morale, ensuring loyalty, and reducing desertions.[1] In this case they operate much like the gifts and countergifts suggested by Marcel Mauss, reflecting the cycle of obligation and reciprocity, although in this case the debt owed might be for life itself.[2]

Conversely, the politics of compensation can also work to exculpate the state, such as when governments readily offer reparation for their action or inaction without mitigating the circumstances that led to loss of life or damage to property. Furthermore, disparities within compensation regimes might deepen existing inequalities among citizens.[3] Disparity between the compensation offered to civilians and to security personnel—including military soldiers and civilian law enforcement officers—is marked not only by what is offered but also by the administrative mechanics through which it is made available. An analysis of this disparity reveals how lives and the accompanying grief of those left behind are valued differently based on how the dead are constructed—as passive, unintended, and unfortunate victims or as active defenders of the nation deliberately sent out in harm's way. Jennifer Mittelstad's study of the US military's welfare policies for its all-volunteer force suggests that the military's ability to secure comparatively generous welfare for its troops lies in its ability to pursue a politics of separation from the civilian.[4] This politics proposes an incomparability between military duty and civilian service in which the former's entitlement to benefits is considered higher because of the risks involved in the line of duty. An examination of this incomparability within Pakistan involves deciphering how the military sets the dead soldier (and his beneficiaries) apart from the dead civilian and dead policeman (and their beneficiaries) and how military compensation regimes are distinguishable from other compensation schemes in their substance, mechanics, and logic.

THE MECHANICS AND LOGIC OF MILITARY COMPENSATION

There has been a steady evolution of compensation policies in the wake of Pakistan's escalating role in the war on terror (WOT) and the resulting high number of casualties of security personnel and civilians.[5] Provincial and federal governments in Pakistan began introducing administrative measures between 2005 and 2008 to compensate civilians, including government officials who were killed in the WOT.[6] These compensation packages are often one-time cash payments that are discretionary, with high variance between provinces. These regimes lack independent budget lines at the federal and provincial levels, which undermine accountability and transparency and also lead to delay in disbursement. Often driven by "political expediency rather than due process and impartiality," there is an absence of comprehensive policy and supporting legislation to govern these systems.[7] These mechanisms are often criticized for complex award procedures, nonuniform treatment of victims, inadequacy of facilitation, and grievance mechanisms available to beneficiaries.[8]

Compensatory regimes for security personnel are more expansive and long term than those offered for civilians. In addition to cash payment, they can include pension schemes as well as allowances for children's education, land allotments, and opportunity of employment for one family member. These schemes have been upgraded considerably even as the disparity between the civil law enforcement and the military persists in what is offered, how it is offered, and how readily it is offered. Unlike the more generous military compensation regime,[9] police departments often have to publicly advocate for upgrade of their compensation packages with provincial governments.[10] Police compensation regimes have been upgraded since the WOT casualties in that department but are still not on par with those given to military soldiers; more importantly, the police force does not have comparable infrastructure in place to assist families in their implementation.[11]

Compensation packages for the families of martyrs in the Pakistan Army began to be enhanced after the Kargil war, according to senior officers interviewed during this study. Public acknowledgment and commemoration of the martyrs in this conflict were slow in coming, but the compensation packages were enhanced, notwithstanding this delay.[12] Another upgrade followed in 2005 as a response to the rise in casualties from operations in the northwest region. In 2009, the army set up the Shuhada Cell under its Welfare and Rehabilitation Directorate to administratively improve compensation mechanisms and reach out more effectively to the families of the deceased. The Shuhada Cell's central office is located in the GHQ, with branches in each of the corps headquarters. These are further supplemented by cells in regimental centers, which in turn are linked directly to the District Armed Services Boards (DASBs) in sixty-two districts of Pakistan. Each DASB reaches down to the local village level with its extensive network of welfare officers. The soldier's parent unit also acts as a contact point for those receiving reparation. The services of the Shuhada Cell and its regimental counterparts include meticulous record keeping, the ceremonial handing over of the dead body, and organizing funerals and regular correspondence and connection with families, including invitations to *Youm-e-Shuhada* (YeS) and *Youm-e-Difah* (YeD) ceremonies. DASBs support these cells in facilitating the compensation process, including helping families to complete the paperwork for claims and settling any disputes that arise regarding the distribution of compensation.[13]

The compensation package provided by the Pakistan Army to its *shuhada* is in two distinct parts, the first comprising emoluments given by the government of Pakistan (GOP)[14] and the second offered by the

GHQ itself.[15] The second portion covers educational, vocational, and health benefits and is funded partly by deductions taken by the military from the salaries of all officers and soldiers during service and from the profits of the military's business activities. Land allotment is reported under GHQ emoluments, and the rationale given for this by officers interviewed is that undeveloped land, which the government releases from time to time, is developed using the military's own funds and as such is owned by the Pakistani military. This division between government and military serves as one explanation for the more comprehensive reparation packages offered to military shuhadas and disabled soldiers compared to those offered to the police, which rely primarily on government funding. Many senior officers interviewed also attributed this difference to the "inefficiency" and "lack of concern" of police management in demanding, procuring, and organizing better compensation packages for *their* martyrs. Soldiers and families are aware of what the government has allotted them and the emoluments they receive from the military. This distinction also strengthens the exclusive kinship bond between the military and its subjects, which stands outside the contract between the government and its soldiers.[16]

Visibility of reparation schemes of civilians and, to some extent, of civilian law enforcement officers exists, and the GOP (including provincial police departments) openly announces its compensatory packages.[17] The deliberate effort to publicize these packages can be seen as an attempt to placate a wounded and suffering public after particularly horrific man-made or natural disasters, and it underlines the importance of preserving the image of a benevolent state. The next of kin also have a visibility and a voice other than those that are institutionally regulated. Dissatisfaction about what is being offered sometimes ensues and is expressed through questions about unfairness or corruption in implementation or through disputes between the deceased's heirs in the corresponding civil court cases. Such events usually receive coverage in the media.[18] There are also regular images of the affected receiving money or in-kind assistance, such as food rations, from politicians and sometimes army officials, as when the Waziristan conflict caused people to be displaced from the Federally Administered Tribal Areas.

Those who receive aid or compensation are presented as helpless, pitiable, and sometimes "suspect" creatures in desperate need of assistance, while the state is portrayed as benevolent and generous.[19] Although the compensation regime may aspire to reflect the obligations of the state to its citizens, reparation can often be arbitrary, especially in the case of civilians, and is presented as an act of charity. It is also presented in full view; in fact, there is a deliberate attempt to ensure that these images go out.[20]

In the case of military deaths, compensation regimes operate according to the logic that what has been lost can be replaced through a combination of material means and affective regulation achieved by commemoration and meaning making. Hence, in addition to material compensation, there is also heavy institutional investment in commemoration. While the latter also exists for civilian deaths, as in commemorative functions for police martyrs or victims of terrorist attacks, these tend to be reactive and one-off events, and they are not as sustained and systematic as military commemoration narratives and events. Interestingly, insofar as both material compensation and commemoration are important ways the military attempts to provide reparation for loss, the military seeks to separate these two functions. Unlike the reparation packages offered by the GOP for civilians and civilian law enforcement, schemes offered by the military are largely missing from the public narrative, almost as though they were irrelevant. In the entire YeS extravaganza, set up to talk exclusively of the shaheed, there is no mention of compensation or the transactional part of this arrangement. No money is handed out and no announcements about the generosity of the government or military are made. The image of the deceased soldier and his family does not inspire pity; instead we have the brave soldier and the stoic family. There is also no behind-the-scenes visibility once the compensation regime rolls out. Instead, all martyrs are folded into the military infrastructure; any dissatisfaction or disputes that arise are managed internally. The military, through its ample administrative apparatus that reaches into the local, goes to great lengths to ensure that the bitter property disputes and family estrangements that flow once this compensation economy kicks in are hidden from public view. Benefits and facilities are received from the paternalistic master (the military) and redressal of grievances is expected from the kinship group (again the military).

If one intent of compensation packages is to appease possible discontent by building the image of a benevolent state that looks after its subjects, the military forgoes this opportunity by veiling the transactional aspect of this relationship. The military as a kinship group is well insulated and its relationship with its constituents firmly entrenched, hence any image building in this regard is deemed unnecessary. Pragmatic reasons for the deliberate masking of military compensation are obvious. The military seeks to downplay the disparity in the value assigned to dying for the nation on the basis of whether a uniform is worn or what color that uniform is, because the compensatory packages for military dead are more generous.[21] The military might also wish to veil these schemes to allow it to compensate victims of more controversial wars such as the one in Kargil. Its ability to mask compensation regimes allows it to appease and recompense NoK that it may not be able to publicly acknowledge.

Within this pragmatism there also lies a more strategic rationale for constructing these schemes as irrelevant to the discussion of the military martyr. The reluctance to foreground this aspect of the relationship is reflective of the Pakistani military's desire to construct death and loss as willing sacrifices that are not regretted, meaning that the figures that now embody that loss are not to be pitied. Imagined as unflinching and resolute, they cannot be depicted as needy, and, more importantly, they cannot be seen as desirous of compensation or engaged in a transactional relationship with the military. Generous and predictable material compensation handed out through systematic policy and local structural mechanisms is at odds with the narrative of *shahadat*, in which the reward is in the afterlife and in which the preciousness of life and limb cannot be brought down to an exchange system that values them in terms of death gratuities and plots of land. Such a dilemma is not intrinsic to this exchange, and in the case of state compensation for civilian deaths, including those of police officers, it seems in fact not to exist if we are to go by the very public displays of the state's "generosity" or the contestations over and demands for redressal by families. In these cases, those who are affected *demand* redressal and compensation and show willingness to openly enter into a system of exchange that can monetize the loss. It is a dilemma that is unique to military death because of the unease that stems from the military's desire to shield the compensation received.

The military's narrative of selfless sacrifice is terrain on which the military is able to command blanket acceptance through the blood of its dead. The military is at pains to not advertise transactions with the families of the deceased because a generous monetized transaction that systematically calculates losses and efficiently delivers compensation is less effective in justifying the narrative of selfless sacrifice that it repeatedly uses to present its image as savior of the nation. Calculating and transacting a loss essentially entails that the price has been paid and the transaction completed. The military must be in a position to *continue* to demand compensation from the nation for sacrifices it has made in its defense that *cannot be compensated*. The relationship between the military and its cannon fodder must not be monetized so that it can be continuously appropriated to maintain the military's image as selfless protector—an image that the military needs to command loyalty from the nation. The reduction of transcendental sacrifice to a monetary exchange between the institution and the family must therefore be avoided and the transaction constructed as irrelevant to the business of sacrifice. The constructed irrelevance of these economies lies at the heart of the military's ability to depict the loss as one that cannot be compensated. Thus the dead and their families can continue to act as conduits for extraction of the nation's support.

The military's desire not to destabilize the image of selfless sacrifice results in a need to distance itself from financial transactions that lie at the core of its ability to sustain recruitment. Ironically, though, these monetized transactions concealed in other spaces must be ever present in the relationships between the families and the military institution if these relationships are to hold. The military establishment oscillates between ideologies of nation and religion, including tropes of honor and sacrifice, and the materialistic drivers of service emoluments and postdeath compensation regimes to cement its relationship with the families of the deceased, emphasizing different ideologies at different times. On the national stage and within public narratives, the invisibility and suggested irrelevance of material aspects of sacrifice are easier to maintain, because these domains are largely about acknowledgment and commemoration of loss. In bureaucratic spaces and local arenas in villages in which these compensation policies are formed and unfold, respectively, this visibility and relevance become harder to escape.

ECONOMIES OF LOSS

Because service in the military and death in combat are possible outcomes in the gamble for a better life, loss, damage, and compensation play out in complicated ways for the families of the deceased. They too are invested in masking this compensation, for reasons that are perhaps more obscure. The overriding trope is one of gratefulness, which is further testament to the district's enduring relationship with the military. These local spaces regard the military as an institution that looks after its subjects from the "cradle to the grave and beyond."[22] But interspersed with these narratives acknowledging the military's generosity are distinct threads of overwhelming grief and residual unease. Imran's father, whose inconsolable grief and unceasing visits to his son's grave are subjects of talk within the village, said to me with a wry half smile, "*Fauj ne to humein paise mein tol diya hai.*" (The army has weighed us [our grief] in money.) Another mother elaborates on this sentiment further, saying, "We have everything now—house, money—but *puttar nahi labda* (I can't find my son)." Yasmin, Nawaz's mother, adds, "He was our *jigar ka tukra* (precious loved one). . . .[23] I feel proud when people say he is a *shaheed*, but my heart also feels *okha* (uneasy); only mothers know how it feels. . . . We used some of the money we received on the village, gave it to the local mosque, and also dug a well for the graveyard." The sense of exchange, of giving up something vital to one's survival to receive something else in return, is palpable in these conversations. There is also a sense of having one's grief calculated on an obscene scale that can somehow assess the damage caused by the death of a loved one. The tone of these conversations is heavy with a grief that, in addition to being overwhelming, is described as okha, signifying an inability to find peace. Mothers and fathers talked about the compensation received and, almost in the same breath, bemoaned losing their sons forever. The loss was referred to almost automatically, the minute they spoke of compensation, as though the knowledge of what was received must continually be contrasted with the impossibility of it being enough to replace what was lost.

To elaborate on this further, it is necessary to first plow through the semantics of loss and compensation in the context of military deaths. Adi Ophir unpacks some of these terms:

> An evil is an injury worsening someone's condition so that no compensation is possible. Compensation assumes the existence of a system of exchange whose terms make it possible to assess the value of the injury. An injury involving losses that are expressible in terms of a system of exchange amounts to damage. Damage is a loss whose value is assessable. Loss is the irreversible disappearance of some irreplaceable thing. A disappearance is the transition of something from "is there" to "is not there" (quotation marks in original).[24]

Here, the disappearance involves the physical absence of a loved one, which leads to the intensely experienced loss of someone who was once dear and is now permanently lost. Damage for a loss can be calculated provided a system of exchange exists that can assess the injury. If there is no system of exchange, then no compensation is possible. Ophir suggests that the response to a condition of loss is mediated through "interest in what has disappeared" and "the impossibility of entering into an exchange cycle and restoring the disappeared." He suggests that "each one of these on its own is a necessary but insufficient condition" for something to be experienced as loss. There are two ways to annul a loss: first, to let go of interest, and second, "to reduce it to the exchange value in some sort of exchange economy."[25] In the case of military death, the former may not be possible due to the sheer investment of affect in the relationship with the deceased. The latter too is never totally possible, for how is one to calculate and put into an exchange system the value of a loved one beyond the economic earning power of his body? Thus, compensation offered for a loss that refuses to fully become damage hangs somewhere in the middle. The loss tries to articulate itself as damage, but the transformation remains flawed. Attempts at annulment of loss are incomplete, because as Ophir suggests, they involve two irreconcilable genres: "the genre of loss is tragedy" and "the genre of damage is the bureaucratic file."[26]

Death in the military is a tragedy made all the more poignant because it is violent, man-made, and preventable but must nonetheless be discussed as necessary, honorable, and meaningful. No questions can be asked, and no responsibility can be assigned, not just because the benevolent military stands at the other end but also because of the affective interiority of the subject. The subject is pained by the grief of disappearance and a sense of irrevocable loss that cannot be fully converted into damage as well as by the "traumatic real kernels" discussed in the last chapter. These are subtle workings of guilt and regret, because the death was not only preventable but also predictable. Service in the military was a choice the family made to improve its economic condition, and insofar as this produces regret, it allows monetary compensation to take on a significance beyond the obvious financial needs it may meet. It stands for what the son earned and what he sacrificed himself for that must now be claimed as a right. The very claim thus becomes an act of loyalty to the lost son. Sohail's mother, engaged in a bitter dispute with his widow over the emoluments received, explained this to me. She said, "He was our blood, our son. Why should we let others [his widow] consume it? Our son earned it, those who raised him, looked after him, his mother and father—it is their right to claim what the *fauj* has given." This symbiotic relationship between the military and its subjects is generated in the almost insufferable moment of separation from a loved one. The very compensation that produces unease and reduces the loss to a monetary transaction becomes pivotal, because demanding it amounts to making the sacrifice count. A terrible price once paid must now be claimed and owned as a symbol of love.

The collusion required to mask these schemes is a result of different sets of desires and anxieties in those who offer them and those who receive them. These anxieties enable the veiling of the monetized aspect of sacrifice for the nation. For the families, the relationship at this juncture is driven by a need to make meaning, reduce guilt, and quiet the unease that comes from entering into a transaction involving the death of a loved one. Compensatory regimes are unable to annul loss, and yet families enter into this transaction, motivated not just because their economic circumstances are desperate but also because taking compensation allows them to claim what their son earned. In doing so they attempt to make the loss worthwhile. For these reasons, compensation regimes come to be defined by loss: a loss that is constructed as noncompensable by the military and a loss that is experienced by the families that cannot be annulled through the schemes offered. These regimes function as economies of loss, with compensation offered by the military and claimed by families for losses that elude reparation.

In addition to being forever marked by loss, these economies are also heavily gendered. Attention to the widow and the mother in these regimes sheds light on the military's uneasy ties to the feminine.

BRINGING IN THE WOMEN
Kausar—The Erring Widow
Sohail was adopted at age five by his maternal uncle and aunt, who were childless. His biological mother and father lived down the lane, only ten minutes away. Kausar married Sohail seven years before his death in Wana. They did not have any children at the time of his death. During the funeral, his biological father was accorded the honor of receiving the flag, as the adoption had never been formalized. Kausar received a full pension and all emoluments in her name after she reassured the DASB authorities that she had no intention of getting married again. Behind the scenes, in consultation with Sohail's adoptive father, she divided all the one-time emoluments (that is, cash payments) she received into three portions—one for herself, one for his biological mother, and one for his adoptive father. She also agreed to give half of the monthly pension she received in her name to his biological mother. With Kausar's consent, the plot of land was allotted jointly to her and to his biological mother. Four years after Sohail's death, Kausar decided to marry his best friend. Although she received the support of her brothers in this decision, Sohail's family and the rest of the village cen-

sured her for moving on and soiling the memory of her shaheed husband. The marriage was duly reported to the DASB by Sohail's biological father, and the full pension reverted to his biological mother. Kausar claims that she returned all the money she was holding to the adoptive father at the time of her second marriage, but both sets of parents claimed that she did not give them anything, causing much acrimony. On my last visit, Kausar claimed she was being pressured to sell the plot of land. Her brothers did not want her to sell, so she was resisting this.

Sumaira—The Wife in Waiting
Sumaira was married at age sixteen to her maternal aunt's son, Tahir. He was injured in Waziristan shortly after that and died six months later in the military hospital in Peshawar. Tahir did not have time to report his marriage, and therefore he was listed as unmarried in the army's records. The initial papers were in the mother's name, but this was rectified at the time of the funeral and all ensuing payments were given to Sumaira, including the Distress Grant (which she immediately handed over to Tahir's brothers). Because of Sumaira's age and the marriage being issueless, it was decided between the family and the military that the pension would be jointly allocated, with a percentage for both the mother and the widow. In the month following Tahir's death, Sumaira was taken a number of times to the DASB in Chakwal for paperwork required by the military. Within a few months of his death, Sumaira's and Tahir's families were discussing the possibility of her being married to the youngest brother. The only hitch was that this brother was already engaged to someone. The village was rife with gossip regarding whether Tahir's family would keep Sumaira or let her go. Most were of the view that if Sumaira could not marry the brother she should forgo her pension and other emoluments in favor of the mother, because a sixteen-year old girl would most likely marry again. Sumaira shifted her stance over the course of our conversations, saying initially that as the widow of a shaheed she would never remarry and then in later interviews suggesting that it would be best if she stayed within the family and married the younger brother. As I was winding up my fieldwork one year later, the family was still undecided about her fate. She

shared a fair amount of weariness and said she would like to go home to her parents' house but that the brothers of the deceased would not let her.

To understand the military's relationship, its obsession and disdain, with its female subjects it may be useful to pick up from the last chapter, which laid out how grieving is gendered as a function of the relationship between the military and its subjects, particularly women. Women, with their excessive emotion, are seen as primitive, irrational, and dangerous, to be managed by both the military and male members of the village. It is to this "subordinate" being that the military turns to formalize the relationship with the soldier's family in contractual and binding ways. The Pakistan Armed Forces recognizes the female dependent as the primary beneficiary in the event of death. If a soldier is unmarried, all emoluments are made out to his parents. In this case, the mother is not specified as a category on paper, but the military will make out the pension and other deeds in her name.[27] If the soldier was married, all emoluments are to be given to the widow, unless nomination by the soldier specifies otherwise. The military, inherited from a colonial past like Pakistan's other state institutions, has chosen to continue the tradition of recognizing the nuclear family (the wife and children) as the primary recipient of the compensation it accords its married subjects in the event of death.

Money exchanges hands right from the beginning, with the salary of the deceased soldier and/or the Distress Grant handed over to the widow or mother to help pay for funeral arrangements. Kausar recounted the following:

> As I walked towards the coffin placed in the courtyard, I started to shiver as if from cold, and I felt faint when I came near the dead body; [then] I fainted. The army man who had come had Sohail's three months' salary with him. He said to my cousin, who was a subedar, "Call his widow." [And] "sign this page, sister," he kept saying to me. He gave me his [Sohail's] things. I told him to give it to my brother; he said, "No, I am not allowed to do that." He is ordered to give it to the widow if he is married and to the mother if not. Later, I gave it to my brother.

This marks the beginning of the compensation process, visible in local spaces, in which the materialist narrative cannot disappear, and hidden in other (national) spaces in which the ideological narrative must remain dominant. The woman suddenly finds herself center stage, and from then on she becomes a visible political subject, a citizen who will now need to engage with the state and its institutions. This may involve getting a national identity card, visiting the District Soldiers Board to be allotted a pension book, collecting pension each month at the local post office, or becoming a litigant in court.

The military's relationship with its two female subjects, the widow and the mother who are recipients of attention, regulation, and emoluments, is not the same. The mother figure is invoked for commemorative practices. She is placed on the higher rung to articulate the narrative of sacrifice and martyrdom, because a mother's love is depicted in popular culture as asexual and pure, whereas the wife is associated with romantic love.[28] The mother represents the archetypal selfless mourner, whose bonds of love are considered more durable and unconditional. It is ties of this kind that need to be emphasized within the militarism project to elicit the kind of nostalgia and emotion that run through the invocation of death and loss for the spectator nation. The wife, however, is an embodiment of romantic and sexual love, her capacity for which continues beyond the soldier's death, creating a set of anxieties. Some of this anxiety has to do with her unsuitability as a figure in commemorative practices that demand more durable and unquestionable bonds. Some anxiety is also linked to the possible attention she can draw to the material aspects of this relationship because of contestations over compensation distribution, especially in the event of her remarriage.

In cases in which a soldier is married, the widow is the legal recipient of benefits given by the GOP to the soldier unless the deceased has nominated another recipient. According to the Joint Service Instructions (JSI) 39/60, soldiers and officers are expected to nominate next of kin during their service from among their legal heirs, defined in order of priority (widow, son, daughter, mother, and father).[29] GHQ benefits, however, are almost always allocated to the widow and children, and soldier nomination is not a consideration unless contested. Deeds for plots of residential or agricultural land are often made out jointly in the name of the widow and her children, with their sale prohibited until the last child turns twenty-one and permission is granted by the GHQ. If the widow is issueless, shares are also allocated to the parents (again mostly the mother) and divided equally.[30] In both categories of emoluments, the widow is clearly preferred over and above the parents of the deceased, especially if she has children. Dispute committees at regimental and GHQ levels can decide distribution in cases of disagreement among heirs. This authority can override nomination by the soldier, based on an assessment of the situation on the ground. Criteria that the DASB and military officers use within dispute committees to decide the suitability of the widow to receive full emoluments are her age, the number of years of marriage, the number of children, the financial conditions of the deceased's parents, and the presence of other sons who can support the parents. If she is older, if she has children, and especially if there are other sons to look after the parents of the deceased, then the widow is protected against other claims to the emoluments. Pragmatism and fairness were the reasons suggested for this by officers I interviewed, because the mother has other sons or a husband to look after her, whereas the wife loses her main source of income. Many officers recognize the vulnerability of the wife in a joint family system after the death of the husband and defend the need to safeguard her against male members of both her husband's family and her own who seek to control her.

In the case of seventeen-year-old Sumaira, described earlier, the family of the deceased fears that she may marry again or move away from the deceased's parents, taking the emoluments with her. They seek to hold on to her by either having her remarry within the family or, as in the case of Kausar, making claims to the DASB or regiment center if she does marry and/or move away. Marriage in rural settings is almost always within the extended family, and these disputes can be especially bitter. Stories of widows such as Kausar who marry again or move out of the deceased husband's home and of parents who thus do not receive a share of military benefits are common in villages. The military is therefore faced with the challenge of trying to appease two distinct sets of next of kin. The primary question is whether the widow will move back in with her parents or stay in the house of her deceased husband. This is not merely a question that lurks in the minds of the deceased's family or that sparks gossip but one that is explicitly asked of the widow when she is taken (because she is not independently mobile) to the local DASB office at the time the property deed and pension book are made out. The military accommodates these anxieties, and policy states that the pension reverts to the mother in cases of remarriage. In situations in which the widow is young and issueless and thus is more likely to remarry, property deeds and pension are allocated jointly.

The Pakistani military prefers to settle disputes through its own internal mechanisms: the DASB and the dispute committees set up at the regimental centers. Disputes have rarely found their way to civil court, but when this happens they are settled mostly in favor of the military compensation procedures. The purported repugnance of the compensation scheme to Islamic laws of inheritance has been cited as grounds for filing a case. These concerns have been addressed by the military and other government departments that offer compensation by labeling the emoluments as gifts or grants by the employer after death, thus excluding them from the heritable estate of the deceased. This distinction between heritable and nonheritable property has been consistently upheld by various reported judgments from courts at all levels, and the law creates a distinction between benefits to which Islamic laws of inheritance apply and those to which it does not.[31]

When disputes are brought to the notice of the military institution, most often at the regimental level, the first step is the verification of the claims made by both parties, which is done locally by the DASB's extensive network of welfare officers (former army soldiers). Based on the recommendation of the DASB, the regimental center makes a decision—often regarding the two most contested emoluments, ownership of land and pension allocation—which is then communicated to the contesting parties. The DASB may play more than just a verification role here and often acts as a mediator between the two groups. A common plea from the dispute committees to both parties is to not tarnish the glory of shahadat by dragging the sacred name of the shaheed through the courts. As the secretary of the DASB in Chakwal, a retired army officer, explained to me:

> I try and talk to them and remind them about their son's sacrifice. I say this [compensation benefits] is your son's sacrifice. These people forget that this is the money of a shaheed. I tell them your son was lucky to have received shahadat. Don't you understand the shaheed lives forever? I tell contesting mothers that they should let the widow take the pension and ask them if it would be acceptable to the shaheed that his widow goes about borrowing money from people for day-to-day expenses.

This theme, often brought up during mediation by the military apparatus, also tacitly runs through the civilian court system. The officer in charge of the Shuhada Cell shared the story of a civil judge who had called to tell him that a shaheed's family had come to his court regarding a dispute over compensation money. When the officer told the judge about the presence of dispute committees right up to the GHQ level, the judge told the families to go to the GHQ. The officer was quite pleased with this, saying that "he [the judge] told them that by dragging the case through a civilian court they insult the shaheed."

The widow is an unpredictable figure as far as the parents of the deceased are concerned. The military acknowledges her vulnerability and her claim to emoluments but colludes with the immediate family of the deceased in attempting to question and ascertain her motives. Unlike the mother, whose devotion to her son is unquestioned, the widow is painted as a somewhat tragic figure, in need of protection but also unreliable, whose sexuality must be watched. Her suitability to receive the emoluments assigned to her as the primary next of kin is conditional and cannot be taken for granted. Such conflicts are usually garbed in talk of the shaheed's honor, and what is often at stake is a set of anxieties of the family (about their inability to stake claim on the emoluments given) and of the military (that the resulting conflict between the two sets of kin might lead to public disputes and contestation). For the latter, control over the management of disputes ensures that these disagreements are addressed internally and do not find their way to the civil courts or the media, a motivation in line with the need for invisibility. The affective tenor of these mediations constantly draws on notions of the sanctity of shahadat. The tales of these disputes are folded in again and again by the military and its local institutions in the district and by the families and the village with the refrain that the sanctity of the shaheed must not be damaged by open talk of money or family disputes over money.

Because of this attention to the female subject and her significant role in compensation regimes, one may argue (or hope) that her entry into the formal institutional mechanisms of the state as a citizen enables more autonomy. The DASB secretary highlighted the need to protect the interests of the female recipient, and the DASB authorities will in principle insist that the mother or widow be present for the pension books to be made, that they must physically make a trip to the post office every month to collect pension, and that they must once again appear before the DASB or at times even the GHQ in case of transfer or sale of land. But a closer look at how these women's lives do and do not change after they lose a loved one in the military perhaps unsurprisingly reveals a different scenario. Like the war widow in other societies, the Pakistani military widow is subject to stereotyping and discrimination and can be abandoned by the state if she decides to remarry.[32] Male members of the family further compound these problems through active control and interference. It is often the father or the brothers of the deceased or male members of the widow's family who will actually control the emoluments and make decisions regarding their use.

Although it would perhaps be easy to attribute the failure of policies to translate into meaningful autonomy for women to the conservative rural environs in which they unfold, the failure lies in part with the logic of the policy itself. In analyzing historical welfare policies for women, Eileen Boris and Peter Bardaglio suggest that the "nineteenth and early twentieth centuries . . . saw not the decline of patriarchy but its transformation from a familial to a state form."[33] In other words, modern social policies protect the status quo, reflecting dominant male interests and regenerating patriarchal norms even as they may unsettle or disturb relations between men and women within families. Building on this finding, Mimi Abramovitz argues that American social policies strengthen a "family ethic" around the position of women.[34] Such policies tend to reward certain kinds of women whose lives include marriage, motherhood, and, in the cases discussed here, fidelity to a deceased husband. Conversely, Theda Skocpol has argued for an optimistic recognition of the "crucial differences" between the "paternalist" British social policy of the early 1900s, which was based on male breadwinning ideals and was devised by men in an attempt to benefit women through male wage-earning capacity, and the "maternalist" early US labor policies, which were based on similar ideals but were advocated for by women and applied directly to women, such as pensions awarded to war widows.[35] I suggest that the transformative potential of modern welfare state policies is severely limited, at least in the case of military compensation for female next of kin, because they are essentially paternalist even when they benefit women directly. In fact, these policies further embed women in sets of gendered relations, which reinforce male domination and control and, in this case, compliance with the militarism project.

The singling out of the female by military policy is not a recognition of female autonomy or the right to claim benefits as the spouse of a soldier who died in service. Instead it is reflective of the patriarchal state that enforces a *family ethic* that recognizes women as dependents who are taken care of when the male breadwinner dies and who if not tended to will be a disgrace and embarrassment to the institution's (and the shaheed's) image. This is in keeping with the trope of the helpless woman whose honor is at stake if the nation is undefended and who needs the masculine military to defend her. Furthermore, women's ability to access these emoluments depends on the benevolence of the state patriarch, here the institution of the military, which determines her suitability as a subject. She must meet a set of conditions, and transgressing those boundaries can result in favors being taken away, as with the reversal of pension in cases of remarriage. The state then turns to a more suitable female subject, the mother. Moreover, even when the widow stays within these boundaries, the male patriarch of the family will step in to control management of these emoluments. As recounted earlier, Kausar handed over the money to her brother almost immediately. This transfer from the state patriarch—the military institution—to the woman for a brief moment and then back to the patriarch of the house is significant.

Thus, it is no surprise that these policies yield limited autonomy to the female subject, even when land deeds and pension books are made out in the names of women. The terms of policy, progressive and affirmative as they may be in principle and in their early implementation, are doomed as much by the status and position of women in rural Pakistan as by the logic of the terms themselves. This logic hands out benefits and services to dependents belonging to the "weaker, more primitive" sex, who are pulled into the project of militarism in ways that further enmesh them in the institutions of the family and the nation-state. The masculine state's erosion of the family patriarch (initially through the grieving processes and then through compensation procedures that name the female as primary next of kin) is to be seen not as a chipping away of patriarchy but as part of its subtle transformation from familial to state form. This transformation neither weakens the structure of relationships between men and women nor translates into visible agency for women but instead positions them as pawns between men, first between the military and the family and then between the male members of the family.

The receipt of emoluments by the female subject serves the military in two ways. First, she is perhaps the ideal subject of a compensatory regime that seeks to remain masked and irrelevant. The giving of monies in exchange for loss through death in battle seems less transactional and materialistic when the recipient is the grief-stricken female subject and also supports the trope of the vulnerable woman (or nation) in need of protection and the narrative of selfless sacrifice that the military holds dear. Second, the pulling in of the female in more binding, contractual ways also serves to bring in a more worrisome subject. This is a subject less readily swayed than the male by the notions of "*izzat* (prestige), *rutba* (status) and *azaz* (ceremony)"[36] and one who articulates the regulation of her affect at the time of the soldier's death as intrusive.[37] The difference is expressed here by Nawaz's sister as she describes the dissimilar responses of her mother and father to the military's commemorative ceremonies: "My father is a political man. He did his matric when very few people in our village had done so. He thinks; he sees things differently. My mother is uneducated. She is emotional; she only feels." This is a difference created not by any essentialist biological variance but by how the female subject is imagined and brought into the militarism project—through ambivalent policies and practices that both espouse and repudiate the feminine. In addition to my fieldwork, I base this assertion on the considerable amount of feminist scholarship supporting the notion that the bonds between women, militarism, and the nation can be more tenuous, because the direct focus of these projects has been men and notions of masculinity.[38] Whereas the sudden attention received by the female subject as the primary next of kin and the meaning this attention and inclusion accords to a senseless death may help bring her closer to this project, what ties her to militarism in more inextricable ways are the myriad social relations that define her in a patriarchal society and that stand to benefit from emoluments. Keeping her invested and complicit becomes the goal not just of the military institution but also of the male members of the family, who need her to access benefits and facilities. The channeling of compensation through her ensures that she is firmly enmeshed in the militarism project and remains a disciplined subject.

Reparation schemes for losses that are essentially irreparable—death, dismemberment, and loss of faculties—struggle with pricing the priceless and demand careful, benevolent management of the subject. Another figure embroiled within these economies of loss, also intractable like the wife (and perhaps even more so), is the disabled soldier. Despite their central placement within compensatory regimes, both sets of subjects are considered unmanageable and burdensome because they are harder to assimilate within the commemorative regimes of the Pakistani military. The next chapter brings into focus the disabled soldier, the other direct recipient of military compensation who lurks behind the more visible tropes of honor and sacrifice.

CHAPTER 7

THE BODIES LEFT BEHIND

IN WAR, violence on the body is sometimes inflicted in ways that do not lead to the most feared outcome—death—but instead to dismemberment or loss of faculties and abilities, a dying of parts of the body even as the self continues to live. Death is permanent, and the dead are silent. It is something that we must all face, and that makes it familiar, intimate, and almost comforting in its expectedness. Death also brings finality and closure. The disabled body continues to live after sacrifice; it continues to breathe even though the life it lived earlier has died. The numbers of those permanently marked by war through disablement of the body began to rise in the twentieth century due to an increase in lethal weaponry deployed in modern warfare and to advancements in medicine and lifesaving technologies available to the wounded.

The ongoing war in northwest Pakistan has resulted in the (declared) deaths of over five thousand army soldiers,[1] with well over two times that number maimed.[2] Newspaper reports of Pakistani military operations carry headlines of those dead, with the many more injured or maimed for life hidden in the fine print. The setting up of difference between the dead and disabled body conveys that the disabled or injured have survived, are going to recover and are not *real* casualties of war, which are defined as those bodies that die. The military's desire to minimize further damage to the body exposed to war and keep war fatalities low is motivated by obvious pragmatics of warfare and sets in motion the massive rehabilitative economy that is dedicated to fixing the damaged body. Guarded visibility has been accorded these incomplete bodies through their appearance as audience members in YeD/S ceremonies beginning in 2012. Sometimes short video documentaries are dedicated to them during these ceremonies and also on military-sponsored TV programs that allow reporters to interview selected disabled soldiers. The *shaheed* is far more visible in nationalist discourse, as is evidenced by the script and craft of these commemorative events. The nation hears constantly of lives sacrificed for the nation but rarely of the much larger number of men who are disabled for life. These representations suggest that although both death and disability are acknowledged as consequences of military service, the Pakistani military assimilates certain kinds of bodies (able bodies and the dead) into its narratives and discards or shields from view other kinds of bodies (disabled). Whereas the image of the military shaheed is carefully crafted through strictly regulated state narratives, the case of the disabled veteran takes on a different significance, largely because of the military's own troubled relationship with a subject that, unlike the shaheed, defies simple categorization.

This discomfort is not new. Unease with the disabled body has been a perennial part of the history of warfare. Joanna Bourke detailed the fluctuations in public and policy attention to the bodies of the disabled in England after World War I. Compared to disabled civilians, constructed as "passive sufferers," the war wounded and disabled were set up as "active sufferers."[3] The "sentimentalization" of disablement in those times constructed the disabled man as "not less but more of a man." The subject of attention from poets, films, and photographers, they were "England's broken dolls," whose absent parts represented "patriotic power."[4] Over time, the special status accorded these disabled veterans faded, and they started to be "identified with passivity—the helplessness of children who needed to be looked after for the rest of their lives."[5]

In the context of the current war in Pakistan, similar fluctuations in representations of the disabled figure suggest that the Pakistani military has only just begun to assimilate this cost of war inscribed onto the living body. Management by the military of the incompleteness of this body, its stubborn persistence in clinging to some form of fragmentary life, presents its own set of dilemmas. Ato Quayson dubs the response to the disabled body by the able and complete body as "aesthetic nervousness" signifying a concealed fear and panic.[6] This affective response is triggered by the uncomfortable recognition of the quintessential contingency and vulnerability of the healthy and whole body. Jeffrey Preston similarly argues that representation and fantasies about disability reflect *normate*[7] fears of human vulnerability.[8] These fantasies include juxtaposing disability with death, with the former being a fate worse than the latter, and setting up disability as a castration both physical, implying impotency, and figurative, implying a sense of emasculation and lack of sexuality. The chapter maps these fantasies of disability onto military representations of its maimed bodies and places them against the lived experiences of the disabled. Furthermore, by offering a comparison between the loss of the disabled soldier and his family and the loss of the dead soldier and his family and the potential (or lack thereof) within disability to offer itself for appropriation by the military, it delineates the military relationship with these intractable subjects.

REPRESENTATIONS AND ERASURES OF THE DISABLED

The disabled in the war on terror (WOT), referred to as War Wounded Persons (WWPs) by the military, have three types of disabilities, largely due to IED (improvised explosive device) blasts: spinal cord injuries, amputations (uni-, bi-, and tri-amputations), and traumatic brain injuries. The military-medical-industrial complex offers the disabled soldier a number of medical, psychological, and rehabilitative facilities through the Pakistan Army Medical Corps. The corps runs over thirty-five Combined Military Hospitals (CMHs) and medical training institutes spread across the country. In addition to the network of CMHs that serve the injured in war, the army has set up specialized centers across the country, specifically in Lahore, Pano Aqil, Malir, Mirpur Khas, Peshawar, and Rawalpindi. Compensation packages for

WWPs were upgraded around the same time as was *shuhada* compensation.[9] The current policy calculates loss based on the degree of disability and assigns one of three categories—A, B, or C—to the soldier, with category A representing the highest level of incapacitation. Discharge with full benefits implies a loss of earning power; the disabled soldier receives a percentage of his salary depending on the category he is in. In 2009, the army announced a new policy whereby WWPs were given the option of returning to their units to be assigned suitable and secure employment with full benefits.

The medical corps, in addition to providing free medical services to army personnel in wartime and in peacetime, also has a mandated role in providing health and humanitarian relief services in times of crisis and disaster to wider civilian populations. This is in addition to the services provided to civilians at a charge through its extensive network of military hospitals. The medical corps has its own set of feeder training institutes and colleges that produce doctors, nurses, and other medical-related tradespeople. The army also inducts civilian medical graduates from time to time as per requirement.

The Armed Forces Institute of Rehabilitation Medicine (AFIRM), the military's largest rehabilitative facility, was constructed in the midst of the sprawling army medical complex adjacent to the GHQ, situated in Rawalpindi, the military heartland. This complex includes a tertiary-level military hospital as well as specialized centers such as a cardiac hospital and the only dedicated department of spine surgery in the country. In addition to surgeries and other medical procedures, services provided at AFIRM include rehabilitation services such as the fitting of prosthetics and other assistive devices, vocational training, psychological support, and hostel facilities.[10] It is an expansive building that, like any other military facility, is marked by army discipline and order. The prosthetic department is a set of rooms fitted with machines and equipment, each with a designated task such as casting, filing, grafting, shaping, and, finally, fitting of the artificial limb onto the body. In the room fitted with machinery to bake the cast, a number of casts are laid out neatly, each bearing the name of the soldier who is to receive the limb. The female medical specialist informed me that the amount of time from the amputation to the fitting of a new limb can vary, because it depends on how skillfully the amputation was done in the first place, which in turn depends on the kind of medical facility the person is taken to after the injury. In some cases, surgery is needed again. Before the final fitting can be done, the wound has to heal and the stub must be formed, as muscles take shape after atrophy. Fittings have to be done periodically, and the entire process can take up to six to eight months, during which time the military encourages the soldier to stay within the facility. Other issues can confound prognosis, such as preexisting conditions like diabetes, the need for more than one prosthetic, or the necessity of a more complicated amputation (such as of the entire leg rather than just the lower leg). The presence of women and children in wheelchairs is a reminder that the facility serves civilians as well. The wards, however, are full of male army personnel. Incomplete bodies, once selected on the basis of exacting physical criteria, honed through grueling training, and further hardened through exposure to combat in severe environments, lie within these rooms, waiting patiently as the rehabilitative economy goes about its business of making them whole again. Far removed from the usual noise, odor, and disarray of public hospitals in Pakistan, this facility is marked by a sense of purpose. There is an aura of efficiency, a quiet going about of tasks in long white silent corridors, in which each step is carefully ordained and leads to the next. This would have been comforting had it not been for the proliferation of maimed bodies that were visible within the facility. Because, after all, this was, to put it crudely, a limb-producing factory in which parts of disposable bodies were produced. These bodies can be civilian, with disability resulting from an accident, but the facility operates primarily to mitigate devastating yet predicable maiming of the body as a consequence of the planned and expected production of violence.

The management of maiming by the military beyond the act of saving and fixing the incomplete body also involves a preoccupation with its representation. The deputy commandant at AFIRM, emphasizing the need for careful handling of the disabled soldier, refused to allow me to speak to the inpatient WWPs at the center. He told me that "all interviews that you see on TV are first approved by the ISPR to see if they are appropriate, and in fact an officer accompanies these people [from the media] when they visit the hospital. They then submit the video or article before they are allowed to screen or publish." In a TV program[11] telecast on Independence Day—August 14, 2015—the presenter, in an obviously scripted show carefully vetted by the AFIRM authorities, sought to impress on the viewer the steadfastness and heroism of the disabled soldier. During the course of the program the presenter asks this of a female doctor in AFIRM: "We should ask a woman's heart, has she seen a weak man in this hospital?" It seems appropriate to seek validation from a *woman's heart*, the primitive ruled by her emotions, and therefore more authentic, who can vouch that the soldier is still a man. The program plays out almost farcically with its emphasis on how brave and unflinching these men are, with negligible attention paid to the actual trials and tribulations disability brings to their lives. It is clear the army does not intend to show other, more realistic representations of the disabled. The psychologist at AFIRM paints a different picture.

> One prepares for death in battle. We as human beings think about death, but no one is prepared for disability. You see everything changes for that person. His standing in life, his position in the house. Marital conflict is common. With time, family support diminishes, and sometimes the family can break up, especially if there are no children. This is especially [true] in the case of spinal cord injuries. Engagement [for marriage] will often break for both the disabled and the spinal cord injured. . . . It is a complete syndrome and will affect their whole life. . . . We see many symptoms of distress: they will range from depression, aggression, noncompliance, [and] wanting to seek revenge. Taking consent for repeated surgeries can be challenging. Many will not inform families. We inform the family so that they can help in recovery. We have to ensure that they accept and harmonize with the new situation [e.g., the artificial limb]. . . . We have to keep them focused on recovery. We have [a] one-hundred-bed facility; we have to have them out in three months, and we have many more patients coming in. We cannot afford that they develop emotional angularities.

In the YeS ceremonies of 2013 and 2014, short documentaries were dedicated to WWPs, but these disappeared from the YeD stage in 2015. This inability to fully absorb the incomplete body into military narratives, with WWPs appearing in some YeD/S programs but not as much in others, is perhaps not surprising. In the military institution, the body is revered; an aspiration of perfection haunts the soldier from the moment he enters the institution and undergoes a series of exacting physical and medical examinations and measurements. The soldier body is paraded around (both literally and metaphorically) to show strength and discipline. The imperfect body can no longer be a representation of hardiness, bravery, and masculinity, and the military's discomfort with it echoes subliminal fears of the normate evoked in its encounter with incompleteness. Anxiety stems from the permanent nature of suffering brought about by this sacrifice and the soldier's capacity to visually represent loss in ways that may not inspire adulation. These features make him less desirable as a subject. When questioned about the periodic disappearance of the disabled from the main stage, the organizers of the YeD/S shows said that was because of time limitations and that they had to prioritize the content and themes selected for the show. Clearly, the disabled are not prioritized as highly as the shaheed. Or more aptly, the uncomplicated affect that the shaheed and his family can invoke is prioritized over the kinds of affect that may be invoked when these disabled bodies are on display. Based on the liberal splashes of the able-bodied warriors that are depicted in these shows, the image the military wants to present is that of the steadfast soldier, undeterred by the loss and wanting to return to the field to continue fighting like a man. So how the disabled body is to be portrayed now that it is imperfect, the very antithesis of all the military stands for, poses a problem. This problem is further compounded by the ability of this casualty of war to cling to life and its capacity to speak and articulate its own version of suffering. This mutilation cannot be shrouded and nailed up in a coffin; this body will be viewed by all, an object of pity, feminized because it can no longer defend itself. While the bodies of dead men serve as "symbolic capital," the mangled bodies of the disabled are not glorious enough to be depicted by the military.[12] Heroism and willing sacrifice are easier to paint on the dead than on maimed, incomplete bodies that can speak. Their inclusion in the narrative is thus less predictable in that they are sometimes allowed a presence and sometimes made invisible.

The concept of biopolitics can be a useful lens through which to view the military's relationship with maiming. Jasbir K. Puar offers an insightful perspective on Foucault's foundational mapping of biopower by giving attention to the suffused relations between living and dying. More specifically, she discusses the maiming of the Palestinian body by the Israeli state. Puar argues that the right to maim implicates vectors of both sovereign and biopolitical power: the earlier right to *take life or let live* and its complementary version, the right to *make live and to let die*. Puar suggests that "debilitation and the production of disability are in fact biopolitical ends unto themselves, with moving neither toward life nor toward death as the aim."[13] She rejects maiming (as opposed to killing) as a humanitarian action that preserves life and contends that maiming poses as *let live* when in fact it is *will not let die*, insofar as the right to maim, much like the right to kill, is exercised as the domain of sovereignty.[14] Whereas the military's role in maiming or killing its own soldier may be indirect, the ability to send soldiers to war to risk death and disability are, in essence, articulations of biopolitics. Within the context of the disabled soldier, including the attempts to minimize further damage to his body, efforts to fix and rehabilitate the damaged body, and his representation within military narratives, these formulations of the third vector of biopower by Puar become useful because they indicate the productive capacity of maiming for the military.

First, the right to *will not let nor make die* ensures that the human cost of war remains low(er) and that only those bodies that die are counted as toll. The recording of the soldier's incomplete body as a casualty of war has to be distanced from the dead, and efforts have to be made to ensure that he does not die and his predicament is downplayed. For this, the military ensures that medical facilities are always provided to its soldiers, which involves heavy investment. Using helicopters, soldiers often must be relocated as soon as possible from war zones to fully equipped medical facilities. This provision of medical aid and expansive services that does not let bodies die (after carefully training them to be willing to risk death and systematically exposing them to the risk of dying) brings to the fore the second productive capacity of this vector. Disablement involves a rehabilitation economy, as is evident by the vast array of rehabilitative services the military invests in and offers its subjects. Investment in the military-medical-industrial complex, often represented by the military as a cost of war that must be borne because of the obligation of the nation and the military to their soldiers, enables the military to enhance its medical and health infrastructure and outreach, including expansion of its medical personnel. It also allows the military to, in times of crisis unrelated to war (such as natural calamities and environmental disasters), be available to civilian populations in a role that strengthens its reputation as a savior going beyond its mandated function to serve the nation in civilian terrains. Third, the management and representation of maiming also shifts focus from why the subject became disabled in the first place to how the sovereign is benevolent in providing treatment and enablement toward a normal life through the fitting of prosthetics and other assistive equipment as well as through making alternative vocational training available. Instead of examining how disability is socially induced, an intrinsic result of modern war and armed conflict in which certain bodies and populations suffer a greater risk of becoming disabled than do others, the management of maiming tries to situate disability within narratives of the benevolence of the military, including some perfunctory and feeble attempts at narratives of empowerment, pride in resilience, and sacrifice for the nation.

INTRACTABLE SUBJECTS AND MASKS THAT SLIP
I did not go looking for the disabled soldiers in the villages of Chakwal; they discovered me through the villagers who pointed them out to me, saying things like, "Why don't you visit Shakeel?" or "Have you heard of Bashir? He just returned; he doesn't have any legs." To the villagers, the connections between my interest in those who had died in the war and in the lives of these disabled men was much clearer. The fact that when I was planning my fieldwork I had not thought I would

also come across them reflects to some extent my own internalization of the grand narrative that spoke only of the shaheed.

I discuss the experiences of the disabled body based on my conversations with an infantry *sipahi* named Shakeel and his family in Kandwal. Shakeel lives with his two sisters and parents in a three-room house on the outskirts of the village. I was introduced to Shakeel through a contact in the village, and I first met him in the marketplace. He wore civilian clothes, and at first glance his disability was not apparent. It was only when he moved and came forward to talk to me that I noticed his unusual gait, an awkward sharp jerk to the left and a hint of instability that disappeared when he took the next step only to return when he moved again. Shakeel had been in the army for two years and twenty-two days when he was maimed in an IED blast in Mahmud Agency in Waziristan. It did not take him long to speak about the battlefield, and the way he spoke about it was in stark contrast to how many other soldiers I had interviewed spoke—he talked of fear, panic, dust, and grime that others often did not mention. He had stayed in rehabilitative care for almost two years after his injury and had undergone a series of operations. When I met him he was training to be a cook and was on leave from his unit. His left leg was amputated at the knee, and the other had a permanent rod inserted in it. The cost of war was inscribed clearly on his body, and during our conversations he felt a constant need to make it visible. During my interviews with him he would often pull up his *shalwar* and take off his artificial leg. Then he would point to the other leg, which had an angry row of scars from his stitches running down the knee. He remembers clearly the day it happened, telling me, "One minute I was standing facing one direction and then suddenly there was dust everywhere. I was lying far away facing another direction. I remember that the major put my head in his lap. It was terrible. I was sobbing, and I was reading the *kalma* (Muslim declaration of faith).[15] I thought I would stop breathing." He also spoke at length of his time in the hospital, the repeated attempts to make him whole again, and his journey back to some semblance of life, including his initial instinct to shield his family from the pain he was experiencing. "I stayed in the hospital for nearly two years. They kept operating on me. I did not tell my family immediately. I wanted to protect them, but later my friend told them, and my mother and older sister came." His fiancée's family broke off the engagement after his injury. The sense of having been changed forever, of a loss that can never be resolved, whether he was in military or civilian environs, was intense.

Shakeel's family also spoke obsessively about the loss; it figured repeatedly in their conversations, and discussion would revolve around the injury. Sometimes his mother and sister would refer to him in the past tense, talking of the way he was, referring to a life and body that were no longer. They expressed how he was different, not complete anymore. This incompleteness was feminized; his sister refers to him as someone who is not much different from women, helpless and no longer able to defend others. "When he takes off his leg, he is defenseless; if someone comes into this house and takes away his leg, he can't do anything. We don't have any male in the house—our father is sick, and he [Shakeel] is like this."

Shakeel spoke hesitantly about how sometimes he was teased in the village and made fun of for no longer being whole. He said the villagers said it jokingly and suggested that maybe they meant no harm, but he reiterated that it hurt him. The tears fell freely. He was able to express sadness for his own loss, and he was able to express fear, emotions that his other brothers-in-arms have difficulty articulating. Shakeel's mother, seizing an opportunity to be private with me as Shakeel stepped out of the room, also spoke about his tears. "He still cries when he looks at his leg. Only a few days ago, he was sitting on the *charpai* and looking at his leg with a mirror. He kept looking and sobbing, looking and sobbing." Her own discomfort with his desolation comes through when she adds, "I walked in and saw him like this and said to him, 'Have you gone mad?'"

Shakeel echoes the shame of being feminized by the injury. The inability to perform and a fear of being found inadequate make him unwilling to return to service. He knows he will be assigned *feminized* tasks: tasks that women can do too, like cooking or gardening.

> I will decide [about staying or leaving the army] after some time. I want a [medical] board.[16] It is difficult to be a *ghulam* (servant) now. Earlier, I was fit. I was a ghulam because I chose to be one. Now I am unfit; now I will choose my own work. . . . Like earlier, if they asked me to do anything, I could perform, I could do it. I can't walk now; I am dependent on others. How can I work for others, follow orders? Others around me will run and do things. It will be difficult to bear that. . . . Earlier, when I went into the army, you are not aware [of the risks]. Somebody says, 'Come join the army; nothing will happen.' But now . . . I have told them [friends and family] that now I will do what I want.

Earlier, the decision to be a ghulam was a choice made freely. Becoming the soldier-subject involved a conscious letting go of control and knowingly becoming an automaton—a not wholly unpleasant experience because it was accompanied by a feeling of mastery and a sense of distance from the primitive, feminine, and civilian.[17] All this shifts with a disability that diminishes the warrior body and emasculates it in its dependency on others. Shakeel no longer wants to be a ghulam, because he fears that his incomplete body will fail him and he will be ridiculed. He says that he will choose his own work from now on. This is an interesting paradox in which the decision to serve and follow orders was acceptable earlier because the body was "fit" but is unacceptable now because it is "unfit" and stands femininized. His mother regrets his decision to join the army. "I wish he had never left for the army, never become a ghulam (servant), even if it meant him working as a laborer. He was our only son, our only support. . . . We educated only him; we did not have money to educate the girls." I notice familiar themes of aspirations for a more comfortable existence and disavowal that the decision to go into the army was in any way promoted or pushed by the family. These are echoes of my conversations with the families of dead soldiers.[18] Shakeel's mother informs me that "he wanted to go; we didn't force him. We thought we would live more comfortably, [that] some money will come into our home, and we will pass our time well."

Shakeel and his family bring up the shaheed in their conversations unprompted, a comparison that seems to gnaw at them and hang over their changed life circumstances. Sometimes these comparisons seem comforting, but at other times they hint at an envy that can be unsettling for the listener, just like the reference to Shakeel's life in the past tense.

> Shakeel: He who is hit by a bullet—he becomes a shaheed, (but) our grief stays and people feel pity for us. They [shaheed] get shot, and they finish. When others see us, they see with what difficulty we are living our lives. When they see them [the shaheed's family], they sympathize with them. Their son is dead; he is a shaheed—all is over. In our case, they will ask us, "How did it happen? When did it happen?" It becomes alive again.
> Sister: We can see his face; at least we can see his face, even if he is disabled. Those who are shaheed—their mother can't look at them; their children can't look at them. They are sad, and we are sad.
> Mother: It is a deep wound. The ones who are shaheed also feel pain, and so do we.

As Adi Ophir suggests, the ability of loss to be annulled depends on either letting go of interest in what has disappeared or entering into an exchange cycle that replaces the loss.[19] Much like the loss of life discussed in the preceding chapter, this loss tries to articulate itself as damage. The transformation remains even more incomplete, though, because unlike families of the dead, WWPs lack recourse to a system of commemoration that helps them make meaning of the loss. Constant comparisons to the shaheed's greater sacrifice, and by default to the disabled's inferior sacrifice, render efforts at reparation ineffectual. The lived experience of sacrifice at times seems to them more painful than death because of an acute sense of continuous loss. Here there is frankness, an immediate ability to express regret about earlier decisions and much less need to constantly refer to the narrative of sacrifice for the nation or religion. Shakeel's sister says, "What happened to my brother is *zulm*" (cruelty, denoting something that is unjust, exploitative, or cruel). This depiction of the soldier's sacrifice of a limb is in contrast to the depictions of families of the shaheed, who in their initial conversations with me referred to the sacrifice of life as a *nazrana* (offering) to the nation. The digressions from disciplined subjects that Shakeel and his family allow themselves are a function of their continuous and visible loss. Shakeel's family has been unable to situate themselves within the military discourse of sacrifice. They hint at equivalence—"They are sad, and we are sad"—but shy away from it, because *at least* the loved one can be *seen*. Part of the reason that the bonds between these families and the military are not as intense is also because the relationship is less direct. In the case of the shaheed, the relationship is directly between the family and the institution, and the family becomes dependent on the military and exposed to its rhetoric. Disabled soldiers serve as intermediaries for their families, who are not invited to commemorative events other than as carers of the disabled, and they are missing from the military narratives that highlight the shaheed's family. For these reasons, the transition from zulm (cruelty) to nazrana (offering) remains unconvincing in the case of the disabled. The two irreconcilable genres suggested by Ophir, loss (tragedy) and damage (bureaucratic file), remain even more estranged here.

In keeping with the strictly regulated image of glorious service and noble sacrifice in the Pakistani military, the military also deems it important that the disabled soldier and his family, like the family of the dead soldier, are provided for and not pitied. Here the third vector of biopower, *will not let die*, is extended to ensure that the disabled soldier lives in a manner befitting the manly military soldier. The military also recognizes that the threat of disaffection, challenge, and claim making from subjects who have sacrificed and do not die but continue to suffer, reflect, and speak is perhaps higher if they stray too far from the military's influence. Within first-world nations there has been collective organizing by veteran organizations demanding state welfare as well as a distinct turn toward disability rights.[20] In Pakistan, where we can trace advocacy for welfare and compensation in the civilian space (both for ordinary public citizens and for law enforcement such as police), such organization remains missing or, at best, concealed within military spheres. This is largely because the military is an institution that thrives on a sense of incomparability and distance from the civilian in Pakistan. The military compensation package in Pakistan for the disabled in war is fairly generous (in comparison to civilian schemes), and since 2009, WWPs have had the option of returning to their units with full benefits. The AFIRM psychologist informed me that depression is common, and patients can initially be noncompliant, but the policy of assured service and benefits helps to alleviate their principal concerns about livelihood. Through this policy, the military attempts to retain the disabled soldier even if that means a greater burden on its resources. It guards the disabled soldier and seeks to keep him close to the institution to safeguard against the possibility of independent organizing and claim making outside military terrain. On my last visit, Shakeel informed me that he had realized that it was better for him to complete at least fifteen years of service, as that allowed him to retire with full benefits. He will also receive full medical support even if he decides to opt out of service, but he recognizes that his chances of receiving better care are higher if he stays in service. He had recently become engaged to a young woman and said he needed to be practical and clearheaded. He said he had been thinking emotionally earlier, and he was thinking more sensibly now. It is, therefore, primarily the compensation regime, or the genre of the bureaucratic file, that supports families in handling this loss. The military recognizes this and ensures that the incentives offered are sufficiently generous that they cannot be refused. As the brigadier at the Shuhada Cell triumphantly informed me, "In case he wishes to retire, we first try and persuade him not to. We show him the benefits of continuing service. If he is adamant then we will let him go. More than 60 percent will continue."

The unease in the military's relationship with disabled soldiers as it acts about discipling and representing their bodies is apparent in this desire to keep them close and in the military's inability to adequately sentimentalize those maimed in war. An institution that thrives on exhaustive regimes of discipline aimed at the careful manufacture of the functional, obedient, and predictable body continues to be confounded by its encounter with disablement. This condition, according to Puar, "stretch[es] the horizon of life . . . and the finality of death into perverted versions of life that look and feel neither like life nor death. . . ."[21] The brigadier at the Shuhada Cell captures this nervousness as he describes the predicament of the disabled: "He is like a *zinda lash* (living corpse). It is a very precarious situation. He suffers the most; everything changes for him." The precariousness mentioned here reflects the life-changing experience of disability and also hints at its uncertain position within military narratives of service and sacrifice. The disabled military subject represents an anomalous category that occupies the spaces of the dead and the living. Still a man and yet as helpless as the dreaded feminine from whom distance has been so carefully created, the disabled soldier is a liminal figure who refuses categorization and thus threatens to destabilize carefully crafted military narratives. A credible commemorative script that holds this figure in place has yet to be developed, although the dangerous and nonfinal nature of affect in the disabled and his family can apparently be disciplined through monetized regimes of compensation.

CHAPTER 8

PRO PATRIA MORI[1]

SINCE 9/11, the Pakistani military has grappled with a new enemy system, fighting a war inside Pakistan's borders against an enemy that is not yet *othered* but whose religious faith is uncomfortably familiar and who brandishes Islam's flag high. Initial support for this war was lukewarm at best, and contestations, including *fatwas* (ruling on a point of Islamic law), against the military were expressed publicly.[2] There was growing unease among troops as well as the general public as military deployment and operations in northwest Pakistan became more intense and, more importantly, as military trucks with coffins on them started to roll into villages.

This is not the first time that the Pakistani military has taken on a Muslim enemy. But the 1971 breakup of Pakistan and the killing of Bengali Muslims did not pose challenges like those faced by soldiers in the war on terror (WOT). For those in West Pakistan, the 1971 war was constructed as a betrayal of East Pakistan, and killing was made possible by othering the Bengali and playing on his supposed affinity with Hindu India. The Pakistan Army labeled the Mukti Bahini, the Bangladeshi guerrilla movement, as a group of *kafir* (nonbelievers). Operations in Baluchistan, especially in the so-called fourth war of 1973–1977, which resulted in substantial loss of Baluch Muslim lives, did not stir up much contention either, as Baluch nationalists were made out to be the enemy.[3] In both these instances, ethnicity trumped religious identity and did not pose a threat to the construction of the Pakistani soldier as a fighter for Islam and the military institution as a defender of faith. In the war in northwest Pakistan, however, religion becomes a site of contestation. At issue was a state-sponsored, undifferentiated brand of Sunni Islam that was devoid of the nuance of the numerous sects that exist within Pakistan and had so far existed as a simple attachment to the state or the military. The subject is faced by two opposing Islamic spaces here: the Islamic state of Pakistan and Islamic militants. For the subject, the dilemma becomes this: How can Islam fight itself?

A cleric from Kandwal in Chakwal District questions the WOT and the soldiers dying in it. He said, "The *qanoon* [law] of the *shaheed* is that one group is defying religion and the other is standing firm on the side of the right, and there is [a] clash between them and a declaration of war. [Only] then is he shaheed. These shaheed are at the orders of America." As is obvious from the cleric's statement, there is opposition to the state narrative on enemies and war. What is also obvious is that whatever unease may have been created by the Muslim enemy, it has been resolved and soothed, because we do not see mass disaffection among troops. Two questions arise here: first, what kind of subjectivities are constructed by the Pakistani state and military that these contentions arise in the first place, and second, how is it that these doubts have had limited impact on soldier loyalty and the district's willingness to contribute recruits and work inside the state-military framework?

Examining these doubts and the dynamics of their resolution provides a useful window through which to understand the relationship between the military institution and its subjects. By looking through the prism of Pakistan's participation in the war on terror, it is possible to strip away the rhetoric of Islam that shrouds this relationship. This is helpful because it lays bare other inducements that may secure service and sacrifice in the Pakistani military. More specifically, this chapter delineates how Islam is positioned within religionationalist subjectivities and how changing narratives about the enemy influence the meaning assigned to dying for the state in two sites: military training centers and local spaces, such as rural Chakwal, long considered the military's labor pool.

LOCATING RELIGION IN THE PAKISTANI STATE

The use of religion as a tool of legitimation has a long and complicated history in Pakistan, and its roots lie in the genesis of the Pakistani state itself. Christopher Jaffrelot describes Pakistani nationalism as such that "the ideological construction of the national project precedes the formation (in sociological terms) of the nation."[4] Like many scholars before him, he suggests that this nationalism has relied heavily on the instrumentalization of Islam, allowing an elite Muslim minority to convince Muslim-majority provinces to participate in the division of what was then British India. That nation, as Salman Rushdie suggested, was not "sufficiently imagined"[5] and was born as a result of what Younus Samad calls "a brief moment of political unity."[6] In his examination of the political idea that lies at the root of Pakistan, Faisal Devji argues that Muslim nationalists nullified history, geography, and even demography to lay the foundation of their political mobilization, focusing instead on an "empty" idea of religion. Religion here was "not an old fashioned theological entity, but an abstract idea and modern idea, . . . whose sense of brotherhood provides a people with the foundations of its nationality. For Muslim nationalism, in other words, religion was conceived of not as a supplement to geography but as its alternative."[7] This was religion "in the peculiarly secular sense,"[8] in which Mohammed Ali Jinnah attempted to construct Islam as an "ethnoterritorial ideology"[9] that could be used for political purposes. Whatever Jinnah may have imagined for the Pakistani state, the indeterminate nature of how Islam was conceived for the purpose of legitimizing the struggle for Pakistan has led to it being exploited by both political and military leaders alike. This exploitation has also played out through alliances with and appeasement of the religious right. Starting with the constitutional debates between the relatively secular Muslim League, which viewed Islam as an identity marker, and religious scholars, who embodied a more Islamist vision, Pakistan's history is checkered with the state's dangerous obsession with the empty idea of religion.

Based partly on the ambiguity just mentioned, the state of Pakistan constructed a Pakistani selfhood predicated on purging the other: the Hindu or the Hindu Indian state.[10] Religion was underlined in this identity as the primary foundation for difference. This was a simpler version of Islam, an internally undifferentiated category that emerged in sharp relief *only* when posited against the enemy, Hindu India. Those building the Pakistani nationhood, which was perceived as under threat from both neighboring India and the internal challenges posed by nationalist movements and ethnolinguistic conflicts after partition, continued the process of deepening its religious character through two routes. First, the culture and identity of a culturally diverse geographical area was forcefully homogenized around a single identity, that of a Muslim. Second, an interrelated trajectory involved strengthening the predominantly Punjabi military over and above other state institutions.[11]

Against this backdrop, religious extremism in Pakistan can be traced to the coming together of two elements in the late 1970s, around the time of General Zia-ul Haq's 1977 takeover.[12] The first was religious sectarianism, involving antagonism between Shia and Deobandi Sunni sects, which intensified largely as result of a mix of domestic and regional factors. These factors included General Zia's 1979 Islamization policy, largely Sunni in flavor, and the dynamics set in motion by the Iranian revolution, with Saudi and Iranian funding trickling in to enhance Sunni and Shia influence, respectively, in the region.[13] It might be useful to clarify here that three of the four dominant sects (Barelvi, Deobandi, and Ahle-Hadith) in Pakistan are part of the Sunni branch of Islam. Within this branch, the Barelvi sect has the deepest roots in Punjab, outnumbering the other two groups. The fourth sect is the Ahle-Tashi Shia minority. What is referred to as the Shia-Sunni conflict is a misnomer, especially in Punjab, and can better be described as antagonism between Shias and Deobandi Sunnis, who are supported by Ahle-Hadith in their anti-Shia stance. This blurring of identities among Sunni sects is important to highlight, for reasons I will take up in the following sections.

The second element that played a pivotal role in rising extremism in the country was the heavy investment in jihadism, a state project to shore up support for the jihad in Afghanistan in the 1970s and 1980s and later in Kashmir during the 1980s and 1990s. The reasons for this investment were firmly rooted in the Pakistani establishment's obsession with India, starting with the strongly felt inferiority and vulnerability that Pakistan inherited at partition in 1947 and reinforced in 1971 when Bangladesh became independent. The route taken by the establishment to ease this sense of inadequacy had consequences that haunt Pakistan to this day. One decision made along this route was to arm jihadist movements to fight in Afghanistan to acquire strategic depth[14] and then in Kashmir in order to bleed India.[15] Another decision was to allow its own soil in the Federally Administered Tribal Areas; in its northern province, KP; and in parts of Punjab to be used to nurture the radical ideologies that supported these groups.[16] The roots of these decisions can be traced back to before the Soviet invasion of Afghanistan. Zulfiqar Ali Bhutto, a civilian ruler, played the religion card both internally, when he pandered to religious parties and used a 1974 constitutional amendment to declare Ahmedis to be non-Muslims, and externally, when he offered his support to Islamist groups fighting to overthrow the pro-USSR regime in Kabul.[17] After the Soviet invasion, under the martial regime of General Zia, the Inter-Services Intelligence (ISI), Pakistan's premier intelligence agency, invested in the Afghan Mujahideen with active support from both the United States and Saudi Arabia. The ISI relied partly on Jamaat-e-Islami (JI), a religious political party, to carry out its strategy, which involved mobilizing young men for jihad in Afghanistan.[18] Once Afghanistan had been "won," the Pakistani jihadist movements turned their attention to Indian Kashmir, with continued support and aid from the ISI and the military.[19] JI, a military ally in this project, claimed the first shaheed in Afghanistan, and a list of hundreds of Afghan and Kashmiri martyrs is posted at the gate of its headquarters in Mansoora in Lahore.[20] It is this same former ally that challenged the Pakistani military's right to claim martyrdom for its soldiers in the current war. These two elements, sectarianism and jihadism, have a natural affinity for each other, although their trajectories in Pakistan may have been different.

Both elements converged and must be viewed collectively if we are to understand how the political use of religion by the state and its proxies, and now by antistate elements, plays out in entangled ways in spaces in which the military claims its subjects.

Since 9/11, pressure from the United States has forced Pakistan to take on the very Islamic militants that it had nurtured and groomed for proxy wars in Afghanistan and Kashmir. This turnabout in military state policy has taken place in fits and starts, as evidenced by the initially small-scale troop deployment and operations in Waziristan as well as by a number of failed peace agreements. It has been suggested that this ambivalence toward sections of the Taliban that promise strategic depth in Afghanistan or toward Islamists that restrict their operation to India continues in current military policy.[21] I do not attempt to add insight to this particular line of inquiry but instead mention this backdrop as essential context for understanding that the subjects produced in these uncertain and shifting frames are bound to be hesitant as well. In other words, ambivalence among those who participate in the militarism project (soldiers, families, and districts) has a social, political, and historical basis.

RELIGION AND NATIONALISM IN THE MAKING OF THE SOLDIER

> Religion and the army have a deep relation. It [religion] warms the blood. Once they shout "Allah-o-Akbar!" (God is great), then they don't think. You say it at a particular point when you are at a certain distance from the enemy or from danger. Then you attack.
> *Jazba* (passion) starts from here; because of this he will go forward, not back.
> —Subedar-instructor, infantry regiment training center, Abbottabad

Since partition, the Pakistani military has relied heavily on the construction of a more ideological and religiously motivated imagining of the soldier who defends against the Hindu threat.[22] Religious influence, or, more specifically, the mixing of religion and nationalism with a military ethos, was a given from the beginning, particularly regarding the imagining of the enemy as a kafir (nonbeliever).[23] This was a shift, as the rhetoric employed by the British Indian Army, which depended on the same regions for recruitment, revolved around the myth of the martial race and loyalty to the Raj.[24] The Pakistani military used religion instead to construct its image as the defender not just of national boundaries but of Islam, and in the four postpartition wars with India, the martyr for the nation and the shaheed for religion have been imagined as one.[25]

The marked intensification of this tendency under General Zia-ul Haq brought religion into the military in more structured and institutionalized ways. During General Zia's time, formal Islamic teaching was introduced in military academies. Within the Educational Directorate, which was headed by a brigadier, he established a Religious Directorate and formalized the position of the *khateeb* (cleric),[26] who until then had been a civilian in the military.[27] The khateeb was inducted through a special recruitment process and became part of the order of ranks. He was given a salary and benefits, and like other soldiers, he was promoted as he grew in seniority. In 1974, General Zia also introduced the *Khutbaat-e-Askaar* (religious military sermons)—twelve designated sermons printed and distributed by the Religious Directorate—in training schools, regiments, and field units for use by the khateeb for Friday prayer congregations.

There are a number of references to Islam in the present-day infantry training center in Abbottabad. Large road signs and stone edifices at the training center are inscribed with sayings from the Quran. There are also four mosques, four imams,[28] and a full-time khateeb on the premises. The days start with recitation from the Quran. According to the khateeb and the course instructor, boys are assessed during the first few weeks on their ability to know the *namaz* (Muslim prayer) and read the Quran. If their ability is found lacking, they are assigned to remedial training during the evening, when they are required to go the khateeb and learn these basic tenets. Regular soldiers who wish to memorize the Quran by rote (*hifz*) can do so with a recommendation from the khateeb and their commanding officer's permission. Soldiers are also *encouraged* to go to the mosque regularly for prayers.

The army is a deeply hierarchal institution, and the khateeb is placed on the lower rungs, subservient to both the commanding officer and the JCOs who act as instructors at the training institution. He is subject to the same disciplinary mechanisms, such as court martials and adverse reports, as the rest of the soldiers. The khateeb thus cuts an interesting and somewhat paradoxical figure, and his treatment by the military is to some extent indicative of how religion is viewed by the Pakistani military. The first clue lies in the fact that the Awareness and Motivation course (the section of the course that deals with Islam) is taught by army-trained NCOs and JCOs (*havildars* and *subedars*), not the khateeb, although he is a full-time appointee at the training center. He has little or no say in the course that is delivered; he may be asked for teaching material and aids, but much of the course's outline, content, and delivery is designed by mainstream army personnel. Despite the khateeb's superior credentials as a religious scholar—ten years of regular schooling followed by eight years in a religious seminary—he is not considered an appropriate teacher for religious sections of the course. According to the colonel at the center, Islam has to be taught in a way that supports the goals of nationalism, and it is important that these classes do not get diverted into pure religious instruction. When I expressed an interest in meeting the khateeb, the colonel was surprised and then suggested I meet with the instructors of the Awareness and Motivation course instead. At my insistence, though, he agreed. As we waited, he told me he had no problem with me meeting him, as "he is a harmless enough chap," but he didn't think I would get anything useful in our talk. At this point both the khateeb and the psychologist walked in (we had called the psychologist in earlier but he had been busy). The psychologist was wearing full army attire and was dressed in combat uniform, including cap and boots, while the khateeb wore a *shalwar kameez* and black waistcoat. I was told to meet with the psychologist first because he might not be available later, and the khateeb was told to wait. When I returned an hour and a half later I found the khateeb waiting patiently for me in the colonel's office.

I was given privacy to interview the psychologist, but I was asked to interview the khateeb in the colonel's office. The khateeb explained his duties to me.

> My job is to fulfill all the religious requirements and needs of this center. . . . My job is *rohani tarbeeyat* (spiritual teaching). Just as a country has geographical boundaries, there are also ideological boundaries that need to be protected. My job is to link this training with the Quran, with namaz and with the *masjid* (mosque). I interact with the recruits during the Friday sermon, or sometimes the *asr* or *maghrib* prayers, where I will say something to them about *iklaqiyaat* (ethics). I also start the day with *tilawat* (recitation) from the Quran in the morning at assembly, and I will often leave them with something to think about.

The khateeb reiterates that his role is vital and positions himself as the spiritual teacher of the recruits. This position is belied somewhat by my earlier description of my encounter with him and his superiors, an impression strengthened by my conversation with other senior army officers. A retired infantry general shared with me how he had confronted the khateeb's influence in the barracks while he was in services. A particular khateeb under his command during the Kargil war was asked to go to a post nearer the combat zone to motivate the troops. The cleric refused on the grounds that certain requirements of jihad[29] had not been fulfilled, so he could not support the effort. "I summoned him and told him, 'You talk of jihad; God will decide what is jihad. This is a war zone, and I am ordering a district court martial of you, and I will ensure that you are put before a firing squad right over here in front of my office.'" He then had him posted out of the area with immediate effect. The khateeb is told here that he is in no position to adjudicate what jihad is, the implication being that the military, in this case the commanding officer, has the right to adjudicate this over and above religious authority, whose only role is to motivate troops in the name of jihad as and when ordered by the military officer. The khateeb is a spiritual guide, then, with no real official authority, an army person but not regular army personnel. He is a "harmless" person yet one who must be monitored, as evidenced by the colonel's initial reluctance to let me talk to him. As another retired infantry general jokingly put it, "He [the khateeb] is uneducated but very motivating." Much like his soldier-class contemporaries, he is regarded by the officer class as somewhat uncouth but nonetheless essential for the training center. He has the specific task of motivating troops and acting as a religious mascot to lend credence to the militarism project.

The twenty-three-week recruitment training course being run at the infantry center I visited can be divided into three units: Physical Training and Discipline, Skills, and Awareness and Motivation.[30] It is instructive to look at this division in terms of the relative importance of each area. Of the 748 classes spread over the twenty-three weeks, the bulk (45 percent) were dedicated to physical training and building discipline. This was in addition to the general organization of the day, the use of space, and the strict rules and regulations regarding movement, language, and dress that had to be followed by recruits at all times.[31] Approximately 41 percent were dedicated to skills such as weapons training, map reading, and so on, with the reminder (14 percent) dedicated to the Awareness and Motivation course. According to the colonel at the center, this was a mix of Islamic teaching and Pakistan studies. Of the nineteen topics offered in the Awareness and Motivation course, twelve were linked directly to Islam. Only seven were about Pakistan's political, geographical, cultural, and military history, and there were liberal references to Islam in those also.[32] This distribution of training courses and particularly the weight given to religious instruction highlights two distinct features of how religious subjectivity in the *jawan* is developed by the military. First, this is just one of the ingredients (and not the most important) that make up the soldier figure.[33] Exposure to religion is deemed an essential element in the potent cocktail offered the soldier, but the correct dose is carefully calculated so as not to upset the balance of factors that drive him. Second, and this may seem contradictory, the idea of Pakistan and the brand of nationalism fed to the soldier to motivate him to fight rely heavily on religion. According to this syllabus, the idea of Pakistan is tenable as a motivator only when attached to Islam.

The military institution considers religious education and alignment important for its soldier, but it also seeks to ensure that it does not delve into what it regards as an unnecessary theological argument and steers clear of complexity or possible contention. The goal is to teach an undifferentiated brand of (Sunni) Islam devoid of the nuance of the numerous subsects that exist within. Here, Islam's purpose is to unify, to act as a bond and a motivator to fight a common enemy. Officers and instructors consider religion a necessary ingredient for motivating the village primitive, who in their opinion holds some notion of religion very close to his heart. Any disavowal of the necessity of religion in training would evoke a strong defensive response in officers being interviewed, but religion would also be viewed as a threat that could get out of hand and hence one that must be controlled and monitored. As officers shared with me, the regularization of the religious teacher during Zia's time was a strategic move, because then the khateeb became just another employee, bound by the same rules, subject to the same code of obedience and disciplinary mechanisms, and, most of all, dependent on the military's generous patronage.

When compared to the religious elements in the curricula of other militaries, what I describe may seem excessive, yet it is important to recognize that it is but an indicator of how religion has been absorbed and appropriated in most public institutions in Pakistan. The nature of the curricula on Islam and the figure of the religious cleric at the training institution are metaphors for the controlled instrumentalization of religion in the Pakistani military, an appropriation akin to the larger state project in Pakistan. The military borrows generously from popular concepts of religion and uses them as fertile ground for instilling particular forms of nationalist and militarist subjectivities in the soldier.

This strict vetting of the kind of Islam allowed at the training center did not prove sufficient when the controversy over Pakistan's participation in the WOT exploded. Soldier subjectivities, so carefully crafted and considered immune to corruption due to strict army discipline, were not able to bear the weight of the ambivalence around the war, its Muslim enemy, and the status of its dead. There were reports of desertions[34] and of refusal to fire on the enemy,[35] and my conversations with officers involved in early military operations (2002–2006) hinted at the same. Interestingly, unlike the officers I interviewed, no *sipahis* admitted to desertions, but nearly all spoke openly about the strong doubts they had had about the Muslim enemy, especially at the beginning of the WOT. Over time, these seem to have been appeased, not so much by religious teaching but, as many soldiers told me, by the increase in the scale of terrorism in Pakistan after military operations began and the large number of casualties, especially among their own brothers-in-arms.

This initial insufficiency is not so much a feature of Islamic radicalization in the army but the result of interaction between forces outside and inside the institution. Inside, the insufficiency stems from how the military positions Islam in its doctrine. In training, soldiers develop ideas of nationalism that are closely tied to religion. Course topics about the state itself nearly always pull in religion, almost as though the state is not viable as an idea without Islam. Thus, when Islam has been pitted against the state, as in the recent WOT, soldier ambivalence has been high. Soldiers found the neutralized version of Islam being taught within the training center insufficient to counter the claims of the more virulent version prevalent outside, which alleged that the war was not jihad and its dead not shaheed. Influences outside the training center—competing religious ideologies—have made significant inroads into local sociopolitical systems and have more power to influence soldiers' subjectivities than the controlled version of Islam, subservient to army authority and discipline, taught at the center. Perhaps outside influences have always been stronger, but this was inconsequential before the WOT, because there was no direct contention between the two. When some religious clergy began to stand starkly counter to the military, things became more complex, and the military and its soldiers were initially unprepared.

This by no means implies that vast numbers have deserted or will desert. It merely sheds light on the high level of ambivalence about the new enemy that existed in soldiers' minds at the start of this war. The military operates as a kinship group, and the bonds that hold the soldier class to the institution of the military are based on systematic, organized, and generous welfare services for troops and their families.[36] Furthermore, soldiers' subjectivities are formed by army discipline and affective regulation, including strong attachment and loyalty to their unit.[37] It is these systems of patronage and technologies of power that keep the soldier in order and in compliance and ensure his loyalty, not controlled instrumentalization of religion within the training institution.

PUNJAB AND SHIFTING ENEMIES WITHIN AND WITHOUT

Since the 1980s, the influence of various competing Muslim alignments and sects has grown steadily in Punjab. These have now become integrated in local spaces through religious and political parties, *madrasas* (religious seminaries), and welfare organizations.[38] Although there are fewer Deobandis than Barelvis in Pakistan, as of 2012 there were approximately 9,500 Deobandi madrasas registered across Pakistan compared to 6,500 associated with other Muslim sects.[39] Deobandi seminaries make up 41.4 percent of the total in Punjab, while the Deobandi population stands at 22.45 percent of the total.[40] Parts of Punjab are Shia dominated, specifically by Shia landlords. Sectarianism has firm roots within the province, and religiopolitical Shia and Sunni identities have often resulted in sectarian violence. Sectarian tensions are rarely restricted to religious grounds but fold into other conflicts—for instance, over land or electoral rivalries.[41] Punjab, especially the south, has also been a recruitment and training ground for jihad in Afghanistan and Kashmir.[42] The specter of the Punjabi Taliban has been repeatedly pointed out by analysts as a formidable force that potently represents the merging of sectarian and jihadist forces made all the more toxic by their past and, many argue, current patronage by the establishment, including state bureaucracy, military intelligence agencies, political parties, and trading communities.[43]

Although the rising Deobandi presence and the interrelated jihadist project has largely been concentrated in southern Punjab, there are also distinct pockets in northern Punjab, where Chakwal is located.[44] Shiites are an influential minority in Chakwal District, but its rural areas are largely Barelvi dominated. Here, Deobandi numbers have increased at a rapid pace, and certain areas, such as the administrative subdivision of Talagang, are more open to this influence.[45] Both Deobandi and Ahle-Hadith religious and militant organizations operate in these areas with support from the business-trading community, religious leaders, and the state machinery.[46] In Chakwal, this steady indoctrination is apparent in the Shiite-Sunni cleavages that have appeared as a result of Deobandi influence. In 2009, a suicide attacker blew himself up inside a *bargah* (a Shiite place of worship) in Chakwal City.[47] Maulana Akram Awan (a former army soldier) of Tanzeem-ul-Ikhwan (The Brotherhood Organization) of Chakwal threatened General Pervez Musharraf with a million-man march to Islamabad to demand the implementation of Sharia law in the country in 2000.[48] In a more recent incident, in 2016, an Ahmedi place of worship was attacked by a mob in Dulmial Village in Chakwal.[49]

Increasing Islamic radicalism in Chakwal, a traditionally martial district, poses the question of how local populations and soldiers from this area may be affected by these local dynamics, which created no dilemmas until Pakistan's participation in the war on terror. The slow but definite turnabout in policies along with the increased deployment of troops and the intensification of operations in Waziristan demonstrates in both dramatic and (more often) undramatic ways the unravelling of the alliance between religion and the military as a result of the inclusion of a new(er) enemy: radical Sunni Deobandi groups that have turned against the state.

THE ENEMY AS ONE OF OUR OWN

Much of my fieldwork took place in five villages in the Chakwal Tehsil of Chakwal District, all of which are Barelvi dominated. There is some Deobandi influence there, but it is not significant in terms of population figures. Findings may indeed be different among Shia populations in urban parts of Chakwal where Sunni-Shia cleavages go deeper or in areas where there is more organized Deobandi influence, such as Talagang Tehsil. Although the conclusions I draw must be analyzed in this context, I believe that many areas of rural Chakwal present a similar picture. Thus the following examination is significant for understanding how the war and the enemy are viewed in areas that are not considered contentious because of their long association with the military and their relatively small Deobandi population. In fact, if contestations about the military's current war exist despite these factors, they are perhaps all the more significant.

A college professor in Chakwal City sets out some of this debate around the war as he discusses the December 2014 attack by Tehreek-e-Taliban Pakistan (TTP) on an army public school in Peshawar that left more than 130 school children dead.

> There are different reactions to this school incident that has just happened. Some people believe that what happened should not have happened; others believe that this is bad but that what happened in the Lal Masjid[50] is also bad. And [then] there are those who say that what has happened is what should have happened. These three perspectives are like stairs. As you go up you move towards extremism—the third stair is the most extreme.

The professor here is highlighting the fact that there is no single way that the local population regards this war. Different perspectives are experienced not as distinct categories but as a continuum, thus permitting a slippery range of positions. He goes on to further qualify this tendency toward extremism, saying that "this extremist thinking is in some Deobandi groups: they think the *fauj* is *murtid* (apostate), those who accept Islam first and then reject it later."

An array of mosques, representing different sects of Islam, dot the landscape of rural Punjab. The most clear-cut division is between Shiite (Ahle-Tashi) and Sunni (Ahle-Sunnat) mosques, which differ architecturally as well as in their adornments. In Palwal, the two dominant subsects are Barelvi and Deobandi, with the former in the majority. There are a total of three mosques in the village, of which two are exclusively Barelvi. The largest and most well-attended mosque is frequented by both Deobandis and Barelvis, and the cleric selected by the largely Barelvi mosque committee is a Deobandi from a neighboring district. Kandwal, the village next to Palwal that is also Barelvi dominated, has a large, well-attended madrasa run by a Deobandi group, to which the local Barelvi population send their children.

During my interviews, adherence to subsects within Sunni Islam was often not expressed outright but emerged only upon direct questioning. Questions about sects are taken to refer to the Shiite and Sunni divide. The *other* was the Ahle-Tashi (Shia), the Marzai (Ahmedi), or, to some extent, the Ahle-Hadith. The blurring between the Deobandi and Barelvi subsects, pointed to in the preceding paragraph in the example of the mosque in Palwal and the madrasa in Kandwal, seemed to cause little contention in the villagers. In keeping with the more pronounced differentiation from Ahle-Tashi, Barelvi parents sending children to an Ahle-Tashi madrasa or Barelvi men going to pray in an Ahle-Tashi mosque would be unthinkable. There was a tendency to regard Barelvi groups and Deobandis groups as being the same, as resting within the folds of the Ahle-Sunnat marker, and my interlocutors generally did not bring up Barelvi or Deobandi identities. When they did, it was often in a pejorative sense, as disapproval of increasing sectarianism in Islam and an almost ostrichlike desire to pretend they did not exist. As the conversation continued, however, differences between the groups would be pointed out by Barelvi villagers, who disapproved of what they saw as Deobandis' insufficient reverence for Prophet Muhammad and Sufi shrines and often alluded to Deobandi ideology as being more antagonistic toward Shias. Although Barelvis viewed Deobandis as somewhat problematic with their more extreme views, they nonetheless regarded them as their own, allowing them clout and space within their environs. Deobandis tended to gloss over these differentiations as weaknesses of the Barelvi groups, who they felt needed reform. The Deobandi villagers I interviewed perceived themselves as more orthodox, disapproving of shrines and grave ornamentation and stressing *tableegh* (propagation of faith) and jihad. Deobandis in villages highlighted similarities between the two subsects and at the same time emphasized differences with the Ahle-Tashi (Shia).

Addressing the question of religious education in Pakistan, Mathew J. Nelson proposes that there is a deliberate effort to emphasize "doctrinal uniformity" rather than religious differentiation when it comes to sectarian difference among Muslims.[51] In the context of the Shia-Sunni divide, Nelson suggests that because Sunnis are in the majority, Sunni Islam's ascendancy is considered justifiable among Sunni populations and is supportive of the belief that there is only one true Islam and that differences are to be abhorred. In the intra-Sunni context, the desire to not acknowledge differences benefits the more organized (minority) Deobandi groups, who are rendered less visible through assimilation within the Sunni sect. This politics of assimilation has consequences for how the war is viewed within these terrains.

Three themes emerged in my discussion with villagers about Pakistan's participation in the war. First, the consensus, even among many Deobandi villagers, seemed to be that rebellion against an Islamic state was not permissible under Islam and that army action in Waziristan was justified. On the surface, the Pakistan card was stronger here, yet it is important to point out that this was only possible within the framework of religion and not on nationalist grounds alone. In other words, the Pakistani state was worth defending only when Islam was attached it. Another justification suggested for putting Pakistan first was that in order for Muslims to thrive, the Pakistani state must be viable, making the antistate rhetoric of the Taliban shortsighted and counterproductive. In both cases, the nationalist argument held only when it was coupled with religious identity. This brand of nationalism is similar to the one taught in military training centers.

Second, support for the military was couched in a language of unease, and the war was often subjected to muted and sometimes open questioning. Villagers criticized the Pakistani state for aligning with the United States and taking on a war that was not its own. This criticism emerged most clearly when the 2007 Lal Masjid operation was discussed. The WOT was seen as a distraction from Pakistan's real enemies: those on the eastern border and those who were weakening Muslim unity. I suggest that only muted criticism was voiced because much of my fieldwork was conducted after the 2014 army school attack in Peshawar. This was followed by widespread state and public condemnation of the TTP and the formulation at that time of the National Action Plan by the government of Pakistan, which promised strict action against extremism and sectarianism, including militancy in Punjab.[52] I can only assume that any sympathy for the enemy I was allowed to witness was a watered-down version of sympathies that actually exist.

Third, there were two common types of narratives about the enemy. The first was a complete rejection of the enemy as Muslim. This narrative projected them as foreign militants, funded by Israel, India, or the United States, and did not see them as Deobandi or aligned with any particular sect in Islam but as mercenaries. Such a belief did away with any angst that may have been provoked by the Pakistani military's killing of Muslims and mirrored the rhetoric used by the military to conflate this enemy with India.[53] In light of the contention that exists around the figure of the shaheed, which I will detail later, it is the second narrative that holds the most sway in these local spaces. This narrative saw the enemy as Muslim but misguided, as being from within and ideologically not at fault but as having a problematic methodology. The enemy was categorized as *gumrah bhai* (brothers led astray) or as sons whose intentions were not at fault but who had an erroneous modus operandi. There was a suggestion that this brother and enemy had been mishandled by the state or the military because of Pakistan's alignment with the West, in particular the United States. Although this narrative categorized the enemy as brothers led astray, it nonetheless did not challenge the war effort outright. There was a tendency to treat the Muslim enemy as an undifferentiated category in terms of religious sect. Discomfort with talking about the enemy's alignment with a particular Sunni sect was an echo of the earlier desire not to acknowledge subsects of the Sunni faith and was a feature of my conversations with both Barelvi and Deobandi groups. The politics of assimilation mentioned earlier influences the (in)ability to see the enemy as an internally differentiated category within the Sunni faith. The enemy is seen as *one of us*, with his religious affiliation only marginally different, unlike Ahle-Tashi or Marzai, who have been more effectively othered.

In discussions of the enemy, his Pashtun and, more specifically, tribal identity would sometimes be brought up instead.[54] As early as

1948, the Pakistani state mobilized militias from Federally Administered Tribal Areas (FATA) to fight in Kashmir.[55] Humeira Iqtidar suggests that the residents of FATA are "enmeshed in a complex web of colonial and post-colonial legal and political regimes that separates them definitively from the rest of Pakistan."[56] This is evident in governance regimes[57] as well as in how the people from these areas continue to be labeled. In Chakwal, othering came more easily in this context. There was often a reference to the Taliban as members of *qabyli* (tribal) areas, and they would be caricatured as uncivilized, uneducated, and barbaric. These accounts were often tinged with grudging admiration for their fierce ability as fighters. Colonial fantasies regarding the fanatic and antistate hordes on the remote frontiers of the empire, further cemented by views of Islamic reformists (such as Sir Syed Ahmed) who painted these border tribes as turbulent and abhorrent of peace, still haunt imaginings around these subjects. Ahmed's response to British historians' categorization of the *Mussalman* (Muslims) as religious fanatics, antimodern, and anti-British is instructive in this regard. Although he defended Muslims, he continued to utilize and build on the category of fanatic masses whose fanaticism he attributed not to religion but to their ethnic and tribal identity, which was constructed as war loving and barbaric.[58] As such, it is no surprise that the unease that haunted these conversations about war hung on the Muslim identity of the enemy, and the qabyli identity helped to soothe this agitation. The othering of the enemy based on their tribal Pashtun identity came easily in Punjab and was reminiscent of the othering of ethnicities such as Bengali and Baluchi. In the war in East Pakistan and the numerous operations in Baluchistan since, the ethnicity of the enemy trumped religious identity and did not pose a threat to the construction of the Pakistani soldier as a fighter for Islam and the military institution as a defender of faith.

ASSIMILATING THE "NEW" SHAHEED

Dying in uniform, and the honor associated with it, has a long history in the village of Palwal, located in the heart of the martial belt. There were shared memories of great-uncles and grandfathers who fought in

Japan in World War II and did not return, tinged with melancholy about never finding out what happened to them or where exactly they died. There was a clear acknowledgment that some of this recruitment happened under conditions of duress, and there were stories of sheer economic desperation that drove many into service and the *pakki mahana amadani* (secure monthly income) that it promised. Many drew a clear distinction between the pre- and postpartition army. The British Indian Army was a *ghair mazhab* (non-Muslim) force, while the Pakistani military was a Muslim force that had fought to save Islam from the Hindu enemy. Participation in the pre-partition British Indian Army was respected; its dead were honored and the reference to it being a nonreligious force was not pejorative. Very few used the honorific shaheed in this context; instead, the dead were referred to as having been *killed* in war.

Postpartition military service, or *pakki naukri*, continues to be referred to as an economic necessity. What has changed, however, is the reverential status accorded the dead. Since here, martyrdom for the state and religion have merged, and the dead are always referred to as shaheed. Dying in military service has become synonymous with dying for Islam, and on the surface, this practice of revering the military martyr continues regardless of whether these men died on the border with Hindu India or in the recent war fighting against Muslims. The dead soldier is a martyr of the Islamic nation-state, a shaheed, to be accorded the highest place in heaven. In the Barelvi-dominated village of Palwal, he becomes something of a saint, with his ornately decorated grave painted with verses from the Quran and fitted with shelves carrying *siparas* (chapters of the Quran). His grave also features state symbols, such as the flag flying over it and the name of his unit and sometimes the operation in which he died carved onto his tombstone. To the occasional visitor, the ideas of state and religion would seem to sit comfortably alongside each other.

In Palwal village, I encountered three types of references to shaheed apart from the military-owned *shahadat*. The first two were typical of what one would find in a rural Barelvi-dominated village. One was a specific reference to Karbala, in which Hussain[59] was mentioned as the preeminent embodiment of shahadat in Islam in both the vernacular and in the sermons of clerics. The other was to a pre-partition Muslim man of the area who had killed a blasphemer and had then been executed by the British, thereby attaining shahadat. The third reference was to shahadat in war. In a sermon given by a local cleric on the occasion of the death anniversary of a soldier who had died in Waziristan, Pakistan was not mentioned. The absence of the state in a sermon given to commemorate the death anniversary of a solider of the Pakistani military is an interesting paradox that brings out the complexities of how the death of a soldier fighting a different enemy in a different war is received in these local spaces. In his hour-and-a-half-long sermon, which blared through the mosque loudspeaker across the village after *zuhr* prayer, the cleric chose to speak instead about the concept of shahadat in Islam, wars in the time of the Prophet Muhammad, and tales of the bravery of Muslim soldiers and their leaders. He described how the shaheed feels no pain at the time of death and talked about the shaheed's reception in heaven. Pakistan was not mentioned, even though the graveyard next to the mosque was decorated with Pakistani flags.

A possible explanation for this omission could be the cleric's own discomfort with the current war as a Deobandi *maulvi*. Perhaps he was displaying a passive antagonism whereby he honored the village's dead without condoning the military's current war. Another explanation given to me by villagers was that the cleric wanted to avoid controversy in case someone did not agree that these men are shaheed. In other words, he was playing it safe. If true, this would imply that unease about these shahadats is an open secret. People may speak of it among themselves in small groups, but they will not openly address it among themselves in larger gatherings or with the military when it comes to the village for the funeral. One way to deal with this unease is to steer clear of the state and discuss only the religious narrative, because that is considered indisputable. But the reverse may not be true. In other words, the idea of shahadat can be discussed without any reference to the state, but the state needs to draw on religion to legitimize itself. In my earlier discussions with villagers about the current war, the nationalist argument for supporting the military operation against fellow Muslims held only when it was coupled with religious identity, a fact that is reinforced in soldier training in which the course on Pakistan makes steady references to religion. The state is worthy of being defended only because it is Islamic. One may suggest in this instance that the reason the religious narrative is foregrounded at the cost of the state is because I am, after all, discussing a religious sermon by the local cleric. But the very idea that a commemoration by the family of a dead soldier is considered incomplete unless it is followed by a religious sermon at the local mosque is an important indicator that Islam must be drawn in, and that when it becomes risky to use the religion-state dyad, it is the state that can be discarded.

The discomfort and anxiety around those who die fighting in this war was not articulated outright but quantified as a comparison with earlier shaheeds. Villagers referred to those who fought and died in wars on the Indian border or on the Siachen Glacier as *asal shaheed* (real martyrs), implying, although never saying outright, that shaheed returning from Swat and Waziristan were not as real. The dead in this war continue to be referred to as shaheed but are differentiated from those who die fighting against Hindu India. Comparing a soldier from Kandwal who died in the 1999 Kargil war with young men in nearby Palwal who had died more recently in the current war, a villager says to me, "There was a lot of feeling generated in the Kargil war; there was a lot of patriotism. They [people in the village] were annoyed when there was a compromise, and the reason was that a dead body from Kargil had come into our village." Referring to the current war, he adds,

> There is more open talk now. . . . There is talk that it is the army's doing that our children are dying. And then it was raised at the national level whether these are shaheed or not. . . . The clash with India is clear; it arouses strong sentiments. It's like the cricket match between India and Pakistan. When the operation started inside the country, people had a different perspective. They say that these Taliban—they are like our sons; they are also taking the name of Islam. Are they [army soldiers] shaheed, or are they [Taliban] shaheed?

In the earlier war with India, the villages rallied around the state more readily, and there was annoyance when Pakistan pulled its troops back in the Kargil war. The death of a soldier from the village intensified the desire to battle. In the current war, doubts around why a war is being fought are aired more openly. There is unease that the enemy is not Hindu or linked to India and is *like our son*, a Muslim, fighting in the name of Islam.

Those currently serving in the army and those who had lost a loved one rarely brought up this differentiation between shaheeds, yet their critique of the war and of army policy was along the same lines. Their challenge was more personal and came from deep grief and anger at being used as cannon fodder in a war that they did not own. For Ayesha, whose son died in this war, it was a particularly painful period when the TTP attacked an army school in Peshawar. She wept as she watched television footage of children's bodies and mothers crying over their losses.

> Ayesha: If we had not provoked them [the Taliban], they would not have done this to us.[60] Musharraf [former chief of army staff] is a dog. He brought this on Pakistan, and he should be kept in jail and never let out.
> Sister: My brother died fighting these people.
> Ayesha [*cutting her short*]: Would Musharraf have got into this war if his son was in the army? He should have sent his son. How many sons have become shaheed because of his decisions?

These affective tones ran counter to and challenged military narratives. These are ruptures in the relationship between the military and the families of the dead that are similar to those mentioned earlier in the discussion of practices and rituals of grieving that go awry.[61]

It is clear from the ambivalence described earlier that the "battle of narratives," to revert to an analogy used by an ISPR colonel,[62] between the institution of the military and the Islamic militants on the legitimacy of this war is still up for grabs in the very constituency the military considers its labor pool: villages in a martial district of Punjab province with dead soldiers from this war buried in local graveyards. What is also obvious in these spaces is continued loyalty to the military. No matter what the nature of contention may be, the village dead are still honored and owned. The village honored its dead in the past when they fought for a *ghair mazhab* (non-Muslim) army, and they continue to honor their dead even when the bonds between state and religion may be questioned. Families display the flag of Pakistan on their sons' graves, and in addition to names and dates of birth, these tombstones carry the names of regiments and the operations they died in. Whatever ambivalence exists in these families about the current war, they continue to attend the YeD/S ceremonies, and they show no sign of tangible disaffection. Also, an overwhelming number of young men turned up for recruitment in the summer of 2015: four thousand young boys aged seventeen and older from Chakwal District who were willing to risk death for pakki naukri and die fighting an enemy they do not consider their own. To explain these seemingly contradictory moves, both toward and away from the military, I now move on to a description of how these contestations about the current war are resolved.

WHISPERS IN THE NIGHT

Saleem, a currently unemployed twenty-three-year old, explains the nature and resolution of tensions around the shaheed of this war.

> When a *fauji* dies he is *majboor* (helpless). He may not be correct in terms of religion, but he has died wearing a uniform we respect so much that we don't look at his character and what he was like; we just look at how he died . . . although the real meaning (of *shahadat*) is that it is used for a person who dies in the way of Allah. . . . The word *shaheed* is used because he was an army man, and we say it to give him respect. Some who are shaheed like this are not very religious, yet we call them shaheed. Those who serve the country and die—their religion is their country. He thinks the land is his mother. This is his intention, and he is *watan ka shaheed* (martyr for the nation-state). *Mazhab ka shaheed* (martyr for religion) is a different category. Those who cannot understand this are more extremist. They will say, "He died fighting in his own country; he is not shaheed. He died while killing other Mus-

lims. . . ." Until after the burial nobody talks. But then in private gatherings people will say this. How can we call him a shaheed? But he is a shaheed, only his level is different, for there are different levels.

Saleem had obviously thought this through, and the reconciliation he proposed was something that also echoed in my conversations with other villagers. He proposed a hierarchy of the shaheed that resonates with the pre-partition understanding of those who died for the British Indian Army. This reconciliation came from the subjects themselves, troubled by the competing narratives around shahadat coming from the military and local discourses. In the village, the resolution is the emergence of a hierarchy of the shaheed that unsettles the link between nation and religion in ways that allow coexistence. This reconciliation is perhaps made possible by the fear that these whispers could strain the relationship between the district and the benevolent army and by the strong affective bonds with the dead, who are easy to identify with, as at some point in their lives most young men in the district will have tried to join or will have been expected to join the military. A sense of affinity made possible by the shared socioeconomic realities of the district and the desire for pakki naukri. This allows a new (for the postpartition era) category to emerge: *watan ka shaheed* (martyr for the nation-state), which is different from *mazhab ka shaheed* (martyr for religion). The cleric cited at the beginning of this chapter, vehement in his criticism of the war, has a son serving in the army. He was unhappy with what he perceives to be an exaggerated reverential status of the shaheed of the village, who he claimed had died fighting "America's war." In response to my question about whether it was difficult for him to accept his son being a soldier in the Pakistan Army, fighting and possibly dying in "America's war," he said,

> It is the rules and regulations of the government [the military] for the one who is serving. God has written down his fate. He can die at home, or he can die there; this is the natural cycle. It is not true that he will only go to heaven if he is a shaheed. You can go to heaven for other reasons too. God has written down how we all will die, so it is futile to argue about this.

In his opinion, our conversation was "futile," because for him, and for Saleem, the "helpless" soldier is simply following orders and is thus absolved of blame. The cleric alludes to the fact that the soldier can still find his way into heaven through his other deeds, suggesting other kinds of shahadat that are not shahadat for *mazhab*.

In the village space, there was an assertion of a new (or a reversion to an earlier) category of shaheed, one who dies because he fights for his country but not necessarily for his religion. To enable this shift, the village pulled in an imagining of the soldier that already existed in the vernacular. This was an imagining at odds with the more public image of the soldier as the determined fearless defender of the nation-state. The village constructed him instead as a simpleton, a yes man who undergoes harsh army discipline and training. Two moves allow this. The first is the claim that he was but a *bacha* (child) or a *larka* (boy) as opposed to a man. Havildar Sohail elaborates on this when discussing those from his area who died in the WOT: "These *bache* were brave boys. Once they were recruited they never looked back. They were brave, but the one who died before in the Kargil war, he was very brave. . . . He was a real man." The second move is an assertion that army discipline does not allow dissent and that the soldier is majboor. Saleem, dismissing these tensions around the war, said to me,

> Many of our [Deobandi] elders are in the army. Everyone knows that the army system is such that one can't say I don't agree and I will not go [to the front]. . . . He is the most majboor person. He has to do his service, and whatever he does, he does because he is ordered. So nobody discusses it if a fauji is Deobandi and he is deployed in Wana. When he comes back, he will not be asked, "What were you doing there?" Because everyone knows he is not fighting there of his own will.

This shaheed, who is less authentic than the asal shaheed, was majboor, only a bacha. He did not fight the real enemy but instead fought the gumrah bhai. He was absolved of any blame; he deserved pity but also respect. In the village imagination, the shaheed was not constructed as the willing soldier but as one who is helpless, infantilized, and unable to desert or reject this war. These tropes of infantilizing the soldier and of helplessness ran through the narratives of soldiers and the families of the dead, an imagining of the soldier that already existed in villages even outside the context of the current war and was actively pulled in to settle doubts and unease as they talked about the deaths of those who died in this war.[63]

The attempts at reconciliation mentioned earlier—the separation of religion and state and the less masculine imagining of the soldier—which permit resolution of the doubt that assails these subjectivities and local spaces, are not those proposed by the state narrative. These attempts directly contradict the state's efforts, which forbid the cleavage between religion and state from appearing and instead assert the religion-state dyad, as in the YeD/S ceremonies. The state does not look for a coexistence that the village has come to accept but desires to revert to earlier unquestioned bonds. The second reconciliation, in which the soldier, caught up in a war that is not his own, is seen as majboor and the dead as bacha or larka, is also a far cry from the masculine and determined solider that YeD/S ceremonies project. Thus, the reconciliations that emerge in these local spaces are often hushed or muted, for they are at odds with military narratives and speak to the dissonances that exist in these seemingly complicit relationships.

BATTLES WON AND LOST

It is unlikely that the army will ever release figures for the number of desertions or court martials within its ranks as a result of the WOT. But the military has formally acknowledged the need to modify the narrative of jihad for the nation-state by incorporating the new enemy into its training curriculum. Sessions on low-intensity conflict (LIC) have been added to the recruitment course, which, in addition to military tactics and strategy linked to countering terrorism, deal with defining the new enemy. These strategy-focused LIC courses were included around 2002 or 2003, with the more specific discussion of the enemy being added after 2006. According to the colonel at the infantry regiment training center, the objective of these courses, in addition to teaching a very different kind of warfare, is to ensure that "there are no doubts, for we cannot afford doubt. So when they leave [after training] they are clear about who is a terrorist and that he is not a Muslim." In keeping with the past, Islam, and the particular version that suits current military policy, is now once again being instrumentalized by the military in its training institutes to shape the subjectivities of the soldiers that are to fight this war.

The parameters of the debate around war continue to be on religious grounds, with the state asserting its right to retain the status of martyrdom for the country as a religious exercise. The military wishes to stand irrevocably aligned with religion, even if the religious frame may have been suitably altered to fit new military policy. Islam comes up repeatedly in YeD/S scripts, and more often than not, the state is predictably mentioned within the folds of faith; the state is Islamic, and the nation has a religion. The Pakistani state and military are haunted by a desire to use religion as a political tool to legitimize their current policies and the original idea of the state. As such, the move in local spaces to separate martyrdom for the state from martyrdom for religion becomes all the more significant, because it threatens the state-religion ideology that the military considers to be foundational to the image of the Pakistan Armed Forces.

The *battle of narratives* on ideological grounds, especially for a narrative that draws on religion as its primary affective repertoire, is far from being won. Doubts and questions are abundant, resulting in a hushed ambivalence. This should cause significant contention, yet we see two opposing moves in the spaces that provide the army's fodder. Ambivalence, doubt, and unease predictably occur, yet we also see continued loyalty, readiness to serve, and honor accorded to the shaheed. So, how are these mutually exclusive moves possible, such that doubt or unease is not followed by disaffection or desertion? When I put this apparent contradiction to the villagers, they responded with bemusement, with a look that seemed to say, "What an odd question to ask!" As Chaudhary Imran, a local district politician put it, "This is a fauji-dominated area. Their livelihoods are attached to the army; they will not turn against the military, and they will continue to serve." To understand this contradiction, we perhaps need to question our own propensity to see these moves as contradictory in the first place. This propensity comes from a view that places Islam and the nation as central drivers in the readiness to serve and sacrifice, a view that the state and the military propaganda apparatus takes pains to project. As a result, we see these moves in a one-dimensional space, in which the state and the now-splintered domain of religion pull at subjects in opposing directions. One way to understand this coexistence is to see that these moves happen on two separate terrains, or battlefields. The military may suggest that it is fighting a battle of narratives on religionationalist grounds, reclaiming the right to martyrdom for religion, and assert that the loyalty that subjects display during funeral rites, their presence at YeD/S ceremonies, and the endless lines for recruitment are signs that this battle has been won. Yet in the hilly tracts of Punjab, where rain is unpredictable and other livelihoods insecure, military service and sacrifice, whether under the British or in the Islamic Republic of Pakistan, has never been about religion or nation alone but also about mundane materialist and affective drivers.

Islam and nationalism—and, more aptly, Islamic nationalism in the case of Pakistan, a state it is hard to imagine without Islam—is a rhetoric offered by the military. It is embraced by the subjects of power in a bid to displace the materialism that makes this readiness to serve and die possible so that claim making to the military on these grounds can continue. It also serves as a way to offset some of the intense grief that accompanies the death of a loved one, a way to make meaning and dispel the discomfort and guilt that accompanies a death that is coupled with material compensation. Contestations remain whispers, a silencing attributable not just to coercive mechanisms of the military or to the huge propaganda apparatus available to the military, such as YeD/S ceremonies, but to bonds of another nature. The district's bonds with the military are held in place by symbiotic relationships that, when threatened, generate a powerful set of anxieties, and a battle that is lost on ideological grounds is won on another other terrain. In local spaces, this resolution is on affective and material grounds, terrain bolstered by the district's history, which keeps the emerging reconciliation very much in favor of the military, even if the military's narrative of the war and the enemy may be rejected.

CHAPTER 9

A POST-MILITARY WORLD?

AT ITS HEART, this book has been an examination of the affective relationships that are crafted within militarism. Foremost, it is an interrogation of the relationship between the Pakistan Armed Forces and its immediate subjects—soldiers and their families. A second relationship, between the military and the citizenry, is studied not directly but as a function of the first relationship, with the bodies and families of dead soldiers serving as conduits for communication with the nation.

In this book, the production, control, and stubborn afterlife of affect emerge as consistent themes running through the relationship between the military and its subjects. A wide range of military practices and policies have been examined that work and rework affect that is considered productive for military interests and affect that is considered counterproductive for the same interests. Affective regulation and the formation of affective attachment are visible in the disciplinary techniques employed in military training institutes, which seek the transformation of the peasant-subject into the soldier-subject. The military demands the acceptance of violence done to one's body and secures this acceptance not just through materialist incentives but also through affective realms, desiring the reimagination of familial attachments according to the concerns of the state. This reimagining allows the emergence of a response of love, loyalty, and attachment to the benevolent benefactor, who has the right to ask you to die or kill in its name. In case of death of the soldier, this affective regulation extends to the family, and militarism also demands that the subject accept violence done to the bodies of its loved ones. Mourning rituals for the dead are meticulously disciplined by the military in local spaces, redrawing the lines between appropriate and inappropriate grief by crafting spectacular funeral ceremonies replete with national and religious meaning making and compensation regimes that are set in motion from the moment the body arrives in the village. During commemorative ceremonies, the grief of the families of the dead becomes material for military scrutiny and crafting. Affective management that seeks to enhance certain kinds of affect and downplay others is evident in the careful preparation of families for their on-stage testimonies at national commemorations. This preparation includes skillful use of the camera and strict control of what is allowed onstage and what is edited out. Collective, predictable, and productive mourning is made possible in these affective spaces, both local and national, in which the military and the family perform for the nation, and the dead body in a coffin is transformed into the revered transcendental figure of the *shaheed*. Thus, an avoidable death is turned into a meaningful sacrifice.

The productive ability of power—in this case the ability of the military to produce certain kinds of affect and response in its subjects—is evident in these appropriations. In the context of grief, subjects perform for the military and reify national scripts of sacrifice, whether in commemorative ceremonies, military funerals, or memorialization sites and practices in local rural environs. Although these reproductions of military rites can be read along the lines of Foucauldian analysis as reiterations of power in which the subject is imbricated, I have claimed that these are not just reflective of power's unchallenged hold over its subjects but also a function of affective residues and effluxes that remain in the interiority of the subject and in the physical spaces in which they reside. This book has documented examples of residues that resist being folded into the militaristic scripts of sacrifice for the nation and hence lie outside them. Grief that has been disciplined by the military spills out again and again in both public and private narratives and refuses to be soothed by religious and nationalistic scripts of *shahadat*. Some other examples of my claim that the afterlife of regulated affect haunts people and spaces are the realizations of what-if (their sons had never enlisted or had left military service) by parents, which induce emotions such as guilt and regret; accounts of the soldiers in training as they knowingly became automatons and experience feelings of numbness and dissociation; and the uneasiness of parents locked in compensation regimes. This afterlife binds the subject more closely to the militarism project, and in order to understand such a contradiction, this book has turned to the role ideologies of religion and nation play (or don't play) in militarist subjectivities.

I have suggested in this book that the apparent complicity of the subject is not just a matter of the appropriations and manipulations invoked by the national script (which in the case of Pakistan is also religious). Instead, a set of materialistic and affective imperatives sustains the relationship between the military institution and its subjects. Within martial districts of Pakistan, the military functions as a modern kinship group that rewards its subjects with pay, pensions, benefits, and land grants. On these martialized terrains, nationalistic narratives of service and sacrifice act as bargaining chips that permit continued membership in the military's kinship group and allow claims to be made from it. The soldier-subject's attachment to all things military, which is nurtured by the military institution, and the regulation of grief at the time of a soldier's death are ways the military uses the control and production of affect to bind its subjects even closer to it. The compliance of the deceased soldier's family and their willing alignment with the military represent not some essentialist, ephemeral, and transcendental love for the Islamic nation-state but rather attempts to make sense of this death and ease the terrible burden of loss. This is also evidenced in the military's ability to largely override the ideological challenges brought about by the shift away from the traditional Hindu enemy and to the new Muslim threat. In these local terrains, the desire to serve in the military is unabated despite deep ambivalence and sometimes outright rejection of the new enemy and war. I have explained this contradiction by positioning Islam and nationalism as rhetoric offered by the military and embraced by the subjects of power in an almost psychological way to displace and offset the reality of the materialism that makes this readiness to serve and risk death possible as well as the grief caused by the death. The repurposing of livelihoods, death, and disability is made possible by the collusion of the subject with the power that forms it, allowing the corporality of the mutilated body to be reconstructed by transforming it into a revered, objectified, flag-draped coffin or by shrouding, veiling, and hiding from view the reasons people volunteer for the military. In the first repurposing, ideology disciplines pain and serves as a way to deal with grief; in the second, ideology masks the material benefits of militarism for the soldier, his family, and the institution.

Moreover, I have argued that the subject is conscious of his or her appropriation and manipulation by hegemonic power. As voiced by the families of the dead, the script of sacrifice and service for the nation-state is a rhetorical crutch from which they feel compelled to read. The phrase *Karna parta hai, kehna parta hai* (You *have* to do this; you *have* to say this) clearly signifies an awareness of the mask, which they are compelled to wear. I have complicated this compulsion through Slavoj Žižek's scholarship on ideology as "fantasy-construction."[1] Families are driven by a need to lessen their intense guilt and regret at losing a gamble taken in order to improve their economic condition. This realization brings its own set of affective residues that trouble them and linger and are assuaged not through subversion or challenge but through further compliance. Affect-laden moments of separation in which there is tension and an ability to decipher disciplinary frameworks become the very sites that permit a reconsolidation of power. My contribution in this book has been to provide two further elaborations of this notion of ideology as *fantasy*: (1) it is affect, both produced and disciplined by the military, that makes these fantasies come alive; and (2) it is also affect—its afterlife and residue—that makes these fantasies forever vulnerable, never still, and therefore in need of constant validation. The affective selves produced in nationalist and religious discourses react to, respond to, and bond with the discourse in more complicated ways than simply by getting duped by ideology or being bought off materially. These symbiotic relationships are fueled by deeply felt affect that leads families to cling to and be soothed by these narratives of sacrifice for and service to the Islamic nation-state. The scripts of nation and religion that are offered then become a language that allows them to stand either on the national stage or in the local space. These scripts become available cultural constructions of sacrifice and honor that can make an intolerable loss breathable.

Specific sites in which the feminine or the female subject of militarism becomes a preoccupation for the masculine military suggest that the militarized self (the soldier) and the military are gendered not just instrumentally because they need to fight wars or defend the nation but because they cannot be imagined without bringing in the feminine. These include depictions of the exalted mother of the shaheed (chapter 2), the desire for distance from the feminine as a rite of passage for the soldier-subject (chapter 4), the military's preoccupation with the ways men and women grieve (chapter 5), and the military's engagement and discomfort with the widow figure and the incomplete feminized body of the disabled soldier (chapters 6 and 7). Without engagement with the feminine, the militarized self and the masculine military are capable neither of delineating their own boundaries nor of capitalizing on affective manipulation.

THE GROWING SHADOW OF THE *SHUHADA* MONUMENT

Every year the chief of army staff (COAS) delivers what can be dubbed a "State of the Union" address at the YeD/S commemoration ceremony.[2] The fact that in a democracy this address can be made by the COAS, broadcast live across the nation by all major private and public news channels, and quoted the next day in the press, electronic media and newspapers alike, and that the subject matter of this address covers issues of governance, the criminal justice system, economic development, foreign policy, terrorism, and corruption without as much as a raised eyebrow powerfully demonstrates how the military establishment positions itself in the polity of Pakistan.

The military's ability to create this space (YeD/S) to communicate directly with the nation and interfere in state affairs may come as no surprise in the context of Pakistan, but what is perhaps significant to note here is the nature of the platform the military uses to assert its power: the stage that pays homage to its dead. An examination of the YeD/S stage, with which this book began as a means of investigating the *hows* of military appeal and its dominance in Pakistan, brings into sharp focus the centrality of carefully crafted narratives of grief and mourning in the messaging the military puts out for the nation.

In 2007, General Pervez Musharraf, Pakistan's third military dictator, handed over the reins of the GHQ to General Ashfaq Parvez Kayani, officially ending military rule (although the retired general still held on as president until 2008). This was followed by a general election in 2008 and the establishment of the first democratically elected government that was allowed to complete its term. General Kayani inherited an army that desperately needed to rehabilitate its image in the wake of General Pervez Musharraf's long and contentious military takeover. The threat of terrorism, directly associated with the WOT, was also increasing, with the military coming under attack from both Islamic militants and Islamic political parties. General Kayani's primary focus during his tenure was to acknowledge the military rank and file, and according to some analysts, there was an unprecedented focus on the welfare of soldiers.[3] It was during his tenure that the *Yadgar-e-Shuhada* monument was built at the GHQ. General Kayani also initiated the *Youm-e-Shuhada* ceremonies and upgraded compensation packages and administrative procedures to improve the GHQ's mechanisms for handling *shuhada* and WWPs. His successors, Generals Raheel Sharif and Qamar Javed Bajwa, have continued these policies. I argue that this inward focus and image building around sacrifice and the shaheed that intensified during General Kayani's time acted as a powerful enabler, legitimizing the military and helping it rebuild its reputation and image. It is this book's contention that the bodies of dead soldiers and the grief of their families are symbolic resources at the disposal of the military establishment that enable it to produce and discipline affect through the tropes of martyrdom, service, and sacrifice. It is a resource that the military zealously and relentlessly deploys in its relationship with the citizenry, especially in times when the country is ostensibly under civilian rule. Much like the soldier trained at the regimental center on tropes of honor, love, and family, the nation is also disciplined and made docile through affective invocations during these constructions of sacrifice.

This book traced the different treatment meted out to the civilian dead and the dead in military uniform as a way to understand how these constructions of sacrifice are made possible. Compensation regimes for civilian dead, often the result of collective organizing, are publicly announced as actions of a benevolent state. In contrast, the more generous and systematic military compensation regimes are seldom brought to the fore in military commemorative spaces or otherwise and are constructed as irrelevant. The masking of military compensation constructs the loss and thereby its sacrifice as one that *cannot be compensated*, and the military seeks a position in which it is able to continually extract compensation from the nation in the form of support and loyalty. Simply put, in cases of civilian death, the purpose of compensation is to assuage the grief and affect around death, and these regimes are a visible means of doing so. With military deaths, there is a deliberate attempt to produce and appropriate grief and affect, which are more potent if compensatory regimes are shielded from view. The transaction of compensation for death in military service involves two sets of relationships. The first is between the military and its direct subjects and involves cultivating a relationship molded by rituals of commemoration in local spaces and on the national stage and accompanied by the *giving* of generous material compensation. The second set of relationships develops between the military and the citizenry, for which the transaction of compensation for soldier death is *extractive* in that it is aimed at extracting legitimacy and unquestioned support for the military institution and its policies.

MEDIATING MILITARISM THROUGH AFFECT

A study of affective relationships crafted within the militaristic project responds to broader theoretical concerns about the working and limits of hegemonic power. The examination of the centrality of affect as a militarist technology of rule in Pakistan extends to those nation-states in which military or militaristic goals may be subsumed under the government. The call to militarism, which in the context of state armies is closely associated with nationalism, can be a project of the nation-state as much as of the military per se.

To decipher the insidious appeal of militarism it is perhaps vital to understand the experiences and motivations of its foot soldiers, those who die and those who let their loved ones die for projects or ideologies by which they may not be duped. This opens up more intimate and perhaps more obscure avenues through which to study the mechanisms that allow the militarism project to work and that sometimes place it beyond meaningful scrutiny. There are two interrelated reasons why a focus on the affective domain represents a much-needed way to understand how militaristic narratives of sacrifice and service to the nation-state have valence with populations. First and foremost, it allows us to recognize that affect is the substance that makes militaristic narratives possible. By attending to this substance, we are able to glimpse the disjuncture between the hegemonic project and its reception at the local level, cracks that are allowed expression through affect. The focus on affect permits us to record the incomplete and fractured processes through which modern militarism claims its subjects. It also allows us to understand how this disjuncture functions as a further reconsolidation of hegemonic power in which anxieties and guilt tightly bound together with economic imperatives underlie the apparent complicity between the powerful and the powerless. Second, it enables an understanding of how affect associated with military death can act as a formidable deterrent to any challenge to or questioning of the militarism project. This ability of affect to stifle dissent, whether among the direct subjects of militarism or within the citizenry, needs more scrutiny. An investigation of antiwar activism will show how criticism is weakened by a desire to show respect for the families of the deceased and the sentiments of soldiers.[4] Even when state policies that have led to combat have been challenged or when movements are fueled by a realization of the unjustness or meaninglessness of war, limits are placed on these critiques by an "emotional pull" that demands that protestors must support soldiers, if not the war, and there remains a concurrent reverence of the troops, who can be pitied for being misled while remaining heroic in the act of sacrifice.[5] In 2007, around the time of the unpopular Iraq War, the British government rolled out a campaign backed by *The Sun* that aimed at gaining some moral ground vis-à-vis the decision to go to war by bringing public attention to the working conditions of military employees. Through this campaign, it "remind[ed] the nation of the debt of honor it owed to the soldiers who fought on its behalf."[6] The campaign helped sever the connection between the army and the unpopular war in Iraq by "separat[ing] the men from the mission."[7] In other words, support for the troops, and by default the army, served to some extent to obfuscate criticism of the war itself. In the context of the US perpetration of the Iraq war, Christophe Wasinski suggests that

> the most important part of the contestation of the war expresses itself as a sort of pity policy, taking an attitude focused on the suffering of the deceased presented only as victims. . . . In this situation, death is not presented as the result of an unjust system but, mainly, as something to be regretted because of the suffering borne.[8]

Does this lead us down a blind alley, in which the challenge to war becomes sealed inside the affect attached to the grief and suffering of death? I contend that this would perhaps be too hasty a conclusion. In the following paragraphs, I address the barriers and potential for challenge in each set of subjects separately.

This book has outlined the many times that, despite overt compliance with affective regulation, the affect of soldiers and families escapes discipline and expresses itself through emotion that frees it to challenge regimes of power. Affect, deemed so appropriate for consolidating militarism's hold over its subjects, instead becomes the very medium that allows subjects to express discontent. Although these may be deeply ambivalent acts of protest that allow subversion to exist alongside complicity[9] and also possibly function as "safety valves,"[10] they nonetheless reveal an interesting trajectory that allows subjects to escape subjection at various points. I contend that understanding these as a "diagnostic of power" is important.[11] I do not suggest that this trajectory leads to resistance and subversion within militarism; in fact, my analysis has consistently recorded otherwise. But I posit that laying bare these mechanisms and recording these dissonances is not just an important theoretical exercise for understanding dynamics of power but also a deeply political one.

In the case of the second set of subjects, the citizens of the nation, modern militarism operates through a blurring and mixing of spaces, so that the lines between the civilian and the military are constantly redrawn.[12] Events that commemorate war martyrs represent an apparent *civilianization of military spaces*, which is opposite what is normally studied in militarism, the *militarization of civilian spaces*. The former is in fact an incorporation of the civilian within military spaces, with civilian subjects participating in the reproduction of military power. This mixing of the civilian with the military creates a powerful illusion of participation, compliance, and support whereby families willingly suffer this violence against their loved ones. This illusion rests on the *manufacture of the authentic*, because it draws on experienced affect and pain of families but is carefully crafted and presented. This seeming alliance between the victims of war and its perpetrators is not questioned, because to challenge these "spectacles of power"[13] is to refute or dishonor both the genuine affect of the families on display and the nation-state, personified by state policy. The state (the military) creates a false equivalence between the affect produced in response to the death of its soldiers and itself as an institution. Just as authentic grief and loss cannot be questioned, the state cannot be questioned. This false equivalence acts as an arsenal at the state's disposal to be used to discipline and control public opinion in its favor.

If we are to understand militarism's ability to establish preparation for war as normal and necessary[14] and to demand sacrifice from its subjects, it is important to expose the mechanisms through which it makes this appeal. Such an appeal is deliberately entangled with the bodies of the dead and the affect associated with them. Any attempt to study it must record the centrality of affect (especially around death) to militarism and how it is deployed to mask the illusory nature of such appeal. There are three sequential ways in which this recognition of affect opens up the possibility of a more potent and political challenge to militarism: first, by understanding that the subjects' complicity in militarism does not reflect a willingness to sacrifice based on some transcendental notion of sacrifice for the nation-state; second, by challenging the false equivalence highlighted earlier that suggests that questioning war or the hegemony of the military state is the same as disrespecting the affect produced in response to the death of its soldiers; and third, and perhaps most challenging, by deconstructing narratives of heroism, pity for suffering, and meaningful death in war and by acknowledging that war can never be glorious and that participation in it is rarely honorable. Thus "the dead soldiers who had participated in that enterprise should not be considered as heroes, should not be mourned for long by the community, and should not be taken as social examples."[15] As long as war is glorious and the dead are heroes, even if they are to be pitied as *bache* or *majboor* (as I documented in chapter 8), and as long as service in the military is not called out for what it essentially is—a viable source of *pakki naukri* for the more economically marginalized (as I documented in chapters 3, 4, and 5)—the state's (military's) ability to depict service and sacrifice as noble and to draw in its foot soldiers will be sustained. This study has shown that the very subjects whose affect is constructed as sacred, a sacredness that is in turn used to stifle questioning and debate, acknowledge at least some of these threads. The political potential of this look at militarism, which adequately deconstructs the moments of disjuncture between the hegemonic project and its reception by its immediate subjects, lies in its ability to trouble the apparent untroubled association between the military and these families. By doing so it reduces to some extent the military's ability to use affect as a technology of rule with both its immediate subjects and members of the general public.

Michel Foucault reminds us that "[power's] success is proportional to its ability to hide its own mechanisms."[16] My intention in scrutinizing these technologies of rule is to contribute to a debate that can resist interrogation because of the reverence and respect accorded to the feelings of the families of the deceased and the tightly knit tropes of service and sacrifice purportedly made possible through ideologies of nation and religion. These ideologies of nation and religion are but an afterthought, and it is in part through the construction of subjectivities via affect that militarism maintains its tenacious hold over the nation-state and its politics. If studies of militarism can document subjects in their lived complexities who are both complicit in and disengaged from these projects and if the affect of militarist subjectivities can be recorded as both manufactured and authentic, then perhaps scholarship on militarism as well as on antiwar activism can begin to challenge the foundations of the carefully manufactured "truth" that men, women, and sacrifice for the nation-state go hand in hand.

> If in some smothering dreams you too could pace
> Behind the wagon that we flung him in,
> And watch the white eyes writhing in his face,
> His hanging face, like a devil's sick of sin;
> If you could hear, at every jolt, the blood
> Come gargling from the froth-corrupted lungs,
> Obscene as cancer, bitter as the cud
> Of vile, incurable sores on innocent tongues,—
> My friend, you would not tell with such high zest
> To children ardent for some desperate glory,
> The old Lie: *Dulce et decorum est
> Pro patria mori.*[17]
>
> —Wilfred Owen

NOTES

CHAPTER 1

1. Fictitious name given to a village in Chakwal District in Punjab, Pakistan.
2. See Gusterson, "Anthropology and Militarism," 156.
3. Examples of macrolevel analysis of militarism include Melman, *Permanent War Economy*; Koistinen, *Military Industrial Complex*; Kaldor, *Baroque Arsenal*; Adams, *Iron Triangle*; Tilly, "War Making and State Making"; Shaw, *Dialectics of War*; and Kaldor, *New and Old Wars*.
4. Lutz, *Homefront*.
5. Lutz, "Military History of the American Suburbs," 901–3.
6. See Vagts, *History of Militarism*; Mann, "Roots and Contradictions"; Shaw, *Post-Military Society*; and Shaw, "Twenty-First Century Militarism." The gendered working of power, in which militant and violent solutions to conflict are inscribed in institutional practices, is important to highlight here. There is evidence that this attitude, coupled with the valorization of violence, spills into civilian spheres and impacts gender relations. See Chenoy, "Militarization, Conflict, and Women"; Enloe, *Maneuvers*; and De Mel, *Militarizing Sri Lanka*.
7. Data provided by the Personnel Administration (PA) Directorate—GHQ, Rawalpindi, January 2015.
8. See Yong, *Garrison State*.
9. The army, the land-based uniformed force within the Pakistan Armed Forces, is the largest branch of the Pakistani military in terms of manpower and the most powerful in terms of resources, political clout, geographical coverage, and public visibility.
10. See Jalal, *State of Martial Law*; Nawaz, *Crossed Swords*; and Shah, *Army and Democracy*.
11. Scholarship on the military in Pakistan has grappled with explaining the institution's dominance in the country. Research suggests, however, that one way to understand it is to pay attention to the military's burgeoning economic empire based on agricultural and property ownership as well as its control of business and industrial enterprises; see Siddiqa, *Military Inc*. Other theorists lean toward institutional theory and path dependence. They suggest that repeated coups in Pakistan have led to the weakening of civil institutions, resulting in the military stepping in directly or interfering with little resistance during periods of civilian rule; see Aziz, *Military Control in Pakistan*. The postcolonial-state hypothesis argues that states that came into being after decolonization were especially vulnerable to an imbalance between military and

civil forces because militaries were derived from earlier colonial machinery. Thus the inherited overinflated military-bureaucratic oligarchy developed more autonomously than other civil institutions; see Alavi, "State in Postcolonial Societies." The influence of the politics of the Cold War and Pakistan's role as a client state to the United States has also been emphasized as a factor; see Ahmed, *Pakistan, the Garrison State*. For more on client states, see Tilly, *Coercion, Capital and European States*; and Wendt and Barnett, "Dependent State Formation."

12. Massad, *Colonial Effects*, 8.

13. According to the notion of a *garrison state* laid out by Harold Lasswell in his book *Essays on the Garrison State*, modern industrial societies that are exposed to the constant threat of war and continual crisis create conditions in which the military establishes supremacy over the state and society through a capture of leadership. In these societies, the population becomes obedient and docile and believes that war is necessary and inevitable.

14. Saigol, *Pakistan Project*, 200–234; and Nayer and Salim, *The Subtle Subversion*.

15. See Khattak, "Gendered and Violent."

16. Saigol, *Pakistan Project*, 248.

17. See Khattak, "Militarization, Masculinity and Identity"; and Babar, "Texts of War."

18. Saigol, *Pakistan Project*, 250.

19. See LalaRukh, "ImageNation."

20. Rizvi, *Military, State and Society*, 15.

21. Long years of military rule in Pakistan have enabled the military to develop enduring roots in the public and private sectors, in industry, business, health care, banking, agriculture, education, communication, and transport. See Rizvi, *Military, State and Society*, 233–39.

22. European Union Election Observation Mission, *Final Report*, 20.

23. Fair, *Fighting to the End*, 5.

24. See, for example, Rizvi, *Military, State and Society*; and Fair, *Fighting to the End*. For in-depth studies of the workings of contemporary military institutions, such as its inner mechanics vis à vis training and disciplining techniques, see Bourke, *Intimate History of Killing*; Ben-Ari, *Mastering Soldiers*; and Ware, *Military Migrants*.

25. Foucault, *Security, Territory, Population*.

26. See Yazawa, *From Colonies to Commonwealth*; Hunt, *Family Romance*, and Banti, "Deep Images."

27. The study of affect has emerged in the last two decades as a way to theorize the social and political. The primary precursors of this interest in affect were a focus on the body, associated with feminist theory, and an interest in emotions, visible in queer studies; see Butler, *Bodies That Matter*; and Grosz, *Volatile Bodies*.

28. See Jenkins, "State Construction of Affect."

29. Foucault, *Security, Territory, Population*, 87–114; and Foucault, "Subject and Power,"

30. Stoler, "Affective States," 9.

31. Traditionally, *affect* is used as the broader term, referring to "states of being," of which emotions are seen as a "manifestation or interpretation"; see Hemmings, "Invoking Affect," 551. *Affect* has also been referred to psychoanalytically as a "qualitative expression of our drives, energy and variations"; see Giardini, "Public Affects," 150. Alternatively, Silvan S. Tomkins suggests that affects are autotelic and insatiable and give depth to our lives by allowing us to narrate our lives to ourselves and others; see Tomkins, *Affect Imagery Consciousness*. Paul Hoggett and Simon Thompson present a robust synthesis of these differences, theorizing affect and emotion as two forms of feelings that can overlap and are not mutually exclusive and yet have different connotations in which "affect concerns the more embodied, unformed and less conscious dimension of human feeling, whereas emotion concerns the feelings which are more conscious since they are more anchored in language and meaning." Anxiety is described as an affect, "experienced in a bodily way," while jealousy is an emotion, directed outward, giving it "meaning, focus and intentionality." The object of anxiety may shift, making it almost arbitrary. But emotion is externally directed, embedded in language and discourse, and more fleeting or transient. Affect remains more abiding, labile, and fluid and is capable of spreading to others; see Hoggett and Thompson, *Politics and the Emotions*, 2–3.

32. How this disengagement is to be acknowledged has been the focus of much debate. Are these acts of protest deeply ambivalent—subversive yet complicit? See Gutmann and Lutz, *Breaking Ranks*. Are these actions limited by available discourses and wrapped up in power that initiates the subject? See Butler, *Psychic Life of Power*; and Mitchell, "Everyday Metaphors of Power." Can they be called counterhegemonic "weapons of the weak?" See Scott, *Weapons of the Weak*. Or are these "safety valves" or acts that reveal the "diagnostics of power"? See Abu Lughod, "Romance of Resistance," 42–47.

33. Theorists have suggested that affects are beyond social, prediscursive states, lying outside social signification. Some of this work sets up affective freedoms and autonomy as a way out of social determinism. See Massumi, "The Autonomy of Affect"; and Bruns, "Laughter in the Aisles." This is a position fiercely contested by constructivist models, which see affect as externally determined, as a social and cultural practice. See Lutz and Abu Lughod, *Language and the Politics of Emotion*; and Ahmed, *Cultural Politics of Emotion*. Clara Hemmings perhaps rightly turns away from what she regards as a misplaced "theoretical celebration of affect" as a way to theorize challenges to social order. She suggests instead that affect presents itself "not as a difference, but as a central mechanism of social reproduction in the most glaring ways"; see "Invoking Affect," 550–51. Laura Berlant has cited the tendency of affective responses to strengthen rather than challenge hegemonic power; see *Queen of America*. See also critical race theorists who have argued that affect plays a role in consolidating structures of power and oppression while also providing the investments needed to challenge these relations: Spivak, *Outside in the Teaching Machine*; and Bhabha, *Location of Culture*.

34. Navaro-Yashin, *Make-Believe Space*, 17–24.

35. Although Lacanian psychoanalysis moves away from this more exclusive connection and acknowledges that subjects are made in relation to other subjects, it still falls short, because the human self or subjectivity remains the primary site for affective energy.

36. Navaro-Yashin, *Make-Believe Space*, 24.

37. Barrier, "Punjab Disturbances of 1907," 376.

38. See Sinha, *Colonial Masculinity*; and Nandy, *Intimate Enemy*.

39. See Chakravarti, "Whatever Happened to the Vedic Dasi?"

40. Saigol, *Pakistan Project*, 98–99.

41. Saigol, 244.

42. See Jaffrelot, "Nationalism without Nation."

43. Dewey, "Rural Roots," 263.

44. A sociological reading of this, especially in the South Asian context, cites the separation of the boy from a feminine world and his removal to a more masculine one, in which "the sexed body [is] imagined and consciously crafted in opposition to the female body"; see Chopra, Osella, and Osella, "Towards a More Nuanced Approach," 25. Expanding these ideas to militarist subjectivities in the context of Hindutva, Dibyesh Anand states that the "militarized/masculinized/nationalized self, however, from its originary moment is fearful of its own fragility and seeks to expunge from within what it perceives as non-masculine and thus weak"; see Anand "Porno-Nationalism," 163.

45. There has been considerable debate within feminist scholarship regarding maternal inclinations toward pacifism and peace movements. See Ruddick, "Maternal Thinking"; and Elshtain, "Mothers of the Disappeared." Sara Ruddick has argued that because of their social (not biological) role, mothers are called on to care for and tend to the young and sick of society and thus develop values and capacities of feeling that affirm peacekeeping and preservation of life. Others have critiqued this move, which claims to establish a link between peace and motherhood, arguing that motherhood is a social and fluid category and citing examples of mothers willingly giving their sons up to the national cause. See De Volo, "Drafting Motherhood"; and Scheper-Hughes, "Maternal Thinking and the Politics of War."

46. Corbridge et al., *Seeing the State*, 7.

47. Biehl, Good, and Kleinman, "Rethinking the Subject," 14.

48. Refers to a soldier below the rank of commissioned officer, namely, sipahi, lance naik, naik, and havildar (collectively referred to as noncommissioned officers) as well as naib subedar, subedar major, subedar, and honorary captain (referred to as junior commissioned officers). Subedars who complete thirty-two years of service may be discharged with the title of honorary captain. This is the highest rank accorded to the soldier class. The anglicized version of the term, *sepoy*, is no longer in common use, but the anglicized plural, *sipahis*, is still common. I also invoke the term *jawan* (young man), which is commonly used in the Pakistani military to refer to soldiers, usually recruits and NCOs.

49. The other two being the air force and the navy.

50. These include commemorative events for war martyrs at the GHQ and the Armed Forces Institute of Rehabilitation Medicine in Rawalpindi, an infantry regiment training center in Abbottabad, and the Army Selection and Recruitment Office and District Armed Services Board in Chakwal.

51. I obtained four types of primary data: transcriptions or notes of interviews, ethnographic notes, photographs I took during the course of my fieldwork, and artifacts, such as video recordings of all YeS shows held since 2010 and of military funerals, the diary of a dead soldier, newspaper clippings announcing deaths of soldiers from Chakwal, and letters from the military that families had kept.

52. This included eight serving soldiers (seven of whom had served in combat), eleven retired soldiers, and five soldiers who had deserted from the army. During the thirteen months of my fieldwork, I was in regular contact with five families of dead soldiers (fathers, mothers, wives, and sisters) in Palwal and Kandwal and in two nearby villages. I also spent considerable time with two disabled soldiers and their families in Palwal and Kandwal.

53. These included local clerics from mosques, the village headman, schoolteachers, NGO workers, a retired general turned politician from the district, two politicians, the district assistant commissioner, a college professor, a local writer, and the caretaker of the district community center.

54. I interviewed officers in charge of designing and coordinating the commemorative events, officers in the Personnel Administrative (PA) Directorate, and officers as well as NCOs and JCOs involved in the recruitment and training of soldiers. These included three generals (two of whom had retired), three brigadiers, eight colonels, five majors, two captains, one subedar, and one havildar.

55. According to current estimates obtained from a local NGO in the adjoining village of Kandwal, the population of Palwal stands at 2,393 (as of 2013), and the number of households stands at somewhere between 420 and 468 (based on records from the local NGO and a woman health worker in Palwal, respectively). Records obtained from the nearest post office suggest that 270 persons from Palwal draw pensions, of which 230 are males and 40 are the wives or mothers of soldiers.

56. O'Reilly, *Ethnographic Methods*, 223.

CHAPTER 2

1. My use of the word *qaum* is taken from the script of the commemorative ceremonies, which constantly allude to the qaum and its relationship with the military, as well as from my interviews with military officers and soldiers. In these texts, the qaum is constructed as a singular homogenous group whose relationship with (and, more specifically, support for and affiliation with) the military is considered vital.

2. See Mosse, *Fallen Soldiers*; Holst-Warhaft, *Cue for Passion*; and Acton, *Grief in Wartime*.

3. Verdery, *Political Lives of Dead Bodies*, 27–33.

4. Jaffrelot, *Pakistan Paradox*, 527.

5. See Gul, *Most Dangerous Place*; and Rashid, *Pakistan on the Brink*.

6. See Haqqani, *Between the Mosque and Military*; and Jaffrelot, *Pakistan Paradox*.

7. South Asia Terrorism Portal—SATP, "Fatalities in Terrorist Violence in Pakistan 2003–2016."

8. See the discussion in the section titled "Locating Religion in the Pakistani State" in chapter 8.

9. Lal Masjid (the Red Mosque) is one of Islamabad's oldest mosques. During the Soviet War in Afghanistan (1978–1989), clerics there played a key role in recruiting and training young men to fight in Afghanistan and enjoyed the patronage of the military regime of the time.

10. See Jaffrelot, *Pakistan Paradox*, 563; Farooq, "Islam in the Garrison"; and Shahzad, *Inside Al-Qaeda*.

11. Jamaat-e-Islami is the oldest Islamist political party in Pakistan. It has traditionally enjoyed a strong alliance with the military and Inter-Services Intelligence (ISI) and played a strategic role in mobilizing young men for jihad in Afghanistan against the Soviets. See Roy, *Afghanistan, from Holy War to Civil War*; and Jaffrelot, *Pakistan Paradox*.

12. Boone, "Pakistani Army Blasts Islamist Party."

13. Raza, "Ideological Fault"; Staff Correspondent, "Controversial Remarks"; Staff Correspondent, "The Martyrdom Controversy."

14. Jaffrelot, *Pakistan Paradox*, 563.

15. Siddiqa, *Military Inc.*, 206–7.

16. The 1965 war with India is looked upon in Pakistan as a decisive victory. Across the border, India too commemorates this war as a victory. Within Pakistan it is regarded as an unprovoked war in which India suffered major losses and the Pakistan Armed Forces won the day for the nation by defeating an enemy far greater in size and superior in technology. History books do not discuss the fact that India's assault on Pakistan's border was in retaliation for Pakistan's initiation of Operation Gibraltar in Kashmir and that there was no clear victor; the war ended after three weeks with the declaration of a ceasefire.

17. These causalities are due to weather extremes and inhospitable terrain in the disputed Siachen glacier region between India and Pakistan. Known as the highest battleground on earth, India and Pakistan have fought intermittent battles here since 1984.

18. This was an armed conflict between India and Pakistan, restricted to Kargil district and along the line of control in Kashmir, between May and July 1999.

19. Dead soldiers from the eastern front—for example, the 2012 Siachen landslide—were also featured on occasion.

20. Staff Correspondent, "President, PM Never Attended."

21. With one exception, the director general of the ISPR has always been from the Pakistan Army, and the more recent appointments have been generals from the army who also act as the official spokesperson for the military.

22. Aretxaga, "Maddening State," 396.

23. Verdery, *Political Lives*, 41.

24. Banti, "Deep Images," 54.
25. Banti, 56.
26. See Khattak, "Militarization, Masculinity and Identity"; LalaRukh, "Image-Nation"; Babar, "Texts of War"; and Saigol, *Pakistan Project*.
27. The analysis presented in this section is drawn from content analysis of video recordings of five YeS shows and one YeD show between 2010 and 2015. When specific examples are drawn from a particular show, the year is provided. When no year is given, examples refer to generalized themes that appear in almost all shows.
28. Rizvi, *Military, State and Society*, 245; Cohen, *Pakistan Army*; Cohen, *Idea of Pakistan*.
29. The appropriation of agency of mothers and wives in military ceremonies that commemorate martyrs in South Asia is common. See Rajan, "Women and the Nation's Narrative."
30. See Chopra, Osella, and Osella, "Towards a More Nuanced Approach."
31. See the discussion in chapter 4 in the section "Kinship and New Families."
32. Reenactments refer to short documentary films that re-create the dead soldier's life using facts from his personal life and professional career, especially the operation in which he died.
33. In talking of the objectivity of belief, Slavoj Žižek suggests that the expression of feelings such as sadness, grief, and mirth, which we often associate with the interiority of the subject, can be delegated to others in an "exteriorization," or "transference," of intimate feelings. An example of this is the act of weeping, which in some societies can be delegated to professional weepers (a common practice in Punjabi villages in Pakistan). The chorus in classical Greek tragedies likewise performed the same function, as does canned laughter in popular TV shows. See Žižek, *Sublime Object*, 31–33.
34. For more discussion on how political spectacles can dominate discourse and constrain challenge to state ideology, see Adams, *Spectacular State*, 3; and Wedeen, *Ambiguities of Domination*.
35. I use the word *collusion* with caution here, recognizing that the relationship between the state and its subject will always be a wildly skewed power equation, with the former wielding far more power and control. To study symbiosis between the powerful and the subordinated is to not disregard the coercive power of the state but to acknowledge the fluidity within power relations and the participation of subjects in their own domination. See Stoler, "Matters of Intimacy," 894.
36. Chapter 7 examines the disabled soldier subject and his relationship with the military in more detail.
37. Chapter 6 addresses the dynamics of military compensation regimes.
38. Compensation regimes for civilian and military deaths are discussed in chapter 6.
39. In an interesting development in 2018, the YeD ceremony, in addition to the traditional COAS speech, also included an address by the prime minister of Pakistan, Imran Khan. The invitation extended in this ceremony to the civilian head of

the government, the first invitation since the YeS was instituted in 2010 and subsequently merged with the YeD in 2015, is in fact a tacit admission that the political setup post–2018 election is a hybrid regime brought to life by Imran Khan's alliance with the military establishment. As such it is just that, an *extension of invitation* by the GHQ, and does not represent civilian ascendancy. See Shah, "Pakistan: Voting Under Military Tutelage."

40. These maneuvers are addressed in chapters in which I discuss the martial district of Chakwal (chapter 3) and village funerals (chapter 5).

CHAPTER 3

1. Darling, *Rusticus Loquitur*, 30.
2. The focus here remains on the Pakistan Army as the most influential branch of the military and the largest recruiter of labor in the district. But in the context of the district, the chapter addresses all three forces (with the proviso that the Army Selection and Recruitment office deals only with induction into the Pakistan Army). This became necessary because the district's population regards the three as a collective, falling within the rubric of military service. In addition, the beneficiaries of some of the institutions discussed in the chapter, such as the District Armed Services Boards- DASBs and the Fauji Foundation, belong to all three services.
3. In this section, unless otherwise specified, Punjab refers to undivided Punjab as it stood before partition. In the subsequent section, *Recruitment in the Post-Colony*, Punjab refers to those parts of the region that fell to Pakistan after 1947.
4. See Talbot, *Punjab and the Raj*.
5. See MacMunn, *Armies of India*.
6. See Mason, *Matter of Honor*.
7. Singh, *Testimonies of Indian Soldiers*, 11–17.
8. Yong, *Garrison State*, 65.
9. Pasha, *Colonial Political Economy*.
10. See Omissi, *The Sepoy and the Raj*, 7.
11. Pasha, *Colonial Political Economy*, 108. He suggests that with the coming of British colonial rule, the precolonial economy experienced three profound changes: "the institution of private property in land, the growth of merchant capital in Punjab and the establishment of cash nexus as the primary form of surplus extraction by the colonial state."
12. The land settlement policy and the Land Alienation Act of 1900 served to create and protect local intermediaries who were loyal subjects.
13. Alavi, "India: Transition from Feudalism," 371.
14. It is important to note here that during wartime, recruitment did not always remain voluntary, and there are numerous accounts of forced enlistment. See Yong, *Garrison State*, 107–8).
15. Saif, *Authoritarianism and Underdevelopment*, 22.
16. E. E. H Collen, quoted in Yong, *Garrison State*, 79.
17. Mazumder, *Making of Punjab*, 258–60.

18. Yong, *Garrison State*.
19. See Salim, "Punjab."
20. Yong, *Garrison State*, 137.
21. See Talbot, *Punjab and the Raj*; and Omissi, *The Sepoy and the Raj*.
22. Ali, *Punjab under Imperialism*, 109.
23. Saif, *Authoritarianism and Underdevelopment*, 39.
24. Yong, *Garrison State*, 91.
25. Mazumder, *Making of Punjab*, 260.
26. A vernacular term used to refer to someone who is regarded as the primary or even sole provider.
27. Yong, *Garrison State*, 142; See also Ali, *Punjab under Imperialism*.
28. Yong, *Garrison State*, 163
29. Pasha, *Colonial Political Economy*, 182.
30. Cohen, "State Building in Pakistan," 318.
31. Kennedy, *Bureaucracy in Pakistan*, 194. Martial districts in the areas that fell to Pakistan were not restricted to Punjab, as parts of Khyber Pakhtunkhwa, then known as the North West Frontier Province, were also used as a labor pool for the British Indian Army. Punjab, however, was the larger supplier of recruits.
32. Saif, *Authoritarianism and Underdevelopment*, 114.
33. In the 1950s, Pakistan signed defense agreements such as SEATO (the South East Asia Treaty Organization) and CENTO (the Central Treaty Organization) that made it one of the earliest Cold War allies of the US power system. These developments facilitated the military's growing ascendancy in state policy and contributed to the first military takeover in 1958. See Saif, *Authoritarianism and Underdevelopment*.
34. The addition of religious factions to build anticommunist frenzy and boost Islam as a bulwark strategy further fueled the already appropriated idea of religion that has haunted Pakistan since its birth.
35. Rizvi, *Military, State and Society*, 62–63.
36. Rizvi, 240.
37. Staff Correspondent, "Punjab's Dominance in Army."
38. According to recruitment data for 2004 to 2013 provided by the Personnel Administration (PA) Directorate at the GHQ, each year an average of 130,000 applicants apply to be a soldier in the Pakistan Army, from which roughly around 38,000 are inducted.
39. Rizvi, *Military, State and Society*, 128.
40. Cohen, *Pakistan Army*, 45.
41. The Bangladesh debacle is a case in point; Bengalis were underrepresented in service and their inclusion was resisted by the army. See Cohen, *Pakistan Army*, 43.
42. Dewey, "Rural Roots," 261; See also Siddiqa, *Military Inc.*, 206–7.
43. The other is the Army Welfare Trust, which is engaged in a number of commercial ventures including banking, insurance, leasing, and others. In *Military Inc.*, Ayesha Siddiqa discusses the Pakistani military's economic empire and its impact on the country's political, economic, and social landscapes.

44. Fauji Foundation, "Fauji Foundation Overview"; Rizvi, *Military, State and Society*, 237.

45. Information based on interviews in 2014–2015 with officers from the PA Directorate; GHQ; the Selection and Recruitment Center, Rawalpindi; and the SRO Chakwal.

46. Six additional provincial directorates exist, four in the main provinces and one each in GB and AJK. These report to the Pakistan Armed Services Board (PASB), which itself reports to the Ministry of Defense. Retired military officers head the national and provincial boards.

47. Information based on interviews with PASB Islamabad and DASB Chakwal, 2014–2015.

48. See Dewey, "Rural Roots."

49. Lieven, "Military Exceptionalism."

50. Dewey, "Rural Roots," 263.

51. Rizvi, *Military, State and Society*; Cloughley, *History of the Pakistan Army*.

52. Two more infantry regiments were raised in this period: Azad Kashmir, or AK (1971), and Sindh (1980). AK had previously been known as the Azad Kashmir Regular Force (AKRF) and had been a territorial force whose recruitment and operations were restricted to Pakistani-controlled Kashmir.

53. This information is based on interviews with a number of army officers, including two retired generals, two serving colonels, and a major interviewed during fieldwork in 2014 and 2015.

54. In 1999 the Northern Light Infantry, a paramilitary force, was designated as a full infantry regiment of the Pakistan Army. Its status was changed as an acknowledgment of its services in the Kargil war. Enlistment had previously been from Gilgit Baltistan, but from that point on, it functioned as a mixed regiment.

55. Staff Correspondent, "Punjab's Dominance in Army."

56. According to officers of the PA Directorate interviewed in 2014, these quotas have been set for the soldier class only. A corresponding policy of increasing the representation of all parts of Pakistan among officers also exists, but there are no strict quotas. Christine Fair and Shuja Nawaz report that the demographics of the officer class are changing, but here too the available data is subject to the problem of numbers reflecting residency in a province rather than ethnicity. See Fair and Nawaz. "The Changing Pakistan Army."

57. Nawaz, *Crossed Swords*, 571.

58. Darling, *Punjab Peasant*, 74.

59. Punjab Lok Sujaag, *Chakwal District, Development and Politics*, 22.

60. Punjab Bureau of Statistics. "Block Wise Provisional Summary Results."

61. Pakistan Bureau of Statistics Pakistan. *Standards Measurement Survey*, 113.

62. Punjab Bureau of Statistics, *Punjab Development Statistics 2017*, 238.

63. This placement is based on Andrew Wilder's division of Punjab into four regions: North, Central, South, and West. His classification is based on a mix of fac-

tors, including geographical boundaries, the borders of older divisions, differences in agricultural patterns, and historical influences. See Wilder, *Pakistani Voter*, 34.

64. Cheema, Khalid, and Patnam, "Geography of Poverty,"168.

65. Cheema, Khalid, and Patnam, 187.

66. See Nelson, "Informal Agencies of Influence in Pakistan." Religious cleavages have played out along political lines, with the Shias of Chakwal supporting pro-Shia Majlis-e-Wahdat-e-Muslimeen (MWM) and Sunni support invested in Sipah-e-Sahaba, later known as Ahle Sunnat Wal Jamaat (ASWJ).

67. Punjab Lok Sujaag, *Chakwal District, Development and Politics*, 34–37.

68. Information based on interviews with local and national politicians and bureaucrats in Chakwal: General Majeed Malik; Chaudhary Imran; Assistant Commissioner, Chakwal; and Ayaz Amir, January–June 2015.

69. Data provided by the Fauji Foundation, Rawalpindi, 2014–2015.

70. Category A reflects boards in areas with a large number of ex-servicemen (over 15,000).

71. This ratio may have changed based on the subsequent population census in 2017.

72. Information based on interviews with an SRO major and a DASB secretary in Chakwal, 2014–2015.

73. This is a reference to the cannon installed by the British government in Dulmial village in Chakwal as acknowledgment of the large number enlisted from this village in World War I.

74. Foucault, *Discipline and Punish*, 194.

CHAPTER 4

1. The literal meaning of this French term is "group spirit." It is often invoked by officers of the Pakistani military.

2. For discussions on the professional disciplined soldier, see Huntington, *The Soldier and the State*; and Perlmutter, *The Military and Politics*. For a discussion on the soldier as armed peasant, see Trotsky, *History of the Russian Revolution*.

3. Singh, *Testimonies of Indian Soldiers*, 4–5.

4. The literal meaning of this term is "youth." It is used in the Pakistani military to refer to the soldier class.

5. Dewey, "Rural Roots, 263.

6. Foucault, *Discipline and Punish*, 135.

7. In her historical reading of the training techniques employed during the two world wars and the Vietnam War, Joanna Bourke traces similar patterns, such as "depersonalization, uniforms, lack of privacy, forced social relationships, tight schedules, lack of sleep, [and] disorientation, followed by rites of reorganization according to military codes, arbitrary rules and strict punishments." Bourke, *Intimate History of Killing*, 67.

8. Foucault, *Discipline and Punish*, 141–54.

9. Foucault, 166.
10. There are three ranks at the subedar/JCO level: naib subedar, subedar, and subedar major.
11. Havildar is the highest rank in the NCO cadre. There are three NCO ranks: sipahi, lance naik, and havildar.
12. Foucault, *Discipline and Punish*.
13. Foucault.
14. See work on resistance by Scott, *Weapons of the Weak*. Scott argues that subjects (peasant classes) are able to penetrate and demystify prevailing ideologies.
15. Butler, *Psychic Life of Power*, 17.
16. Mitchell, "Limits of the State," 92–93.
17. Mitchell, "Everyday Metaphors of Power," 569–71.
18. A considerable amount of scholarship has looked at the ways in which the enemy is dehumanized, objectified, and made into an object of hate so that killing him is easier. See Kennett, *G.I.—The American Soldier*; Ballard and McDowell, "Hate and Combat Behavior"; and Shay, *Achilles in Vietnam*.
19. See Racine, "Pakistan and the India Syndrome."
20. See Nayer and Salim, *Subtle Subversion*; and Saigol, *Pakistan Project*.
21. Anderson, *Imagined Communities*, 141–44.
22. Bourke, *Intimate History of Killing*, 84–87.
23. Bourke, 129–33.
24. Dewey, "Rural Roots," 276.
25. Elshtain, *Women and War*, 206.
26. See discussion in the section titled "The Script" in chapter 2, which discusses the video poem, "Tum ye kaise kar lete ho?" ("How Do You Do This?").
27. Bouhdiba, *Sexuality in Islam*.
28. Rozan, *Understanding Masculinity*, 22.
29. Bourke, *Intimate History of Killing*, 213–20.
30. SSG is a special operations force of the Pakistan Army, known for its grueling training.
31. Macleish, *Making War at Fort Hood*, 132–33.

CHAPTER 5

1. Names of a village and a city, respectively.
2. A large town in South Waziristan, FATA.
3. See Brard, *East of Indus*.
4. This song is also played at the end of the day at army training centers.
5. Ahmed, *Cultural Politics of Emotion*, 3.
6. See Babar, "Texts of War"; Rajan, "Women and the Nation's Narrative"; and Saigol, *Pakistan Project*.
7. Derrida, *Specters of Marx*.
8. A dominant Muslim sect in Pakistan.
9. Foucault, *Discipline and Punish*.

10. Wedeen, *Ambiguities of Domination*; Navaro-Yashin, *Faces of the State*.
11. Berlant, *Queen of America*.
12. Navaro-Yashin, *Make-Believe Space*, 24.
13. Sloterdijk, *Critique of Cynical Reason*.
14. Žižek, *Sublime Object of Ideology*, 27.
15. Wedeen, *Ambiguities of Domination*, 121.
16. Navaro-Yashin, *Faces of the State*, 162.
17. Lori Allen also refers to a similar cynicism in her work on human rights; see Allen, *The Rise and Fall*.
18. Navaro-Yashin, *Faces of the State*, 165–66.
19. Žižek, *Sublime Object of Ideology*, 45.

CHAPTER 6
1. Wasinski, "Post-Heroic Warfare," 116.
2. Mauss, *The Gift*.
3. See Khattak, "Right to Life and Compensation," 43.
4. Mittelstadt, *Rise of the Military Welfare State*, 65.
5. Approximately two thousand Pakistanis on average were killed annually in terrorism-related incidents between 2003 and 2016; see South Asia Terrorism Portal—SATP, "Fatalities in Terrorist Violence in Pakistan 2003–2016." This does not include the number of militants killed in the war. Fatalities have gone down markedly since 2015; see Pakistan Institute of Peace Studies, "Pakistan Security Reports."
6. Prior to 2004, Pakistan's legal system also recognized the principle of civilian compensation, and previous legislation had created insurance funds to indemnify civilians against injuries in 1965 (war with India) and 1971 (war in East Pakistan). There are other precedents, such as compensation regimes and policies in Sindh and Punjab due to rising sectarian and ethnic violence in the late 1990s. See Institute of Social and Policy Sciences, *Compensating Civilian Victims*.
7. Institute of Social and Policy Sciences, *Compensating Civilian Victims*, 13.
8. Khan, "Price of a Life."
9. The institutional and procedural mechanisms described in this section refer specifically to the Pakistan Army, the largest, best-resourced, and most manpower-intensive branch of the Pakistani military. It is also the branch that has incurred the most loss of life, primarily because it is the largest force and because the current war is within a landlocked terrain. Compensatory mechanisms for other branches of the military closely mirror the army package, although some differences exist in both benefits and implementation systems.
10. In case of civilian law enforcement (for example, the Khyber Pakhtunkhwa (KP) police department, which has suffered high causalities in the WOT), there have been a slew of compensation policies since 1995. The 2015 Government of KP, Finance Department notification (No.FD(SOSR-II)4-199/2013) also includes other civil servants killed in the line of duty. Whereas earlier packages were basic, the newer ones also include provisions for cash compensation, pension, education, accommodation,

and health facilities for families. See, for example, Khyber Pakhtunkhwa Police, "KP Police Special Compensation Package"; and Khan, "KP Police Propose Creation of 600 ASI Seats for Family."

11. Khan, "Price of a Life."

12. The losses incurred by the Pakistani military in the Kargil war, which lasted between May and July 1999, were downplayed to mitigate the heavy criticism Pakistan received, both nationally and internationally, for an ill-planned and unprovoked incursion into Indian territory. Official and unofficial casualty figures suggest that between 450 and 1,000 soldiers died. See Zehra, *From Kargil to the Coup*.

13. Much of the institutional and procedural information given here is drawn from interviews with the PA Directorate, Shuhada Cell, and DASB Chakwal during my fieldwork between 2014 and 2015.

14. This set includes pension—100 percent of salary; gratuity—years of service multiplied by monthly salary; death gratuity—twelve months' salary; death compensation—lump sum cash payment based on rank; child allowance; and government-sponsored group insurance.

15. This set includes military group insurance; distress grant; subsistence allowance; child allowance; plot and/or agricultural land—applicable on merit; retention of accommodation for up to five years; education; health facilities; and employment for one family member.

16. See the discussion in the section "Local Recruitment Politics" in chapter 3.

17. See, for example, Staff Correspondent, "Sindh Cabinet Meeting."

18. See, for example, Syed Ali, "Families of '*Shaheed*' Policemen"; and Durrani, "Families of Martyred Policemen Face Hurdles."

19. Khattak, "Right to Life and Compensation," 65.

20. Staff Correspondent, "Martyrs Widows Awarded 11m."

21. I use the word "generous" in comparison to what is offered to other martyrs of the state and not to imply that what is given exceeds the compensation due for loss of life or limb.

22. From an interview with retired brigadier serving in the PASB, 2015.

23. The literal meaning is "piece of one's liver." The phrase refers to a vital part of the flesh without whom survival is not possible.

24. Ophir, *Order of Evils*, 35.

25. Ophir, 90.

26. Ophir, 138.

27. Based on information on a poster titled "Procedure of division of announced dues and facilities for NoK" (translated by author) displayed on the Chakwal DASB notice board, 2015, and on discussions with the DASB secretary and the families of deceased soldiers.

28. See the discussion in chapter 2 in the section titled "The Script."

29. Pakistan Legal Decisions, *Mirza Muhammad Amin etc. v. Government of Pakistan*, 146.

30. Information presented here is drawn from interviews with the PA Director-

ate, the Shuhada Cell, and DASB Chakwal during fieldwork in 2014 and 2015. It is also based on interviews conducted during fieldwork in villages with families of the deceased.

31. According to these rulings, service benefits that an employee can claim from his employer in his lifetime are considered part of his estate upon his death and are heritable. They are to be distributed among all his heirs according to the respective shares allocated to them by Islamic law. Service benefits that can be defined as grants or concessions on the part of an employer are to be distributed only to those members of his family stipulated by the rules and regulations of the service. See Pakistan Legal Decisions, *Mirza Muhammad Amin etc. v. Government of Pakistan*; and Civil Law Cases, *Zaheer Abbas v. Pir Asif and Others*.

32. See accounts of the Israeli war widows in Shamgar-Handelman, *Israeli War Widows*.

33. Boris and Bardaglio, "Transformation of State Patriarchy," 72–73.

34. Mimi Abramovitz, quoted in Skocpol, *Protecting Soldiers and Mothers*, 31.

35. Skocpol, *Protecting Soldiers and Mothers*, 34.

36. See Nawaz's father's testimony in chapter 5 in the section titled "Compliance at the Heart of Ambivalence."

37. See the discussion in the section "Phone Calls, Coffins, and Spectacular Parades" in chapter 5.

38. The link between nation, sacrifice, and men's bodies can be traced back to the wars of the French Revolution and Napoleon, which mark the shift from the career/mercenary officer who served a sovereign king in dynastic wars to the citizen-soldier who drew arms to defend and protect his nation-state. See Ehrenreich, *Blood Rites*, 187; Mosse, *Fallen Soldiers*; and Nagel, "Masculinity and Nationalism."

CHAPTER 7

1. Number announced by the COAS in his address during the YeD ceremony, 2016.

2. Various soldiers and senior officers of the Pakistan Army whom I interviewed suggested this ratio between the dead and the disabled.

3. Bourke, *Dismembering the Male*, 39.

4. Bourke, 56–59.

5. Bourke, 75.

6. Quayson, *Aesthetic Nervousness*.

7. A term coined by Rosemarie Garland Thomson. It refers to an identity position not marked by identifiers of disability. See Thomson, *Extraordinary Bodies*.

8. Preston, *Fantasy of Disability*.

9. This includes disability pensions and one-off disability compensation from the government allocation as well as allotment of land, group insurance, and disability allowance from the GHQ allocation.

10. Information based on interviews with army doctors at AFIRM, Rawalpindi, 2014–2015.

11. Sama TV Network, "Qutab Online."
12. Verdery, *Political Lives of Dead Bodies*, 33.
13. Puar, *Right to Maim*, xviii.
14. Puar, 127.
15. An Islamic declaration of faith mandatory for all Muslims, also read at the time of death to ease the spirit's transition into the next world. Shakeel reading the *kalma* at this point implies that he thought he would die.
16. *Board* here refers to the medical board that can sanction release from army service because of a medical condition.
17. See discussion in the "States of Suspension" section of chapter 4.
18. See the discussion in chapter 5 in the section "Grieving all Wrong."
19. Ophir, *Order of Evils*, 90.
20. The social identity of the disabled could be said to be a product of his interaction with the state, in that veteran organizations have come together to demand recognition and benefits. See Geyer, "Ein Vorbote des Wohlfahrtsstaates." David A. Gerber argues that the identity of disabled veterans was vested in a collective, intensely shared experience and that they desired the right to exist as productive citizens and not just as subjects of pity and charity in addition to demanding better benefits from the state. See Gerber, "Disabled Veterans."
21. Puar, "Disablement and Inhumanist Biopolitics," 7.

CHAPTER 8

1. Latin phrase meaning "to die for one's country." See excerpt from Wilfred Owen's poem at the end of chapter 9 for more context.
2. See the discussion in chapter 2 in the section "The War in Northwest Pakistan and Its Dead."
3. Urmila Phadnis, quoted in Jaffrelot, *Pakistan Paradox*, 139; Titus, *Marginality and Modernity*.
4. Jaffrelot, *Pakistan Paradox*, 189.
5. Rushdie, *Shame*, 87.
6. Samad, *Nation in Turmoil*, 90.
7. Devji, *Muslim Zion*, 47.
8. Devji, 139.
9. Jaffrelot, *Pakistan Paradox*, 459.
10. See Racine, "Pakistan and the India Syndrome"; and Saigol, *Pakistan Project*.
11. See Rizvi, *Military, State and Society*; and Jaffrelot, *Pakistan Paradox*, 123–24.
12. General Zia-ul Haq justified his military coup and subsequent rule (1977–1988) under the pretext of Islamizing Pakistan.
13. See Nasr, "Islam, the State"; Abou Zahab, "Regional Dimension"; and Ahmed, "Roots of Sectarianism in Pakistan."
14. See Cheema, *Armed Forces of Pakistan*, 3.
15. See Rashid, *Pakistan on the Brink*.

16. See Gul, *Most Dangerous Place*; and Rashid, *Pakistan on the Brink*.
17. See Gul, *Most Dangerous Place*.
18. See Roy, *Afghanistan, from Holy War*.
19. Rashid, *Pakistan on the Brink*.
20. Qtd. in Jaffrelot, *Pakistan Paradox*, 502.
21. See Shahzad, *Inside Al-Qaeda*; Gul, *Most Dangerous Place*; and Fair, *Fighting to the End*.
22. See Rizvi, *Military, State and Society*; Cohen, *Idea of Pakistan*; and Saigol, *Pakistan Project*.
23. An example of this are the many war songs and slogans that became popular during the 1965 war that present the soldier figure as a soldier of Islam (see Saigol, *Pakistan Project*, 253).
24. See Mazumder, *Indian Army*; and Singh, *Testimonies of Indian Soldiers*.
25. See Ahmed, *Pakistan, the Garrison State*; and Fair, *Fighting to the End*.
26. Refers to someone who delivers sermons in the mosque. The term is used by the military to refer to a religious cleric who serves with the military institution.
27. Rizvi, *Military, State and Society*, 245.
28. An imam is a prayer leader in a mosque.
29. Here the word *jihad* is used in direct reference to war/combat.
30. Details are provided by instructors at the infantry regiment training center.
31. See the discussion in chapter 4 in the section "Overstating the Automaton."
32. This is similar to the Pakistan Studies courses that were introduced and made compulsory in all schools and colleges across Pakistan during the Zia regime. In these courses, Pakistan and its history are depicted as inextricably linked to Islam and Muslim identity. See Azizi, *Murder of History*; and Nayer and Salim, *Subtle Subversion*.
33. This is mirrored in officer training at the Pakistan Military Academy (PMA), where "Islamic teaching only complements regular professional and academic disciplines." Cohen, *Idea of Pakistan*, 115.
34. See Shahzad, *Inside Al-Qaeda*; Qadir, "Still an Uncertain Future," 167; and Jaffrelot, *Pakistan Paradox*, 563.
35. See Farooq, "Islam in the Garrison."
36. See the discussion in chapter 3 in the section "Recruitment in the Post Colony."
37. See the discussion in the section "Kinship and New Families" in chapter 4.
38. See Jaffrelot, *Pakistan Paradox*; and Siddiqa, *New Frontiers*.
39. Bano, *The Rational Believer*, 70–71.
40. Ramzan, "Sectarian Landscape."
41. See Wasseem, "Sectarian Conflict in Pakistan"; Abou Zahab, "Regional Dimension"; and Nelson, "Informal Agencies of Influence."
42. Siddiqa, *New Frontiers*.
43. Siddiqa, *New Frontiers*; Jaffrelot, *Pakistan Paradox*; Nelson, Informal Agencies of Influence."
44. Siddiqa, *New Frontiers*.

45. Information based on interviews with district officials and local politicians.
46. Siddiqa, *New Frontiers*, 13.
47. Staff Reporter, "Bloodbath in Chakwal."
48. Philippon, "A Sublime, yet Disputed Object?," 160.
49. Dhakku, "Fear Stalks Chakwal."
50. The Lal Masjid operation was a confrontation in July 2007 between Islamic militants and the government of Pakistan, led by President (General) Pervez Musharraf. Pakistan's decision to back the WOT sparked the conflict with the Lal Masjid, whose leadership was openly pro-Taliban. The Lal Masjid (one of Islamabad's oldest mosques) and its adjoining madrasas were the battleground for this operation. Over one hundred casualties, including military dead, were reported, and the response from the general public and the media was ambivalent regarding the use of force by the Pakistan Army.
51. Nelson, "Dealing with Difference," 603.
52. National Counter Terrorism Authority, "National Action Plan 2014 (NAP)."
53. See the discussion in chapter 2 in the section "Elusive Enemy."
54. It is likely that this would be different in KP districts that are Pashtun dominated.
55. The subsequent use of these areas in the Afghan jihad was briefly discussed in chapter 2 in the section "The War in Northwest Pakistan and Its Dead."
56. Iqtidar, "Pakistan's Apartheid Regime."
57. FATA was governed until 2018 under the colonial Frontier Crimes Regulation (FCR) of 1901. The governance framework under FCR consists of political agents, who are selected by the federal bureaucracy and have minimal accountability. Basic rights of a fair trial such as the right to legal counsel, the right to appeal, and the laws of evidence are not recognized within the FCR. This regulation also includes measures such as collective punishment, whereby an entire family or tribe can be punished for the crimes of one individual. The constitutional amendment from May 2018 abolishing FCR is in the process of being implemented.
58. Qadir, "History of 'Dangerous Fanatics.'"
59. Hussain, the grandson of the Prophet Mohammad, along with members of his close family and supporters, was martyred by Yazid's army (Caliph of the Umayyad Caliphate and whose appointment by his father, Muawiya, was the first hereditary succession in Islamic history) as he refused to submit to his rule. Hussain's shahadat and that of his family and supporters at the site of Karbala in Iraq is a significant event in Islamic history and is commemorated as a symbol of brave resistance against tyranny and oppression.
60. The provocation referred to here is the Lal Masjid operation under General Pervez Musharraf.
61. See the discussion in chapter 5 in the section "Grieving All Wrong."
62. This refers to the perceived need to battle the assertion of the religious right (Jamaat-e-Islami and some Deobandi groups) that the military dead are not shaheed.
63. See the discussion in chapter 4 in the section "Chakwal's Retired Soldiers."

CHAPTER 9
1. Žižek, *Sublime Object of Ideology*, 45.
2. Sattar, "State of the Union."
3. Gul, "Armed but Not Dangerous."
4. See Wasinski, "Post-Heroic Warfare."
5. Managhan, "Grieving Dead Soldiers," 439.
6. Ware, *Military Migrants*, 267.
7. Sarah Ingham and Christopher Dandeker, quoted in Ware, *Military Migrants*, 267.
8. Wasinski, "Post-Heroic Warfare," 125.
9. Gutmann and Lutz, *Breaking Ranks*.
10. Abu Lughod, "Romance of Resistance," 47.
11. Abu Lughod, 48.
12. See Lutz and Bartlet, "JROTC"; LalaRukh, "ImageNation"; Enloe, *Maneuvers*; Enloe, *Does Khaki Become You?*; Babar, "Texts of War"; and De Mel, *Militarizing Sri Lanka*.
13. Fahmy, *All the Pasha's Men*, 8. He uses this term to describe images that represent the power of the state. I invoke it to describe commemorative ceremonies organized by the state that are crafted as deeply touching and poignant events that leave the viewer with a sense of awe at the state's ability to summon such sacrifice.
14. Mann, "Roots and Contradictions."
15. Wasinski, "Post-Heroic Warfare," 125.
16. Foucault, *History of Sexuality*, 86.
17. "It is sweet and fitting to die for one's country." Owen and Stallworthy, *War Poems of Wilfred Owen*.

GLOSSARY

bacha/bache: child/ren
barani: rain-fed
bhuq: hunger
chaddar: loose cotton wrap
charpai: traditional woven bed
fauj/fauji: military/military man
ghairat: honor
ghazi: warrior
ghurbat: poverty
janaza: funeral
jawan: young man/soldier
jazbati: emotional/irrational
khateeb: one who delivers the sermon for Friday or Eid prayers—used by the military to refer to religious clerics serving in the military
larka/larke: boy/boys
madrasa: religious seminary
majboor: helpless
maulvi: Muslim cleric
namaz: Muslim prayer
okha: uneasy
pagri: traditional Punjabi headdress worn by men, also a metaphor for honor
pakki naukri: secure government service/job
qaum: nation
rista/riste: relationship/s
sabr: patience
sahulat: facilities
sarkar: government
shaheed/shuhada/shahadat: martyr/martyrs/martyrdom
shalwar kameez: traditional dress consisting of a long shirt over loose trousers
shauq: interest
sipahi/s: soldier/s
sohni: beautiful
vaen: Punjabi mourning ritual

Yadgar-e-Shuhada: Martyrs' Memorial
Youm-e-Difah: Defense Day
Youm-e-Shuhada: Martyrs' Day
zabardast: spectacular
zehen: mind

BIBLIOGRAPHY

Abou Zahab, Mariam. "The Regional Dimension of Sectarian Conflicts in Pakistan. In *Pakistan, Nationalism without Nation?*, edited by Christophe Jaffrelot, 116–29. London: Zed Books, 2002.

Abu Lughod, Lila. "The Romance of Resistance: Tracing Transformation of Power through Bedouin Women." *American Ethnologist* 17, no. 1 (February 1990): 41–55.

Acton, Carol. *Grief in Wartime: Private Pain, Public Discourse*. New York: Palgrave Macmillan, 2007.

Adams, Gordon. *The Iron Triangle: Politics of Defense Contracting*. New York: New York Council on Economic Priorities, 1981.

Adams. Laura. *The Spectacular State: Culture and National Identity in Uzbekistan*. Durham, NC: Duke University Press, 2010.

Ahmed, Ishtiaq. *Pakistan, the Garrison State: Origins, Evolution and Consequences, 1947–2011*. Karachi: Oxford University Press 2013.

Ahmed, Khalid. "The Roots of Sectarianism in Pakistan." *Criterion Quarterly* 2, no. 4 (October–December 2007): 57–85.

Ahmed, Sara. *The Cultural Politics of Emotion*. New York: Routledge, 2004.

Alavi, Hamza. "India: Transition from Feudalism to Colonial Capitalism." *Journal of Contemporary Asia* 10 (1980): 359–99.

———. "The State in Postcolonial Societies: Pakistan and Bangladesh." *New Left Review* 1, no. 74 (July–August 1972): 59–81.

Alcoff, Linda. "The Problem of Speaking for Others." *Cultural Critique*, no 20 (Winter 1992): 5–32.

Ali, Imran. *Punjab under Imperialism, 1885–1947*. Princeton, NJ: Princeton University Press, 1988.

Allen, Lori. *The Rise and Fall of Human Rights: Cynicism and Politics in Occupied Palestine*. Stanford, CA: Stanford University Press, 2013.

Altinay, Ayse G. *The Myth of the Military-Nation: Militarism, Gender, and Education in Turkey*. New York: Palgrave Macmillan, 2004.

Anand, Dibyesh. "Porno-Nationalism and the Male Subject." In *Rethinking the Man Question: Sex Gender and Violence in International Relations,* edited by Jane Parpart and Marysia Zalewski, 163–80. London: Zed Books, 2008.

Anderson, Benedict. *Imagined Communities: Reflections on the Origins and Spread of Nationalism*. 2nd ed. London: Verso Books, 2006.

Aretxaga, Begona. "Maddening State." *Annual Review of Anthropology* 32 (2003): 393–410.

Aziz, Mazhar. *Military Control in Pakistan*. London: Routledge, 2007.
Azizi, Khursheed K. *The Murder of History: A Critique of Textbooks Used in Pakistan*. Lahore, PK: Vanguard Books, 1993.
Babar, Aneela Z. "Texts of War: The Religio-Military Nexus and Construction of Gender Identity in Pakistan and India." *Gender, Technology and Development* 4, no. 3 (2000): 441–64.
Baiocchi, Gianpaolo, and Brian Connor. "The Ethnos in the Polis: Political Ethnography as Mode of Inquiry." *Sociology Compass* 2, no. 1 (2008): 139–55.
Ballard, John A., and Aliecia J. McDowell. "Hate and Combat Behavior." *Armed Forces and Society* 17, no. 2 (Winter 1991): 229–41.
Bano, Masooda. *The Rational Believer: Choices and Decisions in the Madrasas of Pakistan*. New York: Cornell University Press, 2012.
Banti, Alberto Mario. "Deep Images in Nineteenth Century Nationalist Narrative." *Performing Emotions: Historical and Anthropological Sites of Affect: Historein* 8 (October 2008): 54–62.
Barrier, Norman Gerald. "Punjab Disturbances of 1907: Government Responses." *Modern Asian Studies* 1, no. 4 (1967): 353–83.
Ben-Ari, Eyal. *Mastering Soldiers: Conflict, Emotion and the Enemy in an Israeli Military Unit*. New York: Berghahn, 1998.
Berlant, Laura. *The Queen of America Goes to Washington City: Essays on Sex and Citizenship*. Durham, NC: Duke University Press, 1997.
Bhabha, Homi J. *The Location of Culture*. London: Routledge, 1994.
Biehl, Joao, Byron Good, and Arthur Kleinman. "Rethinking the Subject." In *Subjectivity: Ethnographic Investigations*, edited by Joao Biehl, Byron Good, and Arthur Kleinman, 1–24. Berkeley: University of California Press, 2007.
Boone, Jon. "Pakistani Army Blasts Islamist Party for Calling Taliban Chief 'Martyr.'" *The Guardian*, November 12, 2013. http://www.theguardian.com/world/2013/nov/12/pakistan-army-taliban-hakimullah-mehsud-martyr.
Boris, Eileen, and Peter Bardaglio. "The Transformation of State Patriarchy." In *Families, Politics and Public Policy: A Feminist Dialogue on Women and the State*, edited by Irene Diamond, 70–93. New York: Longman, 1983.
Bouhdiba, Abdelwahab. *Sexuality in Islam*. London: Saqi Books, 1998.
Bourke, Joanna. *Dismembering the Male: Men's Bodies, Britain and the Great War*. London: Reaktion Books Ltd., 1996.

———. *An Intimate History of Killing: Face to Face Killing in 20th Century Warfare*. London: Granta Books, 1999.
Brard, Gurnam Singh. *East of Indus: My Memories of Old Punjab*. New Delhi: Hemkunt, 2007.
Brennan, Teresa. *The Transmission of Affect*. New York: Cornell University Press, 2004.
Brewer, John. *Ethnography*. Buckingham, UK: Open University Press, 2000.
Bruns, John. "Laughter in the Aisles: Affect and Power in Contemporary Theoretical and Cultural Discourse." *Studies in American Humor* 3, no. 7 (2000): 5–23.

Butler, Judith. *Bodies That Matter: On the Discursive Limits of "Sex."* New York: Routledge, 1993.

———. *The Psychic Life of Power: Theories in Subjection.* Stanford, CA: Stanford University Press, 1997.

Chakravarti, Uma. "Whatever Happened to the Vedic Dasi? Nationalism, Orientalism and a Script for the Past." In *Recasting Women: Essays in Colonial History*, edited by Kumkum Sangari and Sudesh Vaid, 50–60. New Delhi: Kali for Women, 1989.

Cheema, Ali, Lyyla Khalid, and Manasa Patnam. "The Geography of Poverty: Evidence from the Punjab." Special edition, *The Lahore Journal of Economics*, (2008): 163–88.

Cheema, Pervaiz I. *The Armed Forces of Pakistan.* Karachi: Oxford University Press, 2003.

Chenoy, Anuradha M. "Militarization, Conflict, and Women in South Asia." In *The Women and War Reader*, edited by Lois A. Lorentzen and Jennifer E. Turpin, 101–10. New York: New York University Press, 1998.

Chopra, Radhika, Filippo Osella, and Caroline Osella, "Towards a More Nuanced Approach to Masculinity, Towards a Richer Understanding of South Asian Men." In *South Asian Masculinities: Context of Change, Sites of Continuity*, edited by Radhika Chopra, Filippo Osella, and Caroline Osella, 1–33. New Delhi: Kali for Women and Women Unlimited, 2004.

Civil Law Cases. *Zaheer Abbas v. Pir Asif and Others.* Lahore, PK: PLD, 2011, 1528.

Cloughley, Brian. *A History of the Pakistan Army: War and Insurrections.* 2nd ed. London: Oxford University Press, 2000.

Cohen, Stephen. *The Idea of Pakistan.* Washington, DC: Brookings Institution Press, 2004.

———. *The Pakistan Army.* Berkeley: University of California Press. 1984.

———. "State Building in Pakistan." In *The State, Religion and Ethnic Politics: Pakistan, Iran and Afghanistan*, edited by Ali Banuazizi and Myron Weiner, 299–332. New York: Syracuse University Press, 1998.

Connell, Raewyn. *Masculinities.* Berkeley: University of California Press, 1995.

Corbridge, Stuart, Glyn Williams, Manoj Srivastava, and Rene Veron. *Seeing the State: Governance and Governmentality in India*, Cambridge, UK: Cambridge University Press, 2005.

Darling, Malcolm Lyall. *The Punjab Peasant in Prosperity and Debt.* New Delhi: Manohar, 1947.

———. *Rusticus Loquitur, or the Old Light and the New in the Punjab Village.* London: Oxford University Press, 1930.

De Alwis, Malathi. "Moral Mothers and Stalwart Sons: Reading Binaries in a Time of War." In *The Women and War Reader*, edited by Lois Ann Lorentzen and Jennifer Turpin, 254–71. New York: New York University Press, 1998.

De Mel, Neloufer. *Militarizing Sri Lanka: Popular Culture, Memory and Narrative in the Armed Conflict.* Thousand Oaks, CA: Sage, 2007.

———. *Women and the Nation's Narrative*. New Delhi: Kali for Women, 2001.
Derrida, Jacques. *Specters of Marx: The State of Debt, the Work of Mourning and the New International*. Translated by Peggy Kamuf. New York: Routledge, 1994.
Devji, Faisal. *The Muslim Zion: Pakistan as a Political Idea*. London: Harvard University Press, 2003.
De Volo, Lorraine Bayard. "Drafting Motherhood: Maternal Imagery and Organizations in the United States and Nicaragua." In *The Women and War Reader*, edited by Lois Ann Lorentzen and Jennifer Turpin, 240–53. New York: New York University Press, 1998.
Dewey, Clive. "The Rural Roots of Pakistan Militarism." In *The Political Inheritance of Pakistan*, edited by Donald Anthony Low, 255–83. New York: St. Martin's Press, 1991.
Dhakku, Nabeel. "Fear Stalks Chakwal after Attack on Ahmadi Place of Worship." *Dawn*, December 14, 2016. http://www.dawn.com/news/1302240.
Durrani, Fakhar. "Families of Martyred Policemen Face Hurdles in Availing Welfare Package." *The News*, September 11, 2015. https://www.thenews.com.pk/print/61841-families-of-martyred-policemen-face-hurdles-in-availing-welfare-package.
Ehrenreich, Barbara. *Blood Rites: The Origins and History of the Passions of War*. London: Granta, 1997.
Elshtain, Jean Bethke. "Mothers of the Disappeared." In *Representations of Motherhood*, edited by Donna Bassin, Margaret Honey, and Meryle Mahrer Kaplan, 75–91. New Haven, CT: Yale University Press, 1994.
———. *Women and War*. Chicago: University of Chicago Press, 1995.
Enloe, Cynthia. *Does Khaki Become You? The Militarization of Women's Lives*. Boston: South End Press, 1998.
———. *Maneuvers: The International Politics of Militarizing Women's Lives*. Berkeley, CA: University of California Press, 2000.
European Union Election Observation Mission. *Final Report, General Election, 25th July 2018*. EU Election Observation Mission, October 2018. http://www.eods.eu/library/final_report_pakistan_2018_english.pdf.
Fahmy, Khaled. *All the Pasha's Men*. Cambridge, UK: Cambridge University Press. 1997.
Fair, Christine. *Fighting to the End: The Pakistan Army's Way of War*. Karachi: Oxford University Press, 2014.
———. *The Madrassah Challenge: Militancy and Religious Education in Pakistan*. Washington, DC: United Nations Institute of Peace Press, 2008.
Fair, Christine, and Shuja Nawaz. "The Changing Pakistan Army Officer Corps." *Journal of Strategic Studies* 34, no. 1 (2011): 63–94.
Farooq, Umer. "Islam in the Garrison." *The Herald*, March 2015. http://herald.dawn.com/news/1152791/islam-in-the-garrison.
Fauji Foundation. "Fauji Foundation Overview." About Us. Accessed March 1, 2017. http://www.fauji.org.pk/fauji/about-us/aboutus-overview.

Finer, Samuel. *The Man on Horseback: The Role of the Military in Politics*. Harmondsworth, UK: Penguin, 1976.
Foucault, Michel. *Discipline and Punish: The Birth of Prisons*. London: Penguin Books, 1991.
———. *History of Sexuality: The Will to Know*. Vol. 1. London: Penguin, 1998.
———. *Security, Territory, Population: Lectures at the College de France, 1977–1978*. London: Palgrave Macmillan, 2008.
———. "The Subject and Power." *Critical Inquiry* 8, no. 4 (Summer 1982): 777–95.
Fussell, Paul. *The Great War and Modern Memory*. New York: Oxford University Press, 1975.
Gerber, David A. "Disabled Veterans, the State, and the Experience of Disability in Western Societies, 1914–1950." *Journal of Social History* 36, no. 4 (2003): 899–916.
Geyer, Michael. "The Militarization of Europe, 1914–1945." In *The Militarization of the Western World*, edited by John R. Gillis, 65–102. New Brunswick, NJ: Rutgers University Press, 1989.
———. "Ein Vorbote des Wohlfahrtsstaates. Die Kriegsopferversorgung in Frankreich, Deutschland und Grossbritannien nach dem Ersten Weltkrieg." *Geschichte und Gesellschaft* 9, no. 2 (1983): 230–77.
Ghai, Anita. "Engaging with Disability with Postcolonial Theory." In *Disability and Social Theory*, edited by Dan Goodley, Bill Hughes, and Lennard Davis, 270–86. London: Palgrave Macmillan, 2012.
Giardini, Federica. "Public Affects: Clues Towards a Political Practice of Singularity." *The European Journal of Women's Studies* 6, no. 2 (1990): 149–60.
Gray, Chris H. *Post Modern War: The New Politics of Conflict*. New York: Guilford, 1997.
Grosz, Elizabeth. *Volatile Bodies: Towards a Corporeal Feminism*. Bloomington: Indiana University Press, 1994.
Gul, Imtiaz. "Armed but Not Dangerous." *The Friday Times*, September 16, 2016. http://www.thefridaytimes.com/tft/armed-but-not-dangerous.
———. *The Most Dangerous Place: Pakistan's Lawless Frontier*. New York: Viking, 2010.
Gusterson, Hugh. "Anthropology and Militarism." *Annual Review of Anthropology* 36 (2007): 155–75.
Gutmann, Matthew, and Catherine Lutz. *Breaking Ranks: Iraqi Veterans Speak Out against the War*. Berkeley: University of California Press, 2010.
Haq, Farhat. "Militarism and Motherhood: The Women of the Lashkar i Tayyabia in Pakistan." *Signs, Journal of Women in Culture and Society* 32, no. 4 (2007): 1023–46.
Haqqani, Hussain. *Pakistan: Between the Mosque and Military*. Lahore, PK: Vanguard Books, 2005.
Heathcote, Tony. *The Military in British India: The Development of British Land Forces in South Asia, 1600–1947*. Manchester, UK: Manchester University Press, 1995.
Hemmings, Clara. "Invoking Affect, Cultural Theory and the Ontological Turn." *Cultural Studies* 19, no. 5 (September 2005): 548–67.

Hoggett, Paul, and Simon Thompson, eds. *Politics and the Emotions: The Affective Turn in Contemporary Political Studies.* New York: Continuum International, 2012.

Holst-Warhaft, Gail. *The Cue for Passion: Grief and Its Political Uses.* Cambridge, MA: Harvard University Press, 2000.

Hunt, Lynn. *The Family Romance of the French Revolution.* New York: Routledge, 1992.

Huntington, Samuel. *The Soldier and the State: The Theory and Politics of Civil Military Relations.* Cambridge, MA: Harvard University Press, 1964.

Institute of Social and Policy Sciences. *Compensating Civilian Victims of Conflict and Terrorism in Pakistan: A Review of Policy and Practice.* Islamabad: Institute of Social and Policy Sciences, 2011.

Iqtidar, Humeira. "Pakistan's Apartheid Regime." *Tanqeed*, no. 10 (February 2016). http://www.tanqeed.org/2016/02/pakistans-apartheid-regime/.

Jaffrelot, Christophe. "Nationalism without Nation: Pakistan Searching for Identity." In *Nationalism Without Nation?*, edited by Christophe Jaffrelot, 7–47. London: Zed Books, 2002.

———. *The Pakistan Paradox: Instability and Resilience.* Gurgaon, IN: Random House, 2015.

Jalal, Ayesha. *The State of Martial Law: The Origins of Pakistan's Political Economy of Defense.* Cambridge, UK: Cambridge University Press, 1990.

Jenkins, Janis. "The State Construction of Affect: Political Ethos and Mental Health among Salvadorian Refugees." *Culture, Medicine, Psychiatry* 15 (1991): 139–65.

Kaldor, Mary. *The Baroque Arsenal.* New York: Hill and Wang, 1981.

———. *New and Old Wars: Organized Violence in a Global Era.* Cambridge, UK: Polity Press, 1999.

Kandiyoti, Deniz. "Identity and Its Discontents: Women and the Nation." *Millennium: Journal of International Studies* 20, no. 3 (1991): 429–43.

Kennedy, Charles H. *Bureaucracy in Pakistan.* Karachi: Oxford University Press, 1987.

Kennett, Lee. *G.I.—The American Soldier in World War II.* New York: Scribner, 1987.

Khan, Aurangzaib. "The Price of a Life: Compensating Victims of Terrorism." *Herald*, July 2016. http://herald.dawn.com/news/1153355/the-price-of-a-life-compensating-victims-of-terrorism.

Khan, Javed A. "KP Police Propose Creation of 600 ASI Seats for Family Members of Fallen Cops." *The News*, August 4, 2015. https://www.thenews.com.pk/print/54691-kp-police-propose-creation-of-600-asi-seats-for-family-members-of-fallen-cops.

Khattak, Saba. "Gendered and Violent: Inscribing the Military on the Nation-State." In *Engendering the Nation-State*, vol. 1, edited by Neelam Hussain, Khawar Mumtaz, and Rubina Saigol, 38–52. Lahore, PK: Simorgh, 1997.

———. "Militarization, Masculinity and Identity in Pakistan: Effects on Women." In *Unveiling the Issues*, vol. 1, edited by Nighat S. Khan and Afiya S. Zia, 52–64. Lahore, PK: ASR, 1995.

———. "The Right to Life and Compensation in Pakistan's Tribal Areas." *Identity, Culture & Politics: An Afro-Asian Dialogue* 16, no. 1 (July 2015): 41–69.
Khyber Pakhtunkhwa Police. "KP Police Special Compensation Package." Last modified November 27, 2015. http://kppolice.gov.pk/news/index.php?NewsId=811.
Koistinen, Paul. *The Military Industrial Complex: A Historical Perspective.* New York: Praeger, 1980.
Lagioia, Nicola. "'Writing Is an Act of Pride': A Conversation with Elena Ferrante." *The New Yorker*, May 19, 2016. http://www.newyorker.com/books/page-turner/writing-is-an-act-of-pride-a-conversation-with-elena-ferrante.
LalaRukh, "ImageNation: A Visual Text." In *Engendering the Nation-State*, vol. 2, edited by Neelam Hussain, Khawar Mumtaz, and Rubina Saigol, 75–101. Lahore, PK: Simorgh, 1997.
Lasswell, Harold. *Essays on the Garrison State.* New Brunswick, NJ: Transaction, 1997.
Leigh, M. S. *The Punjab and the War.* Lahore, PK: Sang-e-Meel, 1997.
Lieven, Anatol. "Military Exceptionalism in Pakistan." *Survival: Global Politics and Strategy* 53, no. 4 (2011): 53–68.
Lutz, Catherine. *Homefront. A Military City and the American 20th Century.* Boston: Beacon Press, 2001.
———. "Making War at Home in the United States: Militarization and the Current Crisis." In *The Anthropology of the State*, edited by Aradhana Sharma and Akhil Gupta, 291–309. Cambridge, MA: Blackwell, 2006.
———. "A Military History of the American Suburbs, the Discipline of Economics, and All Things Ordinary." *Antipode* 43, no. 3 (2011): 901–6.
Lutz, Catherine, and Lila Abu Lughod. eds. *Language and the Politics of Emotion.* Cambridge, UK: Cambridge University Press, 1990.
Lutz, Catherine, and Lesley Bartlet. "JROTC: Making Soldiers in Public Schools." *Education Digest* 61, no. 3 (November 1995): 9–14.
Macleish, Kenneth T. *Making War at Fort Hood: Life and Uncertainty in a Military Community.* Princeton, NJ: Princeton University Press, 2013.
MacMunn, George Fletcher. *The Armies of India.* Bristol, UK: Crecy Books, 1984.
Managhan, Tina. "Grieving Dead Soldiers, Disavowing Loss: Cindy Sheehan and the Im/possibility of the American Antiwar Movement." *Geopolitics* 16 (2011): 438–66.
Mann, Michael. "The Roots and Contradictions of Modern Militarism." *New Left Review* 1, no. 162 (March–April 1987): 35–51.
Mason, Philip. *A Matter of Honor—An Account of the Indian Army, Its Officers and Men.* Austin, TX: Holt, Rinehart and Winston, 1974.
Massad, Joseph. *Colonial Effects: The Making of National Identity in Jordan.* New York: Columbia University Press, 2001.
Massumi, Brian. "The Autonomy of Affect." In *Deleuze: A Critical Reader*, edited by Paul Patton, 217–39. Oxford, UK: Blackwell, 1996.
Mauss, Marcel. *The Gift: The Form and Reason for Exchange in Arabic Societies.* New York: Norton, 2000.

Mazumder, Rajit. *The Indian Army and the Making of Punjab*. Ranikhet, IN: Permanent Black, 2011.
Melman, Seymour. *The Permanent War Economy*. New York: Simon and Schuster, 1974.
Mitchell, Timothy. "Everyday Metaphors of Power." *Theory and Society* 19, no. 5 (October 1990): 545–77.
———. "The Limits of the State: Beyond Statist Approaches and Their Critics." *American Political Science Review* 8, no. 1 (March 1991): 77–96.
Mittelstadt, Jennifer. *The Rise of the Military Welfare State*. Cambridge, MA: Harvard University Press, 2015.
Mosse, George L. *Fallen Soldiers: Reshaping the Memory of the World Wars*. Oxford, UK: Oxford University Press, 1990.
Nagel, Joane. "Masculinity and Nationalism: Gender and Sexuality in the Making of Nations." *Ethnic and Racial Studies* 21, no. 2 (March 1998): 242–69.
Nandy, Ashis. *The Intimate Enemy: Loss and Recovery of Self under Colonialism*. 2nd ed. New Delhi: Oxford University Press, 2009.
Nasr, Seyyed V. Reza. "Islam, the State and the Rise of Sectarian Militancy." In *Pakistan, Nationalism without Nation?*, edited by Christophe Jaffrelot, 86–113. London: Zed Books, 2002.
National Counter Terrorism Authority. "National Action Plan 2014 (NAP)." Law and Policy. Accessed December 1, 2018. https://nacta.gov.pk/nap-2014/.
Navaro-Yashin, Yael. *Faces of the State: Secularism and Public Life in Turkey*. Princeton, NJ: Princeton University Press, 2002.
———. *The Make-Believe Space: Affective Geographies in a Postwar Polity*. Durham, NC: Duke University Press, 2012.
Nawaz, Shuja. *Crossed Swords: Pakistan, Its Army, and the Wars Within*. Karachi: Oxford University Press, 2008.
Nayer, Abdul Hameed, and Ahmad Salim, eds. *The Subtle Subversion: A Report on Curricula and Textbooks in Pakistan*. Islamabad: Sustainable Development Policy Institute, 2003.
Nelson, Matthew J. "Dealing with Difference: Religious Education and the Challenge of Democracy in Pakistan." *Modern Asian Studies* 43, no. 3 (2009): 591–618.
———. "Informal Agencies of Influence in Pakistan: The Interdependence of Social, Religious, and Political Trends." In *Mapping Pakistan's Internal Dynamics: Implications for State Stability and Regional Security*, Special Report no. 55, 59–78. Seattle, WA: National Bureau of Asian Research, 2016. https://www.nbr.org/wp-content/uploads/pdfs/publications/special_report_55_mapping_pakistan_february2016.pdf
O'Hanlon, Rosalind. "Recovering the Subaltern Subject and the Histories of Resistance in Colonial South Asia." *Modern Asia Studies* 22, no. 1 (1988): 189–224.
Omissi, David. *The Sepoy and the Raj: The Indian Army, 1860–1940*. London: Macmillan, 1994.

Ophir, Adi. *The Order of Evils: Toward Ontology of Morals*. Translated by Rela Mazali and Havi Carel. New York: Zone Books, 2005.

O'Reilly, Karen. *Ethnographic Methods*. New York: Routledge, 2005.

Owen, Wilfred, and Jon Stallworthy. *The War Poems of Wilfred Owen*. London: Chatto & Windus, 1994.

Pakistan Bureau of Statistics Pakistan. *Pakistan Social and Living Standards Measurement Survey, 2014–2015*. Islamabad: Pakistan Bureau of Statistics Pakistan, 2016.

Pakistan Institute of Peace Studies. "Pakistan Security Reports." 2015, 2016, 2017, and 2018. Publications. Last modified January 6, 2019. https://www.pakpips.com/publications#1512730923805-d52fde57-07fa.

Pakistan Legal Decisions. *Shariat Petition No. 6/R of 1980, Mirza Muhammad Amin etc. v. Government of Pakistan, Federal Shariat Court*. Lahore, PK: Punjab Education Press, 1982, 143–51.

Pasha, Mustapha Kamal. *Colonial Political Economy: Recruitment and Underdevelopment in the Punjab*. Karachi: Oxford University Press, 1988.

Perlmutter, Amos. *The Military and Politics in Modern Times: On Professionals, Praetorians, and Revolutionary Soldiers*. New Haven, CT: Yale University Press, 1977.

Philippon, Alix. "A Sublime, yet Disputed Object of Political Ideology? Sufism in Pakistan at the Crossroads." In *State and Nation-Building in Pakistan: Beyond Islam and Security*, edited by Roger D. Long, Gurharpal Singh, Yunas Samad, and Ian Talbot, 146–65. New York: Routledge, 2016.

Preston, Jeffrey. *The Fantasy of Disability: Images of Loss in Popular Culture*. New York: Routledge, 2017.

Puar, Jasbir K. *The Right to Maim. Debility, Capacity and Disability*. Durham, NC: Duke University Press, 2017.

———. "The 'Right' to Maim: Disablement and Inhumanist Biopolitics in Palestine." *Borderlands E-Journal* 14, no. 1 (2015): 1–27.

Punjab Bureau of Statistics. "Block wise Provisional Summary Results of *6th Population and Housing Census 2017*." Population Census. Last modified January 3, 2018. http://www.pbs.gov.pk/sites/default/files/bwpsr/punjab/CHAKWAL_SUMMARY.pdf.

———. *Punjab Development Statistics 2017*. Lahore, PK: Bureau of Statistics, Government of Punjab, 2017.

Punjab Lok Sujaag. *Chakwal District, Development and Politics*. Sahiwal, PK: Punjab Lok Sujaag, n.d.

Qadir, Shaukat. "Still an Uncertain Future." In *The Future of Pakistan*, edited by Stephen Cohen, 158–71. Lahore, PK: Vanguard Books, 2012.

Qadir, Sonia. "The History of 'Dangerous Fanatics.'" *The News on Sunday*, May 27, 2018. http://tns.thenews.com.pk/history-dangerous-fanatics/#.Ww_r0i-Q3fY.

Quayson, Ato. *Aesthetic Nervousness: Disability and the Crisis of Representation*. New York: Columbia University Press, 2007.

Racine, Jean-Luc. "Pakistan and the India Syndrome: Between Kashmir and the Nuclear Predicament." In *Pakistan, Nationalism without Nation?*, edited by Christophe Jaffrelot, 196–227. London: Zed Books, 2002.

Rajan, V. G. Julie. "Women and the Nation's Narrative: From Imaginations of Femininity to Violence against Women." Special Issue 2, *Femininity, Violence, and the National Narrative, Journal of Postcolonial Cultures and Societies* 4 (2013): 158–65.

Ramzan, Muhammad. "Sectarian Landscape: Madrasas and Militancy in Punjab." *Journal of Political Studies* 22, no. 2 (2015): 421–36.

Rashid, Ahmed. *Pakistan on the Brink. The Future of Pakistan, Afghanistan and the West*. New York: Viking, 2002.

Raza, Shahzad. "Ideological Fault." *The Friday Times*, November 15, 2013. http://www.thefridaytimes.com/tft/ideological-fault/.

Rizvi, Hassan Askari. *Military, State and Society in Pakistan*. Lahore, PK: Sang-e-Meel, 2003.

Roy, Oliver. *Afghanistan, from Holy War to Civil War*. Princeton, NJ: Princeton University Press, 1995.

Rozan. *Understanding Masculinity: A Formative Research on Masculinities and Gender Based Violence in Pakistan*. Islamabad: Rozan, 2010.

Ruddick, Sara. "Maternal Thinking." *Feminist Studies* 6 (1980): 342–64.

———. "Women of Peace, a Feminist Construction." In *The Women and War Reader*, edited by Lois Ann Lorentzen and Jennifer Turpin, 213–26. New York: New York University Press, 1998.

Rushdie, Salman. *Shame*. London: Vintage Random House, 1995.

Saif, Lubna. *Authoritarianism and Underdevelopment in Pakistan, 1947–1958: The Role of Punjab*. Karachi: Oxford University Press, 2010.

Saigol, Rubina. *Knowledge and Identity: Articulation of Gender in Educational Discourse in Pakistan*. Lahore, PK: ASR, 1995.

———. *The Pakistan Project. A Feminist Perspective on Nation and Identity*. New Delhi: Women Unlimited, 2013.

Salim, Ahmad. "Punjab." *Saqafat* 1, no. 1 (Third Quarter 1975): 22–30.

Sama TV Network. "Qutab Online—August 14, 2015." Accessed April 17, 2019. https://www.youtube.com/watch?v=bG1o4hs1ZeE.

Samad, Yunus. *A Nation in Turmoil. Nationalism and Ethnicity in Pakistan, 1937–1958*. New Delhi: Sage, 1995.

Sattar, Baber. "State of the Union." *The News*, September 10, 2016. https://www.thenews.com.pk/print/149153-State-of-the-union.

Scheper-Hughes, Nancy. "Maternal Thinking and the Politics of War." In *The Women and War Reader*, edited by Lois Ann Lorentzen and Jennifer Turpin, 227–33. New York: New York University Press, 1998.

Scott, James C. *Weapons of the Weak*. New Haven, CT: Yale University Press, 1985.

Shah, Aqil. *The Army and Democracy: Military Politics in Pakistan*. Cambridge, MA: Harvard University Press, 2014.

———. "Pakistan: Voting Under Military Tutelage." *Journal of Democracy*, no. 1 (2019): 128–42.

Shahzad, Saleem. *Inside Al-Qaeda and the Taliban.* New York: Palgrave Macmillan, 2011.
Shamgar-Handelman, Lea. *Israeli War Widows: Beyond the Glory of Heroism.* South Hadley, MA: Bergin and Garvey, 1986.
Shaw, Martin. *Dialectics of War: An Essay in the Social Theory of Total War and Peace.* London: Pluto Press, 1988.
———. *Post-Military Society: Militarism, Demilitarization, and War at the end of the Twentieth Century.* Philadelphia: Temple University Press, 1991.
———. "Twenty-First Century Militarism: A Historical-Sociological Framework." In *Militarism and International Relations: Political Economy, Security, Theory,* edited by Anna Stavrianakis and Jan Selby, 19–32. London: Routledge, 2013.
Shay, Jonathan. *Achilles in Vietnam: Combat Trauma and the Undoing of Character.* New York: Scribner, 1995.
Siddiqa, Ayesha. *Military Inc.: Inside Pakistan's Military Economy.* Karachi: Oxford University Press, 2007.
———. *The New Frontiers: Militancy and Radicalism in Punjab.* SISA, report no. 2. Oslo: Centre for International and Strategic Analysis, 2013.
Singh, Gajendra. *The Testimonies of Indian Soldiers and the Two World Wars: Between the Self and the Sepoy.* London: Bloomsbury, 2014.
Sinha, Mrinalini. *Colonial Masculinity: The "Manly Englishman" and the "Effeminate Bengali" in the Late Nineteenth Century.* Manchester, UK: Manchester University Press, 1995.
Sivan, Emmanuel. "Private Pain and Public Remembrance in Israel." In *War And Remembrance in the Twentieth Century,* edited by Jay Winter and Emmanuel Sivan, 177–204. Cambridge, UK: Cambridge University Press, 2000.
Skocpol, Theda. *Protecting Soldiers and Mothers: The Political Origins of Social Policy in the United States.* Cambridge, MA: Harvard University Press, 1995.
Sloterdijk, Peter. *Critique of Cynical Reason.* London: Verso, 1998.
Soss, Joe. "Talking Our Way to Meaningful Explanations: A Practice-Centered View of Interviewing for Interpretive Research." In *Interpretation and Method: Empirical Research Methods and the Interpretive Turn,* edited by Dvora Yanow and Peregrine Schwartz-Shea, 127–49. New York: ME Sharpe, 2006.
Staff Correspondent. "Controversial Remarks: Army Demands Apology from Munawar Hussan." *The Express Tribune,* November 11, 2013. http://tribune.com.pk/story/630232/controversial-remarks-army-demands-apology-from-munawar-hassan/
———. "The Martyrdom Controversy." *Dawn,* November 18, 2013. http://www.dawn.com/news/1056902.
———. "Martyrs Widows Awarded 11m under *Shuhada* Package." *The Daily Times,* July 5, 2016. http://dailytimes.com.pk/khyber-pakhtunkhwa/05-Jul-16/martyrs-widow-awarded-rs-11m-under-shuhada-package.
———. "President, PM Never Attended Youm-e Shuhada." *The News,* May 4, 2014. https://www.thenews.com.pk/archive/print/500505.

———. "Punjab's Dominance in Army Being Reduced." *Dawn*, September 14, 2007. http://www.dawn.com/news/266159/punjab.

———. "Sindh Cabinet Meeting: Package for Martyred Cops Raised to Rs 5 Million." *The Express Tribune*, May 14, 2016. https://tribune.com.pk/story/1103034/sindh-cabinet-meeting-package-for-martyred-cops-raised-to-rs-5-million/.

Staff Reporter, "Bloodbath in Chakwal Leaves 26 Dead 40 Injured." *Dawn*, April 9, 2009. http://www.dawn.com/news/455393.

South Asia Terrorism Portal—SATP. "Fatalities in Terrorist Violence in Pakistan 2003–2016." Accessed January 17, 2017. http://www.satp.org/satporgtp/countries/pakistan/database/casualties.htm

Spivak, Gayatri. *Outside in the Teaching Machine*. New York: Routledge,1993.

Stavrianakis, Anna, and Jan Selby, eds. *Militarism and International Relations: Political Economy, Security, Theory*. London: Routledge, 2012.

Stoler, Anne. "Affective States." In *A Companion to the Anthropology of Politics*, edited by David Nugent and Joan Vincent, 4–20. Cambridge, MA: Blackwell, 2004.

———. "Matters of Intimacy as Matters of State: A Response." *The Journal of American History* 88, no. 3 (2001): 893–97.

Syed Ali, Naziha. "Families of '*Shaheed*' Policemen Being Denied Compensation." *Dawn*, December 22, 2013. http://www.dawn.com/news/1075518.

Talbot, Ian. *Punjab and the Raj: 1847–1947*. New Delhi: Manohar, 1988.

Thomson, Rosemarie Garland. *Extraordinary Bodies: Figuring Physical Disability in American Culture and Literature*. New York: Columbia University Press, 1997.

Tilly, Charles. *Coercion, Capital and European States: AD 990–1992*. Cambridge, MA: Blackwell, 1992.

———. "War Making and State Making as Organized Crime." In *Bringing the State Back*, edited by Peter B. Evans, Dietrich Rueschemeyer, and Theda Skocpol, 169–91. Cambridge University Press, 1985.

Titus, Paul. *Marginality and Modernity: Ethnicity and Change in Post-Colonial Baluchistan*. Karachi: Oxford University Press, 1996.

Tomkins, Silvan S. *Affect Imagery Consciousness*. Vol. 2, *The Negative Affects*. New York: Springer, 1963.

Trotsky, Leon. *The History of the Russian Revolution*, vol. 1. London: Sphere Books, 1967.

Vagts, Alfred. *A History of Militarism: Civilian and Military*. New York: Free Press, 1959.

Verdery, Katherine. *The Political Lives of Dead Bodies: Reburial and Post Socialist Change*. New York: Columbia University Press, 1999.

Vinitzky-Seroussi, Vered, and Eyal Ben-Ari. "A Knock on the Door: Managing Death in the Israeli Defense Forces." *The Sociological Quarterly* 41, no. 3 (Summer, 2000): 391–411.

Ware, Vron. *Military Migrants: Fighting for Your Country*. London: Palgrave Macmillan, 2012.

Wasinski, Christophe. "Post-Heroic Warfare and Ghosts: The Social Control of Dead American Soldiers in Iraq." *International Political Sociology* 2 (2008): 113–27.

Wasseem Mohammad. "Sectarian Conflict in Pakistan." In *Conflict and Violence in South Asia: Bangladesh, India, Pakistan and Sri Lanka*, edited by K. M. de Silva, 19–89. Kandy, LK: International Center for Ethnic Studies, 2000.

Wedeen, Lisa. *Ambiguities of Domination: Politics, Rhetoric and Symbols in Contemporary Syria*. London: University of Chicago Press, 1999.

Wendt, Alexander, and Michael Barnett. "Dependent State Formation and Third World Militarization." *Review of International Studies* 19, no. 4 (October 1993): 321–47.

Wilder, Andrew. *The Pakistani Voter: Electoral Politics and Voting Behavior in the Punjab*. Karachi: Oxford University Press, 1999.

Yazawa, Melvin. *From Colonies to Commonwealth: Familial Ideology and the Beginnings of the American Republic*. Baltimore: Johns Hopkins University Press, 1985.

Yong, Tan Tai. *The Garrison State: The Military, Government and Society in Colonial Punjab, 1849–1947*. New Delhi: Sage, 2005.

Yuval- Davis Nira. *Gender and Nation*. New Delhi: Sage, 1997.

Zehra, Naseem. *From Kargil to the Coup: Events That Shook Pakistan*. Lahore: Sang-e-Meel, 2018.

Žižek, Slavoj. *The Sublime Object of Ideology*. London: Verso, 2008.

INDEX

Italic page numbers indicate material in figures or tables. See also Glossary, page 239.

Abbottabad infantry training center, 87, 89, 98, 182–83
Abramovitz, Mimi, 158
absence of dead from spaces, 124, 126–27, 148
affect: "affective geographies"/physical spaces, 12, 124, 130; "affective munitions," 4–5; emotions of soldiers, 96–98, 106; families acting out real emotion, 39–41, 44–45; mediating militarism through, 213–18; scholarship on, 10–11, 33, 221nn31
affective residues, 130, 134, 136, 208, 210
Afghanistan: border fatalities, 30; FATA as buffer from, 26; jihad against Soviets in, 11, 224nn9; martyrs in, 181; Muslim enemies from, 50; support for Mujahideen in, 6, 181–82, 189
AFIRM (Armed Forces Institute of Rehabilitation Medicine), 164–66, 175. *See also* disabled veteran(s)
agricultural insecurity, 58, 70–71
agricultural land grant to widow, 154
Ahle-Hadith sect, 180, 190, 192
Ahle-Sunnat (Sunni) sect, 191–92, 229n66
Ahle-Tashi (Shia) sect, 180, 191–92, 194
Ahmed, Sara, 123
Ahmed, Sir Syed, 195
Ahmedis, 181, 190, 192
Air Force, 8, 70, 82–83, 85
AJK (Azad Jammu and Kashmir), 65

Akmal, 76–77
Allied Bank Park (Chakwal), 83–84 (*84*)
ambivalence: in acts of protest, 215, 221n32; compliance and, 134–38; and mosaic of affect, 11; in state policy, 28, 44, 85; toward the feminine, 14–15, 160; toward WOT, Taliban, and Shaheed, 182, 187–88, 199, 200, 404, 209
"America's war," 201
amputations and prosthetics, 163–65, 169–70
Anderson, Benedict, 97
antiwar activism, 214, 218
Armed Forces Institute of Rehabilitation Medicine (AFIRM), 164–66, 175
armor of silence, 104
army: COAS (chief of army staff), 30, 33–34, 46, 50, 52–53, 211; as family, 36, 96–100 99; and masculinity, 7–8, 13–15, 35, 102, 122–124, 203, 211; national integration of, 6, 68–69, 73, 82; providing livelihood, 36, 55, 58, 70–71, 81-82, 135-137, 204; as volunteer force, 6, 63, 67. *See also* disabled veteran(s); Pakistan Armed Forces
army recruitment (Pakistan): first phase of, 66; second phase of, 67–68; third phase of, 68; centralization of, 82–83; in Chakwal District, 74–75; district quotas, 73–74, 82; DSBs (Dis-

army recruitment (Pakistan) (*continued*) trict Soldiers Boards), 60, 62, 65, 73; as kinship privilege, 77–78; pressure from parents, 75–76; recruits running home, 91–93, 100
asal shaheed (real martyrs), 198, 202
Aslam: anniversary ceremonies, 128–29; video of funeral, 117–22
Attock District, 57, 62, 70
audience for YeD/S shows: as active participants, 23–24; families' emotion transferred to, 2–3, 9, 32, 41; live and TV, 42; YeD versus YeS, 29
authenticity: maintaining illusion of, 38–39, 43; manufacture of, 216, 218; of woman's heart, 166
automatons, soldiers as, 94–95, 102
Awan, Maulana Akram, 190
Awareness and Motivation course, 184, 186
Ayesha (mother of martyr), 115, 139, 199
Azad Jammu and Kashmir (AJK), 65; Azad Kashmir (AK) regiment, 228n52
Aziz, Maulana Abdul, 26

bacha/e (child/ren), soldiers/shaheed as, 93, 119, 202–3, 217
Bajwa, Qamar Javed, 212
Baluchistan province, 26, 46, 63, 65, 67–69, 177, 195
Bangladesh, 67, 177, 181, 227n41
Banti, Alberto M., 32–33
Bardaglio, Peter, 157
Barelvi sect, 128, 180, 190–92, 194, 196
barsi (death anniversary), 111, 126
Bashir, 169
battlefield emotions, 96–97, 103. *See also* fear
battle of narratives, 30, 199, 204–5
battle over mind, body of soldiers, 99–101, 106–7, 112
Bengali Muslims killed, 177, 195

Bengali units mutinying, 67
Berlant, Laura, 221n33
bewakoof (fools), 93
bhagoras (runaways from army service), 91–93, 100
bhuq (hunger) as motivation for service, 55–56, 133
Bhutto, Zulfiqar Ali, 67, 181
biopolitical power/biopower, 168, 174
bodies of deceased soldiers: *aam janaza* (regular funeral), 115; battles over, 99–101, 106–7, 112; bodies of enemy, 104; controlling access to body of deceased soldier, 114–16, 122–23, and "dead-body politics," 24; military funerals, 17, 27, 53, 114–24; mourned before burial, 113–14; photographs of, 126, 131; sacredness of, 17, 32–33, 87, 125, 155; as "symbolic capital," 167; as "symbolic vehicles," 25, 212. *See also* disabled veteran(s)
Boris, Eileen, 157
Bourke, Joanna, 105, 162, 229n7
brand martyrdom, 29–32 (*31*)
British Indian Army: colonial influences of, 6, 13, 56–62, 226n11; as *ghair mazhab* (non-Muslim) force, 196, 200–201; and Indian soldiers, 13–14, 85, 87–88; as kinship group, 60, 76–78; myth of martial race, 62, 67, 87–88, 183; phases of recruitment by, 66–68; and Punjab, 16, 55, 57–59, 205, 227n31; and World War I, 58, 60, 80, 85, 162, 229n73; and World War II, 64, 80, 97, 196
brothers led astray *(gumrah bhai)*, 194, 202
"bureaucratic file" and damage, 149, 174
burial: cementing of grave, 112; corpse in inner sanctum before, 113; denial of Islamic, 26; women do not attend, 114. *See also* funeral(s); military funerals

camaraderie, 99–101
Chakwal District, 55, *61*, 62, *71*, 74, 80; Allied Bank Park memorial, 83–85 (*84*); building of new memorials, *79*, 83, *84*; Chakwal Mega Family Festival, *81*; creation of, 70, 72; Dulmial Village, 190, 229n73; graveyards, 80, 127, *127*, 196; history of, 56–58; Islamic radicalism in, 189–90; martial traditions in, 80–81, 85; military recruitment in, 73–80 (*74*); political landscape of, 72; retired soldiers in, 107–10; SRO in, 73–75, 78; Talagang Tehsil, 73, 190; terrain and climate, 70, 81; views of Taliban and WOT in, 178, 191, 195. *See also* Pakistan Armed Forces; Palwal village; Punjab
charpai (traditional woven bed), 118–19, 126, 171
children: disabled considered as, 162; of martyrs, 31–32, 35–36, 141, 152–54; participation in commemorating dead, 129; victims of Peshawar school attack, 191, 199
civilianization of military spaces, 53, 124, 216
civilians: compensation to as charity, 144; compensation regimes for, 140–144; disabled, 162; killed in terrorist attacks, 51–52, 141, 145, 191, 199, 213; as raw material, 87; transition/distance from in military training, 87, 90 91, 100, 102
class and unequal sacrifice, 46–47
CMHs (Combined Military Hospitals), 163
COAS (chief of army staff), 30, 33–34, 46, 50, 52–53, 211
compensation to families: Ayesha on, 139; compensation regimes for civilians, 140–144; for disabled soldiers and WWPs, 163–64, 175; family disputes over, 144, 149; masking of compensation, 45, 139, 144–46, 147–49, 213; monetary, 139, 141–47, 175; as paternalistic contract, 140; for soldier death, 213; as system of exchange, 148, 213; two parts of, 142–43; 149
court martials, 28, 100, 184–85, 203
critical race theory, 221n33
crying: of audience, 41–42; of bereaved parents, 34, 38–39, 131, 199; at funeral, 115–17, 119; of MC on stage, 41; over dead comrades, 104; in school skit, 129; of Shakeel, 171; of soldiers in training, 92; during vaen, 111, 131

Darling, Malcolm L., 55, 228n58
DASBs (District Armed Services Boards): in Chakwal, 73; as civil-military bridge, 65–66, 108; mediating inheritance claim disputes, 142, 155–56; support for mothers, daughters and widows, 150–51, 154–57
death: versus disability, 161–63, 166, 173–74, 166; framed as meaningful sacrifice, 24, 113, 136–37, 149, 208–9
death of a soldier: versus *aam* (regular) death, 113–115; eternal life and, 130; fight for control over, 112–13; controlling access to body, 114–16, 122–23; as necessary, honorable, meaningful, 24, 113, 136–137, 149; no mourning for shaheed, 115; as willing sacrifice, 145. *See also* script of willing sacrifice
debilitation as biopolitical end, 168
Defense Day. *See* YeD
democratically elected government, 9, 53, 211–12
Deobandi sect, 180, 189–94, 197, 202
depersonalization, 89, 105, 229n7
depression among disabled soldiers, 166, 175

Derrida, Jacques, 124
desertions/deserters, 223n52; after 2004 fatwa, 28; compensation to reduce, 140; family's thoughts about, 132–33; home worries leading to, 103; over fighting Muslim enemy, 187–88, 202–4; as "wastage," 68
Devji, Faisal, 179
disabled veteran(s), 44, 160; AFIRM facility, 164–66, 175; amputations and prosthetics, 163–65, 169; compared to shaheed, 173–74; disability as a castration, 163; disability versus death, 161–63, 166, 173–74; as feminized, 167, 171–72, 211; military management of maiming, 165–66; production of, 168; rehabilitative economy due to, 162, 169; welfare, compensation for, 163–64, 174–75; of World War I, 162; in YeD/S shows, 44, 167
Discipline and Punish: Birth of the Prison (Foucault), 89, 230nn12–13
dissociation and numbness, 17, 105–7, 209
Distress Grant, 151–52, 232
doubts regarding war, 178, 188, 199, 203–4
DSBs (District Soldiers Boards), 60, 62, 65, 73, 153. *See also* DASBs

East Bengal Regiment, 67
East Pakistan, 177, 195, 231n6
economic backwardness and recruitment, 58, 69
economies of loss, 147–50
emoluments: from government or GHQ, 142–43; inheritance laws and, 155; male relatives' control of, 157–59; military relationship with female recipient of compensation, 152–59. *See also* compensation to families

enemy/enemies: anger against in YeD/S, 44–45, 49; dead bodies of, 104; Hindus as, 97, 180, 196; India as, 224n16; Muslims as, 25, 30–31, 50, 52–53, 177–79, 187–88, 190, 194, 199, 203, 209; shaping of, 49–50; Sunni Deobandi groups, 190–95, 197; as un-Islamic, 50, 183, 187; in YeD video reenactments, 51
enframing, 95–96
England, English as modern, 13, 51
esprit de corps, 87, 98–99
ethnicity over religious identity in war, 67, 178, 195
examination, physical and medical, 74–76, 167
ex-servicemen, 64–66, 68, 73, 78, 85, 107–110

families of martyrs: at YeD/shows, 2, 23, 25, 33, 38–43, 124; bonds with family weakened, 36–37, 100; boycotting military funerals, 27; compensation packages for, 45, 142–50; conduits/symbolic resources/capital, 10, 25, 34, 207, 212; disputes over compensation, 45, 152–56; family pressure to enlist, 76–77, 92–93; guilt over son's service, 133, 138; as semi-militarized, 42
fathers of martyrs, 18, 19, vii; at funeral, 116, 120, 130–31; guilt over son's service, 133, 138; prepping for YeD, 2, 38–39. *See also* YeD/S shows
fatwas against military operations, 26, 28, 177
Fauji Foundation, 64–65, 72–73, 108
faujis (military men), 78, 88, 94, 109; always deserving respect, 200–201; as automatons, 94–95, 102; learning not to show fear, 103–4; as majboor/bache, 200–2, 217; as not feminine, civilian, primitive, 102–3; recruits

socialized into, 88, 101; and religion, 200, 205; in retirement, 108–10
fauji zehen (army mind), 94, 109
fear: control of as masculine, 14; of dead bodies, 25; by families of combat soldiers, 132; of forgetting, 48, 104; of maiming, disability, 163, 167; management of, 87, 90, 97, 102–4, 107; soldiers' descriptions of, 103–5, 170; of speaking out, 136
Federally Administered Tribal Areas (FATA), 25–26, 181, 236n57; representations of people from, 143, 195
feminization of WWPs, 167, 171–72, 211. *See also* disabled veteran(s)
flag: draped over coffin, 116, 118–19, 210; at funeral, 119–20; marking graves, 80, 86, 112, 127–28, 196–97, 200; presented to father, 120, 122, 150; in schools, 129
Foucault, Michel, 9, 12, 89, 92, 95, 130, 168, 217, 230nn12–13
funeral(s): *aam janaza* (regular funeral), 53, 115, 118–19, 121; of Aslam, 117–22; boycotting military funerals, 27; DASB coordination of, 142; fathers of martyrs, 120; flag at, 119–20, 122, 150; military funerals, 17, 27, 53, 114–24, 134, 150, 208; money for, 152; of Nawaz, 134. *See also* burial; military funerals

garrison state concept, 59, 220n13
gender, 33, 211, and emoluments, 157–60; female affirmation of male, 35, 166; and governing practices, 9–10; in grief and mourning, 113, 121–26, 129; patriarchy and masculinity, 13, 117, 157–60; and power, 219n6; religion and kinship, 33; research fieldwork and, 18–20; in war, 7–8, 13–15
ghairat (honor), 14, 97–98, 103
ghazis (warriors), 44, 48, 51

GHQ (General Headquarters): attack on, 29; and centralization of recruitment, 82–83; DASBs and, 66; emoluments granted by, 142–43, 153–54, 156–57, 233n9; Shuhada Cell in, 142; "wastage" and quotas, 68, 77; *Yadgar-e-Shuhada* monument at, 27, 29, 212; YeD/S ceremonies at, 30, 46, 53
ghurbat (poverty) as motivator to enlist, 55–56, 86, 133
Gilgit Baltistan (GB), 46, 65, 228n54
graves: cementing of, 112; in Chakwal, *127*; of shaheed in Palwal, 127–28; of war dead marked with flag, 80, 86, 112, 127–28, 196–97, 200
grief: appropriate and inappropriate, 130–34, 208–9; as gendered, 113, 116, 122–23, 126, 152; management of, 10, 24–25, 34, 37–39, 113, 115–16, 122–24; military's ritualization of, 137; public and private, 131; Sajjida's, 111–12, 131, 133; weighed in money, 147–49. *See also* men and masculinity (grief as gendered); phases of grief; residues of grief
guilt: over compensation money, 136, 138, 149, 205, 214; of parents of dead soldiers, 132–34, 209; script of sacrifice to alleviate, 137, 210; survivors', 104
Gulf States, migrant labor in, 17, 70, 81
gumrah bhai. *See* brothers led astray

hakumati (governmental) policies, 78–79
"The Handsome Young Men of the Country" song, 128
Hassan, Syed Munawar, 27–28
hate or love, amplification of, 97–98
hauntology/hauntings, 124, 137
havildars (NCOs), 82, 109, 184, 222n48, 230n11; Nasir, 92–93, 101, 104; Sohail, 94, 109, 202
heaven, 125, 196–97, 201–2

hegemonic power of military, 9, 11–12, 136, 210, 214–17, 221n33
Hemmings, Clara, 221n33
Hindu/Hinduism: Bengalis and, 177; as the enemy other, 13, 31, 97, 180, 196; martial races in, 57; threat, 53, 97, 180, 182, 209; wars with India, 53, 196, 198; womanhood and manhood in, 13
Hoggett, Paul, 221n31
honor, 14, 35, 97–98, 103, 217
"How do you do this?" video poem, 36–37
"Humara Naam Ghazi Hai" ("We Are Warriors"), 51
Hussain, 196–97, 236n59

ideology, 9; battles of, 188, 204; as cynical, 133; disciplines pain, 210; duped by, 194, 211; extremist sectarian, 28; as fantasy, 137, 210; functions of, 136, 153, 210; khateeb on, 185; as a mask, 135–37, 145, 147; of nation or religion, 48, 146–47, 179, 218; Sloterdijk on, 135; Žižek on, 135
IED (improvised explosive device) injuries, 163, 170–71
Ijaz, 105
illusion: of authenticity, 38–39, 43; and ideology, 136; of willing sacrifice, 216
Imran, Chaudhary, 204
Imran and father, 130–31, 147
India: All India Muslim League, 8; division of, 179; as funder of mercenaries, 194; and Kashmir, 181–82, 189, 195, 224n16; true shaheed in clash with, 198–99; wars with, 7, 29, 50, 53, 128, 196, 198–99, 224n16. *See also* British Indian Army; Hindu/Hinduism; partition and aftermath
Iqbal, Allama, 13
Iraq war, 105–6, 215

Islam: battle imagery of, 33; and battle of narratives, 204–5; conflict within, 177–78, 198–99, 212; defining "soldier of Islam," 26, 195–97; as "ethnoterritorial ideology," 179; inheritance law and emoluments, 155; militants in North Waziristan, 27–28; military training and, 182–89; and Pakistani self-identity, 13, 50, 125, 178, 198–99, 205; Sunni/Shia sectarian tensions, 72, 180, 189–94, 229n66. *See also* religion; *shahadat*
ISPR (Inter Services Public Relations), 19, 224n21; on "battle of narratives," 30, 199; managing YeD/S shows, 30–31, 34, 37;
Israel, 168, 194
izzat (prestige), 14, 97, 134, 159

Jaffrelot, Christopher, 179, 222n42, 223n4, 234nn3, 4, 9
Jamaat-e-Islami (JI) party, 27, 181, 224n11, 236n62
janaza. See funeral(s)
jawan (young man, subaltern soldier), 13, 14, 85, 88, 94, 99, 186, 222n48
jazba (passion), 134, 182
Jhelum District, 56–58, 62, 70, 73, 78
jihad/jihadism: 26, 181, 185, 188, 189, 192, 203, 224n11
Jinnah, Mohammed Ali, 179
journalists as martyrs, 51

kafir declarations, 177, 183
Kandwal, 55, 170, 178, 192, 198, 223nn52
Karbala, 196, 236
Kargil war, 224n18; disagreements over, 185; Northern Light Infantry in, 228n54; treatment of war dead, 116, 142, 145, 198–99, 202, 232n12; and YeD, 29
karna parta hai (you *have* to do this), 135, 137, 139, 210

Kashmir (AJK), 65, 181, 182, 189, 195, 224n16
Kausar (widow), 116–17, 150–52, 154, 159
Kayani, Ashfaq Parvez, 29, 212
Khan, Imran, 225–26n39
Khan, Sepoy Khudadad, 84
Khan, Sikandar Hayat, 59
khateeb (cleric), 183–87
Khutbaat-e-Askaar (religious military sermons), 183
Khyber Pakhtunkhwa (KP)/North West Frontier Province, 46, 63, 181; under British rule, 14; DASBs in, 65; as good recruiting grounds, 88, 227n31; police casualties in, 231n10
kinship group: metaphors of nation, military, 36, 78; military functioning as, 66, 77–78, 86, 96–101, 145, 188, 209

labor policies, British versus US, 158
Lacanian psychoanalysis, 136, 222n35
Lahore Resolution (1940), 8
Lal Masjid (Red Mosque), 26–27, 191, 193, 224n9, 236n50
Land Alienation Act (1900), 226n12
land allotment, 64, 141, 143, 150, 154–55, 157
larka (boy), shaheed as, 202–3
Lieven, Anatol, 66
loss of limbs, faculties, 139, 160, 161, 173
low-intensity conflict (LIC), 203
Lutz, Catherine, 4, 237nn9, 12

maa baap (mother-father), military as, 60, 76, 99
Macleish, Kenneth T., 105–6
madrasas (religious seminaries), 189, 192h
maimed soldiers: biopower of, 168; care, management of, 165, 169, 175; downplaying of, 44, 167–69; numbers of, 26, 161; Shakeel, 169–75, 234n15.

See also disabled veteran(s); WWPs (War Wounded Persons)
majboor (helpless), 200, 202–3, 217
Malik, Majeed, 72
manufacture of the authentic, 38–39, 43, 216–18
Mard-e-Momin (the Male Believer), 13
martial race doctrine, 56–58, 62–63, 67, 87–88, 183
martyrdom: branding of, 29–32 (*31*), 53; of civilians, 51–52; controversy over, 27, 50, 181; desire for, 36, 125; for nation-state versus religion, 52, 196, 200–202, 204–5; right to claim, 26–27, 181, 205; school skit portraying, 129; songs glorifying, 7, 128. *See also shahadat; shaheed;* YeS (*Youm-e-Shuhada*)
Martyrs' Day. *See* YeS (*Youm-e-Shuhada*)
Marzai (Ahmedi) sect, 192, 194
masculinity. *See* men and masculinity
materialist motivations for service, 146, 153, 159, 205, 207, 209–10
maternalist versus paternalist policies, 158
maulvi (local cleric), 76, 121, 197
mazhab ka shaheed (martyr for religion), 200–202
Mehsud, Hekimullah, 27
memories: of dead comrades, 104; of dead family members, 122, 124–26; and fear of forgetting, 48, 104; of previous generations, 195–96
men and masculinity: disability as emasculation, 163; formed in contrast to women, 8, 102, 113, 115–16, 123; grief as gendered, 113, 116, 122–23, 126, 152; loss of masculinity, 13, 167; military instilling sense of, 57, 88, 92, 96–97; Muslim, 13; role of, 7, 160; as thinking over feeling, 160. *See also* gender

militant religious groups, 27, 81, 178, 182, 194, 199, 212. *See also* Islam
militarism: challenges to, 21, 217; legitimizing of, 212; mediating through affect, 213–14; militarization of civilian spaces, 53, 56, 124, 216; military as benevolent figure, 60, 76–77, 169, 213; military as kinship group, 78, 96–101, 145, 188, 200; military as savior/*muhafiz* (protector), 9, 45, 146, 169; scholarship on Pakistani military, 219–20n11; as source of *pakki naukri*, 55, 63, 86, 93, 137, 196, 200, 201, 217. *See also* WOT (war on terror)
military funerals, 114–24; boycotts of, 27; bureaucracy of, 114–15; displays of grief discouraged, 115–17; family's lack of access to body, 116, 123–24; as grand performance, 17, 113, 116–18. *See also* burial; funeral(s)
military-medical-industrial complex, 163, 169
Mitchell, Timothy, 95–96
mothers of martyrs, 24; as *azeem maan* (great mother), 34; as *maadar-e-watan* (the mother of the nation), 34; and military engagement with feminine, 211; government benefits to, 152–53, 160; grief of exalted but managed, 34, 44, 47, 153; ordered not to touch body, 116, 122; told not to cry at funeral, 115–17, 122–23; vaen by Sajjida, 111
Mujahideen, Afghan, 6, 26, 181
Mukti Bahini labeled as *kafir*, 177, 183
murtid (apostate), 191
"*musalsal zehni koft*" (continuous mental irritation), 94
Musharraf, Pervez, 190, 199, 212
Muslim League, 8, 72, 179
Muslims as enemies: ambivalence, unease regarding, 177, 188, 199, 209; America cannot declare, 178; battle of narratives, 30–31, 50, 52–53, 194; Mukti Bahini declared *kafir*, 177; in WOT, 25, 177, 187–88

Nasir, Havildar, 92–93, 101, 104
nation: cultures and narratives of, 32–33; as female, 35, 42; nationalism and religion in military training, 182–89; as spectator, 32, 42–43; as third vector, 24, 32, 168–69, 174
National Action Plan, 193–94
National Integration Policy, 6, 68–69, 73, 82
Navaro-Yashin, Yael, 12, 130, 135
Nawaz, 3, 9, 47–49, 132–35, 147, 159
Nelson, Mathew J., 192–93
9/11 attacks on US, 26, 177, 182
NoK (next of kin; families of dead soldiers). *See* fathers of martyrs; mothers of martyrs; YeD/S shows
normate fears of vulnerability, 163, 167
North Punjab demographics, 70–72
North Waziristan, 51
North West Frontier Province, 46, 63. *See also* Khyber Pakhtunkhwa (KP)
northwest Pakistan, war in: deaths and injuries in, 25–28, 161, 177; and embellishing of graves of deceased soldiers from, 127; shifting to new enemy, 30, 177, 194–95, 198–99; YeS instead of YeD, 23, 29–30, 83. *See also* WOT (war on terror)

okha (uneasy), 116, 147
Omar, Sipahi, 94
"One force, one family, one nation," 36
Operation Gibraltar, 224n16
Operation Radd-ul Fasaad, 26
Operation Zarb-e-Azab, 26
Ophir, Adi, 148–49, 173–74
othering, 97, 106, 177, 195
Owen, Wilfred, 218, 234n1, 237n17

paband (restricted), 93
Pakistan: after partition, 177–79; as an ideology, 33, 186; Hindu/Hinduism as the enemy other, 13, 31, 97, 180, 196; religionationalism of, 33, 178–79, 183–88, 193, 198, 205, 209–11; religious extremism in, 180, 190. *See also* WOT (war on terror)
Pakistan Armed Forces, 207, 219n9; Act of 1952, 28, 63; Army Medical Corps, 163, 164; Army Selection and Recruitment, 65–68; *fatwa* against operations, 26, 28, 177; functioning like a kinship group, 66, 77–80, 96–100; ISPR (Inter Services Public Relations), 19, 30, 166; as percentage of government budget, 62, 66; Punjab as recruitment area for, 13, 63, 70–71, 88, 189; as volunteer force, 6, 62, 63, 67; war against India, 224n16. *See also* army; Chakwal District; WOT (war on terror)
Pakistan Day, 8, 25
pakki mahana amadani (secure monthly income), 196
pakki naukri (secure government service), 55, 63, 86, 93, 110, 196, 200–201, 217
Palestinians, 168
Palwal village, 1, 55, 223nn52; author's contact with, 17, 19, 118, 126; civilians as militarized, 130; graves of shaheed in, 127–28; other references to shaheed, 196–98; recent shaheed in, 1–2, 49, 195; school skit of shuhada, 129; subsects in, 191–92; views of pre- and post-partition army, 196; views of proper and inappropriate grief in, 130–34. *See also* Sajjida
partition and aftermath, 26; DSBs becoming DASBs, 65; Hindus as enemy, 97, 179–80, 182; homogenization under Islam, 13, 196; India/Pakistan wars, 183; Pakistan's vulnerability, 181; Punjabi domination, 62; recruitment in army, 62–70. *See also* pre-partition Muslim deaths in colonial army
Parveen, 116
Pasha, Mustapha Kamal, 61, 226n11
Pashtun, 194–95
passive, male family members as, 122–23
"passive" versus "active" dead and sufferers, 45, 140, 162
patriarchy, 13, 117, 157–60
patronage politics, 66, 70, 72–73, 77–78, 83, 187–89
pension, 60, 153, 155, 157
performances: of grief, 3, 24, 48, 134; manufacture of the authentic, 38, 43; script for, 32–38
Peshawar school attack, 191, 193, 199
phases of grief, 113
photographs of dead, 104, 126, 131
poetry, 36–37, 111
police as martyrs, 26, 51–52, 140–45, 174, 231–32n10
politicians as martyrs, 51
politics: of "as if," 135; of assimilation, 193–94
Potohar, 17, 70
power: Foucault on, 130, 217; modes of, 95–96; productive ability of, 208
pre-partition Muslim deaths in colonial Army, 196–97, 201
Preston, Jeffrey, 163
"pricking" to draw out emotion, 39
professional weepers, 114, 225n33
pro patria mori, 177, 218, 234n1
prosthetic limbs, 164–65, 169
proxy wars, 182
Puar, Jasbir K., 168, 175–76
Punjab, 6, 226n3; DASBs in, 65; as good recruiting grounds, 55, 63, 70–71; grief and mourning in, 113; ma-

Punjab *(continued)*
  jority of Pakistan Army pre-2001, 63; military as primary employer, 64, 68; objections to enlistment quotas, 82; pre-partition, 58–59; Salt Range region, 64; support for jihadist movements in, 181; and United States, 62. *See also* Chakwal District
Punjab Regiment, 67
puttar nahio labda (I can't find my son), 139, 147

qabyli (tribal) areas, 195
qaum (nation), 24, 36, 42, 46, 223n1
Quayson, Ato, 163
Quran, the: memorizing by rote *(hifz)*, 183; on shaheed, 33, 50, 120–21, 183, 196; in YeD/S videos, 118

Raj, the, 13, 57, 87, 183
Rawalpindi district, 62; army medical complex in, 164; GHQ in, 9, 23, 46; recruitment depot in, 57–58, 70–71; YeS commemorations in, 23
recruitry ki photo, 126, 131
regiment centers, 65, 67–68, 77, 83, 154
religion: as empty idea, 179; ethnicity trumping, 178; and military, 33, 187, 190; and nationalism, 182–89; as political tool, 182, 204; religious education in military training, 183–89, 192–93; religious right, 179, 236n62; versus state, 198, 203–4. *See also* Islam
religionationalism, 33, 178–79, 183–88, 193, 198, 205, 209–11
Religious Directorate, 183
remarriage of widows, 35, 151–55, 158
remittances from abroad, 71–72, 81
residues of grief, 130, 134, 136, 208, 210
retired soldiers of Chakwal, 107–10
rista/riste (relationships), 33, 36, 52

rituals: attempted discipline of, 199, 208; of commemoration, 213; for military death, 114–22; of mourning, 11, 24, 112, 114, 122; for newborns, 76; of truth, 85. *See also* funeral(s); YeD/S shows
rohani tarbeeyat (spiritual teaching), 185
romantic love, 34–35, 153
Rushdie, Salman, 179
Rusticus Loquitur (Darling), 55
rutba (status), 134, 159

sacredness of war dead, 17, 32–33, 87, 125, 155, 217
Saigol, Rubina, 8, 225n26, 230n6
Sajjida, 111–12, 131, 133
Saleem, 200–202
Salt Range, 57–58, 64, 70
Samad, Younus, 179
sarkar (government): as benevolent, 62, 77; loyalty tied to, 78; vestiges of British, 80
Saudi Arabia, 70, 81, 181
script of willing sacrifice: around dead soldiers, 3, 11; and disabled soldier, 161–62, 167–69, 173–76; and families of *shaheed*, 26, 42, 113, 125, 130–34, 136–37; and monetary compensation, 145–46, 213; and physical space, 80–86, 124–26, 128; and religion, 121, 205; as salve, 210; women's role in, 153, 156, 159
script of YeD/S ceremony, 32–33, 36–37, 39–41, 43–45
sectarian ideologies, 28, 180–81, 189–94, 203–4
Selection and Recruitment Office (SRO), 65, 69, 73–75, 78, 226n2
September 11 attacks and aftermath. *See* 9/11 attacks on US
shahadat (martyrdom in the name of Islam): battle of narratives regarding,

30–31, 33, 131, 133–34, 145; desire for, 125; hierarchies regarding, 128, 196–97, 200–202; family pride in, 125–26; *fatwas* regarding, 26, 28; graves in Chakwal, *127*; of Hussain, 236; rewarded in afterlife, 145, 156; sermon on, 197

shaheed (martyr): adornment of graves, 127–28; from Afghan and Kashmiri jihad, 181; *asal shaheed* (real martyrs), 198, 202; continued loyalty to, 204; designated next of kin, 153–54; developing hierarchy of, 128, 196–97, 200–202; establishing legitimacy for, 178, 196–98, 202; and feeling of pain, 117, 173, 197; as helpless, infantalized, 202–3; as *larka* (boy), 202–3; as lucky, 156; no mourning for death of, 115, 125–26; non-military meanings of, 196–97; as still alive, 116–17, 120, 156; who counts as, 27, 52, 167, 197–98, 200–201. *See also* fathers of martyrs; mothers of martyrs; *shahadat*

Shakeel, 169–75, 234n15

shame, 14, 93, 102–4, 107, 171

Shamil, 107–8

Sharif, Mian Nawaz, 27

Sharif, Raheel, 212

shauq (interest) as motivation for service, 55

Shia/Sunni sectarian tensions, 72, 180, 189–94, 229n66

Shuhada: Cell, 142, 156, 175–76; monument, 33, 52, 211–12

Siachen Glacier, 19, 29, 198, 224nn17

Sikhs, 57, 60, 76

Sindh: Infantry Regiment, 67; province, 46, 63, 65, 67–68, 228n52; regiment, 228n52

sipahi (soldier), 16, 222n48; NCOs and JCOs, 17; as "occidental soldier," 87; Sipahi Omar, 94, 109–10; Sipahi Shakeel, 170; viewed as simpletons, 109; on WOT, 188; WWI correspondence of, 60. *See also* soldiers

Skills training course, 186

Skocpol, Theda, 158

Sloterdijk, Peter, 135

Sohail (martyr), 149–52

Sohail, Havildar, 94, 109, 202

Sohaila (mother of martyr), 49

soldiers: asking to return home, 132–33; battlefield experiences, 103–5; challenges of interviewing, 19, 88–89; homesickness of, 92, 98; welfare of soldiers, 60, 66, 72–73, 212. *See also sipahi*; training

soldier training: of body, mind, and heart, 90–91; homesickness and isolation during, 92, 98; in LIC (low-intensity conflict), 203; mental effects of, 95; poverty encouraging resilience during, 93; punishment, 92; in religious nationalism, 182–89; units of, 186

sons, death of, 35–36, 132

South Asia Terrorism Portal, 26

South Waziristan: debate over shahadat in, 27, 198; disaffection within, 26–27; displacements from, 143; injuries, deaths in, 151, 170, 197; Nawaz (martyr), 3; reenactment of Zarb-e Azab operation, 51; support for army action in, 193; war on terror in, 25–27, 182, 190. *See also* Ayesha; Nawaz

spinal cord injuries, 163–64, 166

SRO (Selection and Recruitment Office), 65, 69, 73–75, 78, 226n2

SSG (Special Services Group), 105, 230n30

subedars (JCOs), 222n48, 230n10; in Chakwal, 107–9; joke by, 101; jokes about, 108–9; in retirement, 108; as simple-minded, 109; standing out from villagers, 109; statements by, 82, 182; on trainee transition, 91

Sumaira, 151–52, 154
survivor's guilt, 104, 132–33
Swat district, 25, 130, 198

Tahir, 151
Tahir, Rao, 72
Taliban, 26–27, 182, 189, 191, 193, 195, 198–99
Tehreeke-Taliban Pakistan (TTP), 27, 50, 191, 193, 199
television: footage of school casualties, 199; issues debated on talk shows, 27; YeD/S commemorations, 23–24, 28–30, 42
terrorists: as non-Muslims, 203–4; portrayal of, 50; portrayal of victims of, 51, 144;
testimonies by families of deceased soldiers, 2–3; audience reaction to, 41; content of, 32–37, 44–45; from different areas, 46; family reactions to YeD/S shows, 46–47; as manufacture of the authentic, 38–39; prescreening, rehearsing for, 37, 38, 43–44, 208. *See also* YeD/S shows
thumbs-up from grieving father, 38–39, 48
traumatic brain injury, 163
traumatic real kernels, 136–37, 149
tribal identity, 77, 143, 181, 194–95

United States: criticism of alliances with, 178, 193–94; "maternalist" early labor policies, 158; military welfare policies, 140; supporting Afghan Mujahideen, 181; US drone, 27
unskilled migrant labor, 17, 70–71, 81

vaen (mourning ritual), 11, 111–12, 114–15, 131
value of life, health, 147–50
Verdery, Katherine, 24

videos: as documentaries in YeD/S shows, 33, 36–37, 40–43, 50–51, 122, 162, 166; of military funeral, 117–19
volunteer force, Pakistan army as, 6, 13, 62, 67, 210

war on terror. *See* WOT
Wasinski, Christophe, 215
watan ka shaheed (martyr for the nation-state), 200–201
"We Are Warriors" ("*Humara Naam Ghazi Hai*"), 51
Wedeen, Lisa, 135
Welfare and Rehabilitation Directorate, 142
welfare officers (WOs), 65, 73
West Pakistan, 67, 177
"When I cry" poem, 111
widows of martyrs, 24, 31–32, 34–35, 150–57
"wild animals," new recruits as, 87, 90
women: becoming visible political subjects, 153; female love causing weakness, 98; as irrational, primitive, 113, 122–23, 152, 160; professional weepers, 114; helplessness of, 35, 158–59. *See also* gender; mothers of martyrs
World War I, 58, 60, 80, 85, 162, 229n73
World War II, 64, 80, 97, 196
WOT (war on terror): compensation packages for deaths and disability in, 141–42, 163–64, 231n10; controversies around *shahadat*, 26–28, 198–203; desertion, refusal to fire during, 187–88, 203; disabled from, 163; as distraction from real struggle, 193; fellow Muslims as enemy, 25, 31, 177–78, 236n50; General Kayani and, 212
WWPs (War Wounded Persons), 44, 163–67, 173–75, 212. *See also* disabled veteran(s)

Yadgar-e-Shuhada monument, *79*; COAS address at, 52; families laying flowers at, 33; installation of, 29, 80, 83, 212; lighting up of, 1; Sharif's visit to, 27

Yasmin (mother of Nawaz), 3, 9, 47–48, 132, 135, 147

YeD *(Youm-e-Difah)*—Defense Day, *31*; author attending, 1–4, 47–49; documentaries dropped from, 29, 167; and India, 31. *See also* YeD/S shows

YeD/S shows: audience response to, 2–3, 23, 32–33, 38; as branding of martyrdom, 30–31; as commemorations, 29–31, 51; as civilianization of military spaces, 53, 124, 216; depiction of soldiers, 24, 36, 40, 51, 97; disabled bodies in, 44, 162, 167; families as participant-spectators in, 23, 40–42; invoking/weakening bonds of kinship, 37, 100; monetary compensation not mentioned, 45, 144; religion in, 33, 203–5; script of, 36–37, 39–41, 43–45; selection, coaching of family members, 37–39; "State of the Union" address at, 211–12; videos in, 33, 36–37, 40–43, 50–51, 122, 162, 166; YeD/YeS merger, 53; YeS compared to YeD, 29–31, 53, 144–45

YeS *(Youm-e-Shuhada)*: COAS speech, 52–53; national ceremony discontinued, 30; origin and purpose of, 23, 29, 212. *See also* YeD/S shows

Zarb-e Azab operation, 26, 51

zehen (mind): affected by grief, 122; home/military parallel worlds, 105–6, 109; during military training, 91–92, 94

Zia-ul Haq, Muhammad: and Afghan Mujahideen, 181; approving Chakwal District, 70, 72; compulsory Pakistan Studies courses under, 235n32; Islamization under, 180, 183, 187, 234n12; and Sindh Infantry Regiment, 67

Žižek, Slavoj, 135–36, 210, 225n33

zulm (cruelty), 173–74

ALSO PUBLISHED IN THE SOUTH ASIA IN MOTION SERIES

In the Name of the Nation: India and Its Northeast
Sanjib Baruah (2020)

Faithful Fighters: Identity and Power in the British Indian Army
Kate Imy (2019)

Paradoxes of the Popular: Crowd Politics in Bangladesh
Nusrat Sabina Chowdhury (2019)

The Ethics of Staying: Social Movements and Land Rights Politics in Pakistan
Mubbashir A. Rizvi (2019)

Mafia Raj: The Rule of Bosses in South Asia
Lucia Michelutti, Ashraf Hoque, Nicolas Martin, David Picherit,
Paul Rollier, Arild Ruud, and Clarinda Still (2018)

Elusive Lives: Gender, Autobiography, and the Self in Muslim South Asia
Siobhan Lambert-Hurley (2018)

Financializing Poverty: Labor and Risk in Indian Microfinance
Sohini Kar (2018)

Jinnealogy: Time, Islam, and Ecological Thought in the Medieval Ruins of Delhi
Anand Vivek Taneja (2017)

Uprising of the Fools: Pilgrimage as Moral Protest in Contemporary India
Vikash Singh (2017)

The Slow Boil: Street Food, Rights, and Public Space in Mumbai
Jonathan Shapiro Anjaria (2016)

The Demands of Recognition: State Anthropology and Ethnopolitics in Darjeeling
Townsend Middleton (2015)

The South African Gandhi: Stretcher-Bearer of Empire
Ashwin Desai and Goolam Vahed (2015)

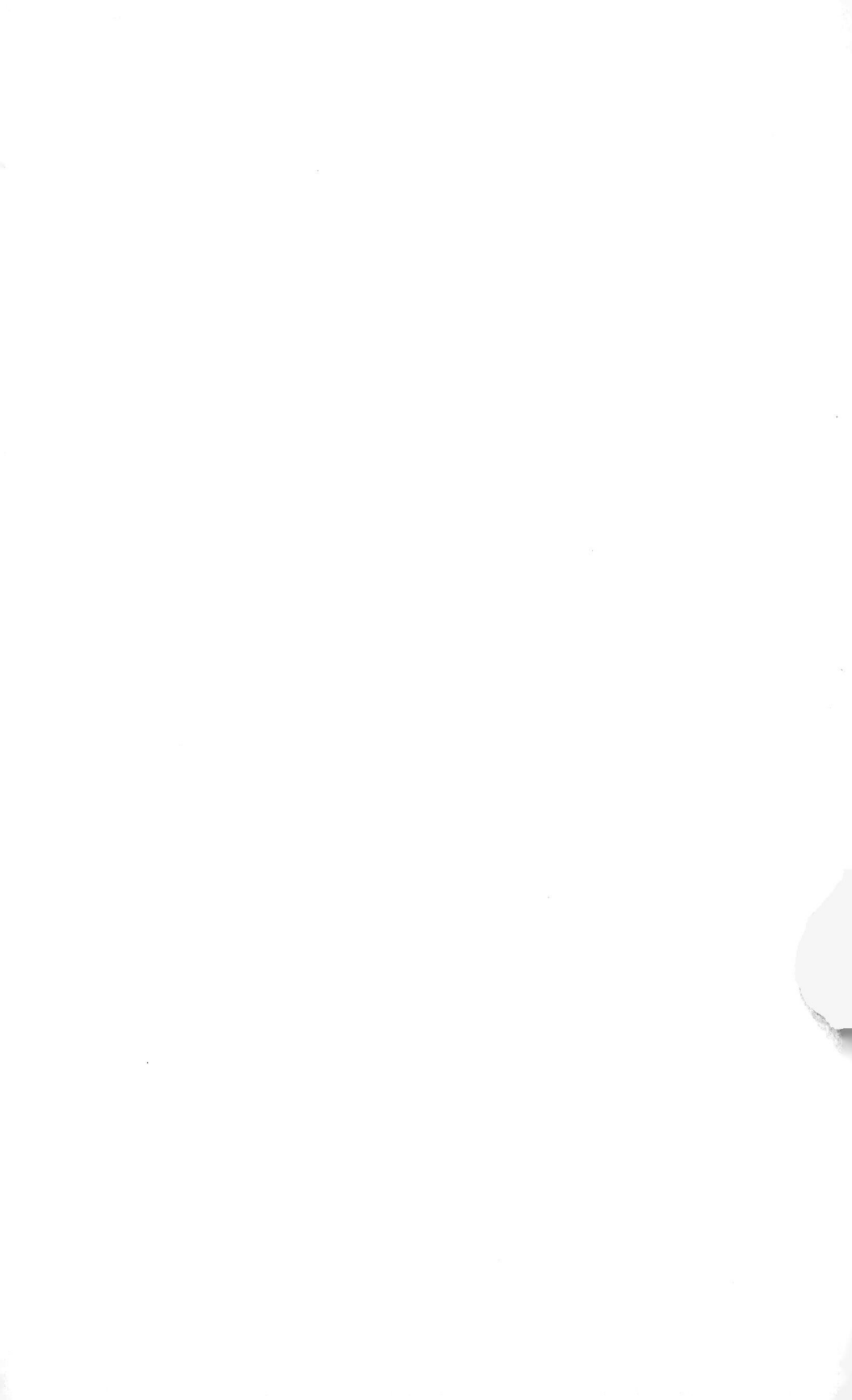